WESTERN ONTARIO
AND THE
AMERICAN FRONTIER

THE CARLETON LIBRARY

A series of Canadian reprints and new collections of source material relating to Canada, issued under the editorial supervision of the Institute of Canadian Studies of Carleton University, Ottawa.

Fred Landon

Western Ontario
and the
American Frontier

The Carleton Library No. 34 / McClelland and Stewart Limited

*The following dedication appeared in
the original edition*:

TO MARGARET LANDON

Western Ontario and the American Frontier was first published
in 1941 by the Ryerson Press, Toronto, and Yale University Press,
New Haven; one of the series of the Relations of Canada and the
United States prepared under the direction of the Carnegie
Endowment for International Peace, New York.

The Canadian Publishers
McClelland and Stewart Limited
25 Hollinger Road, Toronto 16

FC
249
L32
1967
Cop.2

PRINTED AND BOUND IN CANADA
BY
T. H. BEST PRINTING COMPANY LIMITED

CONTENTS

Introduction to the Original Edition

I

This volume in the series of historical studies bearing upon the relations between Canada and the United States was planned at a time when the sort of ordered freedom which prevailed so conspicuously on both sides of this international boundary seemed assured in the world for generations to come. The peril which now overclouds the whole English-speaking world lends a poignancy altogether unforeseen to this whole series and particularly to this volume.

There is scarcely a parallel in history to the friendly and beneficent intercourse which has prevailed between what is now Western Ontario and the contiguous states of the American union. Certain passages in their common history are not pleasant to reflect upon – the fratricidal strife of a century and a half ago, the bitter War of 1812, and more than one crisis in the thirties and again in the sixties when antipathies rather than affinities seemed the order of the day. But these have come and gone; while environments of peace and many common interests have demonstrated for more than a century the blessings of neighbourliness and a common way of life. Strangely enough, as Dr. Shotwell has pointed out elsewhere, this series is the first comprehensive attempt to deal with these relations; and this particular volume goes to press at a time when this whole structure, regarded for so many years as almost too commonplace for comment, is threatened by a new and devastating world order.

At no part of the international boundary, perhaps, has geography come so directly into play as in the peninsula which juts down into the American union from the flanks of the Great Lakes. Southwestern Ontario is farther south than most of New England, than "up-state" New York, than Minnesota, North Dakota, Montana, and the State of Washington. It is farther south than most of Michigan, Wisconsin, South Dakota, Wyoming, Idaho, and Oregon. It is as far south as portions of Pennsylvania, Iowa, and Nebraska. It is nearer the population centre of the United States than thirty-five states of the union.

London, Ontario, is south of Madison, St. Paul and Minneapolis, Portland, Oregon, and Seattle. It is less than one degree of latitude from Albany and Boston, and less than five from Washington and San Francisco.

But not only is the Ontario peninsula a central continental area geographically; its geology and topography have made it a highway for more than one of those people-wanderings which have reached and submerged the American frontier. The New England pre-revolutionary and Loyalist migrations radiated by sea to the historic frontier of New England, the old Province of Nova Scotia. For up-state New York and Pennsylvania, however, the Loyalist frontier was across the St. Lawrence and Niagara rivers. Following hard upon this semi-political migration chiefly into what is now eastern Ontario was a movement which Lieutenant-Governor Simcoe invited upon other grounds for the western reaches of the province. Contrary to Loyalist traditions, it was Simcoe's conviction that free grants of two-hundred-acre farms – prototype of the free homestead – ought to replace, in British policy, the prodigal grants to promoters, and that the ideal settler for the Upper Canadian wilderness was the American frontiersman. Simcoe's delusion that reserves of loyalism still to be found in the original colonies would reinforce and dominate this movement does not impair this forecast for the early settlement of Upper Canada. The bearing of this post-Loyalist migration, both before and after the War of 1812, upon the life of the new frontier across the international boundary forms one of the most interesting chapters of the story which Professor Landon unfolds in this volume.

II

There is a second reason why regional studies of this and other areas across Canada would seem to form a necessary approach to their present relations. There was a national government from the beginning in the United States, but for nearly half the period since the American Revolution, disintegration and sectionalism rather than union was the order of the day for the British provinces.

In the Maritimes the contacts with the Canadas were far less intimate than those with New England. For ten years after the War of 1812 only a single ship from the Maritimes passed the Montreal customs, while Lord Dalhousie in Nova Scotia noted that "the connection between the respectable inhabitants of this Province, and the States, is yet very intimate; scarcely is there a family that has not Fathers, Brothers, and near relations settled there."[1] Even the Canadas themselves were separated by

[1] W. M. Whitelaw, *The Maritimes and Canada Before Confederation* (Toronto, 1934), p. 60; Public Archives of Canada, C.O. 217, 160, 59.

imponderable barriers of race, language, and religion, and within two decades the legislative union between them in 1841 had become intolerable. Farther west, the Red River Settlement after the triumph of "the Bay" over "the River" in the coalition of the North West Company with the Hudson's Bay Company in 1821, had disappeared from the Canadian scene, and the next impact upon the Red River district was the approach of American migration from the south, canalized by the prodigious technique of the land-grant railways. West of the Rockies was a fifth region of isolated settlement overshadowed by the potential expansion of Oregon and California.

The official relations of the United States with these isolated areas are easily woven into a uniform state policy, though even here the less tangible intercourse of ideas and frontier life are not so easily resolved into a uniform pattern. The relations of these isolated regions with the United States, on the other hand, were subject to all sorts of contingencies and vicissitudes. While the Upper Canadian Loyalist regarded the War of 1812 as the last round of the Revolution, the Nova Scotian Loyalist went on trading with his New England neighbour, and Dalhousie University was afterwards founded from the customs revenues collected at Castine to accommodate the commercial intercourse between them. A quarter of a century later the policy of the United States for New Brunswick during the "war of pork and beans" over the Aroostook boundary could be integrated with policy for the Red River Settlement in Rupert's Land or for the prospective settlement of Oregon; but the British provinces continued to face their problems piecemeal, and any attempt to integrate them was apt to have unfortunate local consequences, as Sir John Harvey in New Brunswick discovered at the hands of Sydenham and Lord John Russell. As late as Confederation the repeal agitation in Nova Scotia raised for the first time in that province the bogey of annexation to the United States, but the problem of annexation in British Columbia remained so remote that Howe was almost unaware of its existence.

This would seem to mean that the local approach to relations with the United States tends to remain sectional or regional on the Canadian side to the point where a common destiny became the accepted faith of the British provinces. In truth this regionalism is traceable far into the federal period of Canadian history. This is particularly true of the extremities of the long line of Canadian provinces – the Maritimes and British Columbia. It is less obvious perhaps in central Canada which is nearer to the political centre of gravity for the whole Dominion; and if Professor Landon's survey stops short of the present century in many respects it is chiefly because the prevailing trends have been swallowed up in national policies which in Canada as in the United States are traceable in "horizontal" studies, so to speak, across the whole Dominion.

III

In this regional study of Western Ontario and the American Frontier Professor Landon has had a congenial and perhaps a somewhat exceptional task. He has sought to reconstruct the mosaic of frontier life as it was affected by the ebb and flow of ideas as well as living people across the international boundary. This is a more elusive task than the computation of numbers or the charting of demographic trends. It has already been possible from adequate historical evidence to reach sound conclusions about many aspects of frontier settlement. The volume on *The Mingling of the Canadian and American Peoples* compiled by the late Dr. Hansen is a brilliant demonstration, as Professor Brebner says in the Foreword, of "what rich harvests of significant knowledge may be reaped from the study of population movements by insight, intelligence, and hard work." In a further volume Dr. Coats of the Dominion Bureau of Statistics and Dr. Truesdell of the United States Census Bureau bring the technique of the statistician to bear upon those elusive eddies and currents of population which have been flowing to and fro across the boundary since the spring tides of mass migration to the agricultural frontiers of the continent came to an end. But the recapture of the imponderables, the ideas that were brought along or left behind, the tools and fashions and habits of daily life, the barn-raising "bees," the camp-meetings, the taverns, the commonplace tale of spelling-books and newspapers and politics – these things, as Stevenson once remarked at the end of his travels, are sometimes to be found, after all our research, awaiting us at home beside the stove.

For many of these mass migrations to the agricultural frontiers of the continent during the nineteenth century, the contemporary record has been almost irretrievably lost. It was during the last of these frontier "swarmings," so to speak, ever to be seen, in all probability, on this continent – that into Western Canada – that Dr. Isaiah Bowman and a group of colleagues conceived the idea of observing these elusive features of frontier settlement by scientific field-work while it was still in process. The economist and the historian were to fill in the background, while the sociologist could record the vital evolution of the frontier from the experience of those still living who participated in it. The volumes published in the "Canadian Frontiers of Settlement" series have done for Western Canada before it was too late what may never now be possible for those receding agricultural frontiers of the past.

It is already too late to apply this method to the district which under the name of Upper Canada, Canada West, and Western Ontario, has had the most direct and continuous contacts in Canada for nearly a century and a half with the social and cultural influences of the United States. But Professor Landon has attempted the next best thing. From an unrivalled range of knowledge in this field he has brought to light, over a long range of years, the pattern of frontier development; and in many respects he has brought it not only to light but almost to life again.

CHESTER MARTIN

Foreword to the Carleton Library Edition

There is no country in the world, including Great Britain, to which Canada is tied so closely by blood and geography as she is to the United States. On a front of nearly 5000 miles, if Alaska is included, two of the world's great democracies face each other, . . . The only major country in the world with but a single limitrophal neighbor, Canada has been subjected to the cultural, political, economic and social influences of that neighbor to a far greater extent than are nations bounded by two or more ethnically diverse peoples. Canadians have long been aware of the overwhelming importance to them of this relationship.

ROBIN W. WINKS, *Canada and the United States, the Civil War Years* (Baltimore, 1960) vii.

This is not a history of Western Ontario but is, as its title suggests, a study of the influences exerted upon this particular area of old Upper Canada (Ontario) by neighbouring American communities. In general, it is the period preceding Confederation which has been examined since, by the time the British North American provinces had achieved a partial federation, the American frontier was a thousand miles farther to the West. Comparisons or contrasts with the earlier American frontier were no longer valid.

Studies of Canadian-American relations, whether written in either country, have tended in the past to record the connections chiefly in terms of state policy. The series of volumes of which this is one sought to demonstrate that relations involve much more than the activities of organized governments. Account had to be taken of the movements of peoples across international boundary lines and, of even greater importance, of the movement of ideas across these boundary lines.

In the decade of the 1850's when John A. Macdonald spoke of the voters in the Western Ontario of his day as "Yankees and Covenanters, the most yeasty and unsafe of populations" he was not the first, and certainly not the last, to express such a political judgment. Western Ontario was then, and continued to be, an area marked by political uneasiness and an uncertainty as to where its support would go in any particular political situation. It is the purpose of this book to examine the historical background of the population inhabiting the peninsula between Lakes Huron and Erie and the western end of Lake Ontario and to determine the relations of their geography and their history as determining factors in their attitudes.

When Macdonald used the term "Yankees and Covenanters" he was incidentally recalling the racial origin of the earlier settlers in this area: Loyalists, driven from their homes in New York State by their support of the English cause during the Revolution; land-hungry American immigrants who entered Upper Canada at the invitation of Governor John Graves Simcoe; and Scottish immigrants who arrived soon after the close of the War of 1812 and occupied land in the western townships.

The characteristics of these elements have been retained by their descendants. The American strain in the population is still alert to any business opportunity, while the Scottish element has shown remarkable tenacity in holding on to its land. Even today many farms, in Elgin county for example, remain in the hands of descendants of the original owners. Moreover, these Scottish Canadians have preserved their racial habits and way of life to a remarkable degree, as Kenneth Galbraith has so ably recorded. However, both American and Scottish elements had one common characteristic in Macdonald's day, namely, their leaning toward Reform principles. It was their adoption of "Clear Grit" ideas in the fifties that stirred Macdonald's ire. Their demand for a widely extended suffrage, the secret ballot and a broad extension of the elective principle indicated their belief that the United States represented the ultimate form of democracy. One man was as good as another. This phase of Canadian politics corresponded to Jacksonian democracy or the later Lincoln republicanism. This challenge to Macdonald's political views came from a characteristically agrarian community. Geography and the historical background combined to explain its uneasy, restless disposition.

Colonel John Graves Simcoe, the first governor of Upper Canada, was an admirer of monarchy, aristocracy and the established Church of England. He aimed to set up in the Canadian wilderness a replica of these three institutions which he regarded as the most perfect that man's mind had ever conceived. Their acceptance and adoption might, he believed, lead to the reunion of the separated states with the mother country. To this end he welcomed settlers from the republic and granted them land on their taking the oath of allegiance. The writings of British travellers who visited the province before the War of 1812 abound with references to the "Yankee" character of the common people and the prevalence of "Yankee" manners and habits of speech, even among those of other than American origin.

Governor Simcoe might dislike the "Yankee" twang and the crude manners of his American settlers but he must have known and appreciated the fact that they were experienced North American farmers. To some observers their methods seemed inefficient and shiftless but their energy and practical ability were quite as noticeable. The American settler knew how to clear the heavily wooded land, build himself a log house and barn, harness any nearby watercourse and provide for himself and neighbours a sawmill or a grist-mill. He was so adept at making satisfactory tools that American scythes had a distinct superiority over those brought from abroad.

Simcoe must also have realized that the American immigrants, whether Loyalist or non-Loyalist, had recently passed through a great social, economic and political revolution which they had heard discussed in its every aspect. Whether they approved or disapproved of the outcome, they had been subjected to such unsettling ideas as the equality of men, freedom of religion and hostility to any special privilege. These liberalizing concepts, North American in character, permeated the thinking of the Upper Canadian community and contributed to the unrest and desire for change which affected the province during its first half-century.

Simcoe's admiration for monarchy did not greatly trouble the American immigrants, many of whom had earlier lived under King George III. Nor was the concept of a republic as yet deeply rooted in their minds. With the prospect of ownership of good land it mattered little to them whether they were under a royal governor or under the appointed representative of the republic. As for aristocracy, they were fortunately spared its creation. Simcoe could not find enough "gentlemen" in the province to set up an elite class on the British model.

Much more dangerous for the future peace of the province was the claim, accepted by Simcoe and his successors, that the Church of England was "established" in Upper Canada just as it was in England. Establishment meant financial support, a close connection with government and a primacy over other church bodies. This conflicted with American ideas of freedom of religion and special privilege. It became one of the basic grievances of the Rebellion era and continued to bedevil provincial politics even beyond that date.

For more than a generation after its official entry into Upper Canada the Church of England was a stranger to the scattered settlers. Its growth in numbers and influence was retarded by the pioneer's dislike of ritual and by its claims to be established. On the other hand, the missionaries sent in by American Protestant church bodies, Methodist, Presbyterian and Baptist, more truly met the religious needs of the province. Moving about on horseback, they reached the population as no settled ministry could have done. American settlers also had a broad concept of what was meant by freedom of religion – not merely the right of believers to worship in their own manner without interference of any kind but also the right of the individual to change from one church body to another for any reason that might appear good in his eyes. This American freedom of church affiliation contrasted sharply with the lifelong adherence to one belief commonly observed in older lands. Travellers in Upper Canada frequently noted this early version of modern ecumenicism.

When war came in 1812, disturbing the hitherto comparatively peaceful relations between Upper Canada and the United States, it was inevitable that the province would be the chief battleground. With a population of little more than 100,000, four-fifths of whom were Americans, the government had reason for worry and the American settlers were themselves placed in a difficult situation. Some left the province and went back to the United States, others were expelled by the authorities, and a few were openly traitorous. There was disloyalty even in the Assembly and two members were formally expelled in 1814. Three years of war left deep feelings of resentment against the United States in the minds of Upper Canadians and the process of Americanization received a severe check.

The reaction to peace when the Treaty of Ghent was signed differed as between the antagonists. In the United States it did much to dispel the lingering colonial complex and uncertainty in foreign affairs. Freed from external entanglements, the republic now turned to the opening up and development of its West.

Six new states entered the Union in the first seven years after the war, five of them carved from frontier territory. By 1820 the new West had 27 per cent of the country's total population. Upper Canada, on the other hand, suffering considerable material damage in a war for which it could see no reason and which it had certainly not itself provoked, was now in a mood to demand reform of abuses under which it had been suffering. Political groups began to emerge. Further immigration from the United States had been forbidden at the end of the war and Canadian businessmen were aggrieved over the drying up of land sales. Of the great trek to the American West only a trickle came into Upper Canada though this trickle was of a superior type, including as it did men with capital and technical skills, also professional men such as doctors who had hitherto been few in number. The majority of the physicians entering Upper Canada at this time had received their training at the Fairfield Medical School in Herkimer County, New York State.

The outbreak of political violence in 1837-38 registered the pent-up feelings of a considerable element among the common people. It was really an epoch in the struggle between the democratic forces of the Upper Canada frontier and the official effort to impose a class society and a privileged established church. Unfortunately, the American people in their own land largely mistook the character of the uprising, regarding it as a definite struggle for independence. This mistaken idea led to the rise of "Patriot" movements in the mid-western states which by invasions and raids along the border sought to free the "enslaved Canadians." Frequent alarms, necessitating the rousing of the militia and other defensive measures, disquieted the province for more than a year.

The background for the widespread unrest in the province lay in the abuses of the government land policies, in the character and actions of the Family Compact at the capital and lesser local compacts elsewhere, and in the claims of the state-supported church. Permeating all was the democracy introduced by the early settlers. These factors acting together produced a Reform party after the War of 1812 which battled for its claims in the Assembly and on the hustings at election times. What is not always realized is that there was no general uprising in Upper Canada. Though eastern districts were subjected to "Patriot" invasion they themselves had little part in the attempt to overthrow the provincial government at York. In the London

District there was a secondary uprising under Dr. Charles Duncombe while elsewhere unrest showed itself in forms ranging from plain fist fighting to the passing of mere resolutions or refusals even to protest. Lesser known features of the uprising were the arrests and imprisonment of hundreds of persons against most of whom no charge could be proven, senseless militia raids on Quaker settlements and the use of Indians in tracking down Duncombe's scattered contingent. Canadian-American relations were much worsened by the uprisings in the British provinces, partly because of the widespread suspicion that the Washington administration condoned the "Patriot" threats and invasions. The inheritance of anti-American prejudice from the War of 1812 was added to and strengthened by the events of 1837-38. On the other hand Upper Canada gained a large accession of British population during the twenties and early thirties when the British government was able to release the masses of people carefully conserved for "cannon fodder" during the Napoleonic Wars. The province took on a more British colouring as the American tinge faded.

The British government, alarmed by uprisings in both Upper and Lower Canada, hastened to make inquiry as to the causes and Lord Durham was commissioned to make the necessary investigations. Though he spent only a few months in Canada he proposed a union of the two provinces and the adoption of the principle of responsible government in their future administration. United Canada's legislators gradually, but not painlessly, learned what responsible government meant during a decade in which American influence upon Canadian affairs was lessened by the preoccupation of the republic with the expansion of slavery into the new territories admitted into the Union and the problems associated with this movement.

Closely related to the American religious ideas and practices which entered Upper Canada in its pioneer era was a later contagion of interest in the humanitarian and moral reform movements which agitated the republic from the thirties. In the northern states almost every department of life was being examined and given a new evaluation. The old Puritan theology was fading away and in its place there was a rising interest in such matters as temperance, prison reform, care of the insane, labour conditions, education and anti-slavery. National societies interested in such fields were increasing their memberships by thousands yearly.

Temperance was one of the first such moral issues to enter Upper Canada and received enthusiastic Methodist support. In the early thirties there were twenty such societies with a membership of ten thousand. Better treatment of the insane and prisoners in jails had been proposed as early as 1836 by Dr. Charles Duncombe after a visit to New York State but not until 1850 were his recommendations carried out. His ideas on prison reform received attention earlier when an experienced American prison administrator was appointed to supervise the first provincial prison established at Kingston.

The anti-slavery movement in the United States was of particular interest for Western Ontario because, ever since the War of 1812, fugitives from the Southern slave states had been making their way to freedom in the province. When Congress passed the infamous Fugitive Slave Act in 1850 the Negro migration to Upper Canada became a torrent and friends of the fugitives at once organized the Anti-slavery Society of Canada. This body functioned until the Civil War ended and slavery in the republic disappeared.

Public education, so important for the welfare of any people, made little advance before the period of the rebellion. Governor Simcoe had dreamed of a university but thought little of the education of the children of common folk. Nor did the Assembly produce any worthwhile measures. As for the Church of England, it continued to seek full control of education. No real advance came until 1844 when the Rev. Egerton Ryerson, Methodist leader and educator, was appointed Superintendent of Education for Upper Canada. Ryerson, who was well acquainted with United States educational practices, made his investigations chiefly in the British Isles and in European countries. His findings were embodied in the Common School Act of 1846. From the United States was drawn the guiding principle that every child was entitled to an education provided by the state. This aim, Ryerson felt, could only be realized through the provision of well-qualified teachers, suitable buildings and equipment, regular inspection and uniform textbooks. Ryerson's inclusion in his system of various American ideas was questioned but when secondary education was also established in 1853 it was noticeably modelled on the American example. Ryerson's findings and methods continued to dominate the education of the province for the better part of the next century.

The fifties and early sixties saw the development of the

movement earlier suggested by Lord Durham of a union of all the British provinces in North America. Canadian historians have at times seemed reluctant to admit that the United States could have had anything to do with bringing about Confederation. Today, however, it is generally recognized that fear of the course the United States might follow at the end of its civil struggle was probably one of the greatest influences in bringing the British provinces together in a new nation, the Dominion of Canada.

By 1865 both the United States and Canada were moving into new phases in their history. Reconstruction in the United States after the Civil War, and the creation of a transcontinental dominion and a national economy in Canada introduced new issues into the historical evolution of each country. In the changed conditions that prevailed after 1867, the social institutions and attitudes of a region such as Western Ontario played their part in determining the character of a greater whole.

Inspiration for the writing of this volume came from the late Professor James Thompson Shotwell, long a member of the Department of History at Columbia University and for almost fifty years one of the most dedicated protagonists of internationalism in the United States. His death at the age of 90 occurred in July, 1965. From 1917, when he became an adviser to President Woodrow Wilson, Professor Shotwell was closely associated with the presidential problems of war and with the ensuing problems of peace. He was present as an adviser at the Paris peace negotiations and during the next eight years arranged for the writing by the most competent authorities, many of them cabinet ministers and statesmen, of the 150-volume *Economic and Social History of the World War*, a project sponsored by the Carnegie Endowment for International Peace.

When this gigantic task was nearing completion Dr. Shotwell suggested an examination by Canadian and American scholars of the international relations of Canada and the United States. In 150 volumes there had been chronicled the ambitions, the jealousies and the collisions of European nations, culminating in the two most disastrous wars in all history. Canadian-American relations had long been under discussion in both countries and it was Dr. Shotwell's belief that an inquiry into their past economic and social relations might prevent future misunderstandings and bad judgments. Twenty-five volumes, of which this was one, were comprised in this second Carnegie-sponsored enterprise. Dr. Shotwell had a personal interest in the volume dealing with Western Ontario because this area had been the home of his ancestors as well as the scene of his own youth. The occasion of this reprinting of *Western Ontario and the American Frontier* seems an appropriate time to pay tribute to the memory of a great citizen of Canada and the United States.

The text which follows is unchanged from that of the original edition of *Western Ontario and the American Frontier*. All the notes appearing in the original edition are reproduced here. The Author's Preface in the 1941 edition of the work has been replaced with a new Foreword, and two maps in the first edition have been omitted. The Bibliography has been revised to add material on the subject published since 1941.

FRED LANDON
London, Ontario
February, 1967

1: Two Experiments in State Building

The great mutual blessings of superior soil and of climate, British freedom, British union and the experienced loyalty of those who inhabit this province will speedily raise it up to an unexampled height of prosperity and permanent security.

—JOHN GRAVES SIMCOE (1795)

The movement that carried American civilization beyond the Appalachians was essentially individualistic. . . . In the main, the great West was conquered by individuals or, to speak more accurately, by families.

—CHARLES A. BEARD

On July 15, 1788, at Fort Harmar, the present site of Marietta, Ohio, Governor Arthur St. Clair read his credentials and proclaimed the new government of the Northwest Territory. On July 8, 1792, at the little town of Kingston, Lieutenant-Governor John Graves Simcoe took the oath of office and inaugurated for the new Province of Upper Canada a constitution which he described as "the most excellent that was ever bestowed upon a colony."

These ceremonies set in motion two experiments in colonial government and state-building, carried on in areas that were contiguous, possessing many common physical characteristics and separated only by a chain of navigable lakes and rivers, the use of which was shared. Into these areas, one American and the other British, there came during the next quarter-century large migrations of people from the older states of the Republic and some people from across the sea. Between 1788 and the outbreak of the war in 1812 the population of the Northwest Territory increased from 6,000 to 300,000. In the same period the population of Upper Canada grew to 75,000, of which number about one-fifth were Loyalists and their children, a lesser number British immigrants and their children, and the remainder non-Loyalist Americans. Apart from the Loyalist movement into Upper Canada after the Revolutionary War, it was chiefly one common westward movement of land-seekers which peopled both the British province and the neighbouring American territory.

The presence within the province of these two American elements greatly influenced the earlier history of Upper Canada.

Records of Loyalist numbers are inaccurate and confusing since some of the later arrivals from the United States, with no valid claim, found it profitable to pose as victims of republican injustice in order to participate in the material benefits provided for Loyalists and their children. Including those who settled along the north shore of Lake Erie and on the Detroit River there were probably not more than 12,000 Loyalists at the turn of the century. Immigration between 1790 and 1812 was chiefly from the United States, but in this period it was free land which was the chief attraction and the oath of allegiance was often an unimportant and lightly regarded prelude to its possession. Upper Canada was essentially an American community under British law and British forms of government down to the period of the war with the United States.

The Northwest Territory comprised the great area lying between the western boundary of Pennsylvania and the Mississippi River, northward from the Ohio River to the waters of the Great Lakes. The population which flowed into the territory in its early formative period settled chiefly on the banks of the Ohio and its tributaries. It was a population of diverse origins, drawn from New England, the Middle States, and the South, as well as from the backwoods of Virginia, Pennsylvania, and Kentucky, common folk of the older states and including many revolutionary veterans. It was a population imbued with democratic ideas and impatient to put those ideas to the test of experience. At the beginning, however, it was under an administration not unlike that of a Crown colony, though there was an assurance of autonomy whenever the population became sufficiently numerous.

The western portion of the Province of Quebec, which after 1791 received the name Upper Canada, consisted of the area between the Ottawa River and Lake Huron, northward from the St. Lawrence River and Lakes Ontario and Erie. Early settlement was confined to lands along the southern boundary waters. The Loyalists were established chiefly on the St. Lawrence and in the Niagara district, though there were some also at Long Point on the north shore of Lake Erie, and on the Detroit River. For a brief period they formed a majority of the population but were eventually outnumbered by others from the United States. The western section of the new province received only a minority of the Loyalists but it attracted a majority of the later American immigrants, thereby developing a viewpoint more democratic than that of the eastern section and in its social and economic conditions becoming more akin to the region to the south. The Loyalist families tended to view the later immigrants with a condescension based upon an assumption of their own superiority. They felt that they were an aristocracy, even if they were not wealthy. They had been persecuted and they had kept the faith; therefore such offices and emoluments as they received were but the payment of a debt. They tended to be conservative, and in the more select groups were often reactionary towards political change. Their presence in the midst of the restless land-hungry immigrants contributed to the unrest which prevailed in the period before 1812.

It is significant that to the new Province of Upper Canada, originally created as a home for Loyalists, there was appointed as its first Lieutenant-Governor a man of that same type which in the older colonies had contributed so largely to the spirit of independence. Had fate placed Simcoe in one of the earlier colonial administrations he would have been found contending valiantly for the King's authority against all local claims and pretensions. In his official position in Upper Canada there was something almost childish and confiding in his belief that every jot and tittle of the British constitution should have its place in the life of the frontier community. His duty, as he conceived it, was to establish "on immutable foundations" His Majesty's American Empire in Canada, and to interpret the constitution provided for the province, "the very image and transcript of that of Great Britain by which she has long established and secured to her subjects as much freedom and happiness as it is possible to be enjoyed under the subordination necessary to civilized society."

Simcoe had served in the Revolutionary War and amid much mediocrity of command had displayed both ability and energy. Steadfastly devoted to the British cause he had spared himself not at all and when he was paroled to England after the surrender of Cornwallis his health was much impaired. Quiet and rest in the homeland brought recovery and for ten years he lived the life of a country gentleman, developing his small estate, participating in local affairs and in 1790 taking a seat in Parliament as the member for St. Mawes, Cornwall. During the first session which he attended at Westminster the Canada Act was passed, making provision for the division of Quebec into the two provinces of Upper and Lower Canada. Soon thereafter he was appointed to the office of Lieutenant-Governor of the new western Canadian province.[1]

The appointment stirred his imagination. An empire in America had been lost. Might not that empire be recovered? This was the high ideal to which he proposed to devote his energies. Given the opportunity, he would create in Upper Canada a colony so conspicuous by its freedom, by the purity of its laws, by its gradations of society, and by its generally prosperous and happy condition that the lost colonies would be drawn back as prodigal sons to seek a place within the British family. Writing to Dundas, before leaving for Canada, he said: "It is in the hope of being instrumental to the Reunion of the Empire, by sowing the Seeds of a vigorous Colony that I prefer the station I am appointed to and its fair prospects to any post in His Majesty's Dominions of whatever Emolument."[2] To Sir Joseph Banks he wrote: "I would die by more Indian torture to restore my King and his Family to their just Inheritance and to give my country that fair and natural accession of Power which an Union with their Brethren could not fail to bestow and render permanent."[3]

Simcoe's general attitude towards the United States was characterized less by hatred than by contempt. His outlook was coloured by his prejudices and by the frustration of his hopes during the war. He believed that incompetent generalship had brought defeat to England and had permitted a cause to triumph that had neither reason nor justice. Those who had advocated independence and guided the "wild and phrenetic democracy" were, in his opinion, traitors. Washington he once described as "among the most treacherous of mankind and most hostile to the Interests of Great Britain," and he expressed the wish that "with adequate force and on a just occasion" he might meet him face to face.[4] The Revolution was "the most scandalous and swin-

---

[1] There are biographies of Simcoe by David B. Read (Toronto, 1890), Duncan Campbell Scott (Toronto, 1905), and William Renwick Riddell (Toronto, 1926). E. A. Cruickshank edited the correspondence and allied documents relating to Simcoe's administration of Upper Canada, published by the Ontario Historical Society in five volumes (Toronto, 1923-31). These are hereafter described as *Simcoe Papers*.

[2] Simcoe to Dundas, August 26, 1791, *Simcoe Papers*, I, 53. Henry Dundas was Secretary of State for Home Affairs.

[3] Simcoe to Banks, January 8, 1791, *Simcoe Papers*, I, 17. Sir Joseph Banks was President of the Royal Society and a liberal patron of science.

[4] Simcoe to Portland, December 20, 1794, *Simcoe Papers*, III, 233. The Duke of Portland had by this time become Secretary of State for Home Affairs.

dling transaction that has disgraced the annals of mankind," the Americans were "at once a most avaricious and ambitious people" and their leaders "totally destitute of Public or Private Morality." He even played with the idea that Upper Canada and its Indian allies might have entered into a "compact" with the forces of the Whisky Rebellion in western Pennyslvania and thereby have presented "a most systematical and formidable opposition to the United States."[5]

Mingled with this contempt for the government of the United States was his apprehension of war between England and the Republic. He was much exercised over the defenceless character of the province, particularly the western portion which he regarded as the more important and more valuable section. It was here that he proposed to place his capital and he brought forward from time to time elaborate schemes for forts, blockhouses, naval stations, and other aids to security. La Rochefoucault, the French nobleman who visited Simcoe in 1795, says of this interest: "He is acquainted with the military history of all countries; no hillock catches his eye without exciting in his mind the idea of a fort, which might be constructed on the spot; and with the construction of this fort he associates the plan of operations for a campaign, especially of that which is to lead him to Philadelphia."[6]

Simcoe was a soldier by profession but he had remarkably clearcut views on many matters of economic character, and particularly as to the place of the fur trade in the province. This deeply entrenched and monopolistic business, with a long experience in dealing with governments as well as with Indian hunters, was generally regarded in official circles as the basis of the country's prosperity. But Simcoe did not think so. "I consider the Fur Trade on its present foundation to be of no use whatever, to the Colony of Upper Canada,"[7] he informed Dundas, and in various communications to the home authorities he set forth plainly the reasons for his opposition. The fur trade was a monopoly, necessarily so because of the huge capital investment that was required. It added nothing to the agricul-

---

[5] Simcoe to Portland, December 20, 1794, *Simcoe Papers*, III, 233.

[6] *The 13th Report of the Bureau of Archives*, Ontario (1917), contains that portion of La Rochefoucault's journal which relates to Canada, translated and edited by W. R. Riddell. See also the notes to chapter XIX of the biography of Simcoe by Riddell.

[7] Simcoe to Dundas, April 28, 1792, *Simcoe Papers*, I, 141.

tural population; indeed, the fur trade was opposed to settlement. It was demoralizing to the social life of a colony and it could never be the staple of a settled country such as Upper Canada, in Simcoe's opinion, was destined to be.

Simcoe planned to exclude the fur trade so far as possible from that portion of the province which lay between the Great Lakes, restricting its field of activity to more distant northwestern regions. Upper Canada was to be a land of homes, not the preserve of Montreal fur traders. He realized that there would continue to be some hunting and fur trading even in the areas destined for settlement; very well, let the trading be confined to the towns, to which the Indian hunter would bring his furs, "become his own carrier," and "be more industrious in his hunts." Wheat, not furs, was to be the staple that would support Upper Canada's population and bring prosperity. Through Simcoe's correspondence during the five years which he spent in Upper Canada may be traced his steadily growing interest in agriculture as the basis of material well-being in the province and his gratification at finding others sharing his belief.

The considerable space devoted to military matters in Simcoe's correspondence and papers, and the fact also that he was a professional soldier, has tended to obscure his constant concern for the economic development of the province placed under his care. Whatever place military matters might have in his mind, they were never an end in themselves but only means to an end. The prosperity and well-being of the British province was his responsibility, and he desired that in due time he might make good report of his stewardship. It is easy to see that he had no real appreciation of the strength of the democratic forces in the United States, and he would have been horrified at the thought that Upper Canada might ever be similarly contaminated. He had in view another future for Upper Canada, namely, that it should "dilate itself into an increasing and majestic support of the British Empire."[8] This destiny was to be achieved through measures chiefly economic in character: by increasing the agricultural population, by the growth of towns as centres of trade, by opening up roads and other means of communication, and particularly by the development of the St. Lawrence waterway, thereby making Upper Canada the channel for British trade with western portions of the United States and

[8] Simcoe to Dundas, August 12, 1792, *Simcoe Papers*, I, 50.

even with the Spanish possessions beyond the Mississippi. But in his plans time was the important element. The control of western trade, if not secured now, might be lost forever, and so through his official correspondence runs a note of impatience, and eventually of disappointment and frustration, over the failure of the home government to seize the opportunities for commercial domination of important sections of the United States.

In contrast to Lieutenant-Governor Simcoe, let us view Arthur St. Clair, who was Governor of the Northwest Territory during the whole of Simcoe's régime in Upper Canada. St. Clair was born in Scotland and became an ensign in the British army in 1757. He served with Amherst in Canada but resigned from the army in 1762 and purchased a large estate in western Pennsylvania. When the Revolution came he espoused the American cause but had an unfortunate military record. After the war he was a member of the Continental Congress in the years 1785-87 and President of that body in the latter year. At the creation of the Northwest Territory he was appointed Governor and served in that office until 1802 when he was removed by Jefferson. He was described by Jacob Burnet as "plain and simple in his dress and equipage, open and frank in his manners, and accessible to persons of every rank," in these respects exhibiting, says Burnet, "a striking contrast with his secretary, Colonel Sargent."[9]

St. Clair came to his new duties in 1788 with considerable prestige as a former President of the Continental Congress, but he was not generally popular. Some of the difficulties which attended his régime may be attributed to his frequent and prolonged absences from the territory and to the highly dictatorial manner of Secretary Winthrop Sargent who was left in charge during these absences. Sargent in 1798 computed that St. Clair had not been present in the territory during more than five and a half years out of nine. These absences drew a sharp reprimand from the Secretary of State in 1794 and a very plain intimation that he should attend more strictly to his duties.[10] During the first seven years of his governorship Indian problems gave St. Clair constant concern while in the later period he found himself in conflict with the rising democracy of the Northwest which in the end pushed him aside.

[9] Jacob Burnet, *Notes on the Early Settlement of the North-Western Territory* (New York, 1847), pp. 374-5.

[10] Randolph to St. Clair, Philadelphia, May 15, 1794, *Territorial Papers of the United States* (Washington), II (1934), 479. See also pages 647-8 for Sargent's tabulated record of St. Clair's absences.

Compared with the unceasing activity of Simcoe in Upper Canada and the highly paternal attitude which he assumed towards the province and the people under his jurisdiction, there was a more casual character about the administration of the Northwest Territory under St. Clair. In the earlier years Marietta was the seat of government, but St. Clair and Sargent exercised the executive functions wherever they happened to be. There was no designated place of deposit for official papers and Sargent was accustomed to take necessary records, and at times even the great seal, about with him. Because of St. Clair's frequent absences the more distant parts of the territory were left unvisited. Only once did either the Governor or Secretary journey to the Michigan region, the recorded visit being that of Sargent to Detroit in 1796 to organize the government after the departure of the British garrison. Administration could not fail to suffer in effectiveness by such absent control since frontier conditions so frequently produced situations demanding prompt and intelligent action.

The form of government for the Northwest Territory was determined by the Ordinance of 1787, which, with the Land Ordinance of 1785, formed the basis of this American colonial experiment. There were to be three definite stages in the development of the territory. In the beginning there was to be a temporary administration, consisting of a governor, a secretary, and three judges, all appointed by Congress. In the second stage, when there were five thousand free male adults, a local legislature might be elected which could make laws, while representation would be given in Congress by admission of a delegate who might take part in debates but have no vote. The final stage was to come with the growth of population to sixty thousand in any portion of the territory, which would then become a state equal in powers with the original states. It was contemplated that from the Northwest Territory, might eventually come five new states. The hardy American stock which entered the territory did not take kindly to the autocratic government under which they were to serve their apprenticeship, and when drafting their new state constitutions they repudiated its chief features. In place of the restricted suffrage of territorial days came manhood suffrage. The governors became mere figure-heads "with scarcely power to do more than draw the meagre salaries constitutionally assigned to them" and courts and judges were brought under the thumb of the legislatures.[11] Three states in which such democratic ideas prevailed were in existence by 1818.

In Upper Canada there was set up by the terms of the Canada Act a system of government patterned outwardly as closely as possible after that of Great Britain. The Crown had its counterpart in the appointed Lieutenant-Governor, the House of Lords in the appointed Legislative Council, and the House of Commons in the elected Legislative Assembly. The attempt to reproduce the institutions of the older land went even beyond this, however. It was proposed to create a colonial aristocracy by conferring titles which might elevate the holders to hereditary membership in the Legislative Council, thereby emphasizing further the similarity between the Council and the House of Lords. A more dangerous provision in the Canada Act was that which contemplated the setting up in Upper Canada of the Established Church of England and the granting to it of privileges which would not be given to other religious bodies. In this concern for a religious establishment may be found one of the more striking differences between the British and American experiments in government. The provision for hereditary titles proved harmless since no one other than Simcoe appears to have viewed it seriously. The provision for a church establishment became, however, in after years a most prolific source of political contention and did incalculable harm to the very church body which it was intended to aid. Any such religious turmoil and bitterness was avoided in the Northwest Territory by the provision in the federal constitution that Congress should "make no law respecting an establishment of religion or prohibiting the free exercise thereof," and by the first article of the Ordinance of 1787 which guaranteed freedom of religion.

The system of government established in 1791 for Upper Canada lasted for exactly half a century, but within fifteen years after its inauguration there were visible indications of unrest arising out of the autocratic and aristocratic nature of the administration. Though the war with the United States, with its demands for unity in defence, quieted the unrest for a time, it broke out with new intensity after 1815 and grew in volume year by year until the armed uprising under William Lyon Mackenzie at the end of 1837. That dramatic incident, coming in the first year of the reign of the young Queen Victoria,

[11] See T. C. Pease, "The Ordinance of 1787," *Mississippi Valley Historical Review*, XXV (September, 1938), 167-80.

focused British official attention upon the affairs of Upper Canada, prompted an official inquiry into the causes of unrest, and led to an experiment in self-government that has since profoundly influenced the development of the British Empire.

The American experiment was worked out in a shorter time and with more spectacular results than those that flowed from the Canada Act. Ohio was the first section of the Northwest Territory to be organized as a state. It was admitted in March, 1803. The Territory of Michigan was set off from the Territory of Indiana in January, 1805, while Indiana and Illinois were admitted to the Union in 1816 and 1818 respectively. Michigan attained statehood in 1837, leaving only the most westerly portion of the Old Northwest to be organized. This was done in 1848 when Wisconsin entered as a state and the fragment that still remained was incorporated in Minnesota Territory. The rapidity of the growth of population in these western states and territories during the early nineteenth century was striking. Ohio, with a population of 45,365 in 1800, grew to 230,760 by 1810 and to 580,434 by 1820.[12] Development of settlements in the West was so rapid that it seemed to threaten the economic and political power of the older communities in the East.

The states which were formed from the Northwest Territory came into the Union on terms of complete equality with the older states. Each was self-governing in all those matters which by the federal constitution were assigned to state control, and each, by its representation in Congress, had a share in the shaping and control of national affairs. In 1828 these frontier states helped to send to Washington the first frontier President in the person of Andrew Jackson. They had their particular local reasons for supporting him, but their support also had in it elements of revolt against the monopoly of control in national affairs by eastern leaders. These western people were citizens of states but they were also citizens in a larger national union and could influence its affairs. In Upper Canada there was no similar larger allegiance. England was far away and nothing that was done in Upper Canada could have any influence upon its national affairs. Interest centred, therefore, upon the little provincial capital at York where, for more than a generation, the Governor's party and the reform groups strove for mastery. And because the stage was so small, political bitterness was the more intense.

[12] *Statistical Abstract of the United States* (Washington, 1911), p. 40.

2: The Early American Immigration

In the Upper Province the population is very scanty, and, with the exception of the Eastern District, are chiefly of American extraction. These settlers have been suffered to introduce themselves in such numbers that in most parts they form the majority, and, in many, almost the sole population.

—COLONEL EDWARD BAYNES (1814)

For twenty years after the conquest of Canada the western portion of the present Province of Ontario, save the Detroit River settlement, remained an unexploited and little known portion of the King's domain. Between 1763 and 1774 it formed a part of the closed Indian territory into which settlers might not enter. Imperial legislation in 1774 incorporated it in the Province of Quebec, the boundaries of that province being then extended to the Mississippi and Ohio rivers. When peace came in 1783, ending the struggle between England and her revolting colonies, the cession of the Northwest to the independent states reduced Quebec's area, the new western limits being Lake Huron, the St. Clair River, Lake St. Clair, and the Detroit River. The peninsula lying between Georgian Bay, Lake Huron, and Lake Erie now became the most westerly portion of Quebec and remained so until the creation in 1791 of the new Province of Upper Canada. Although the treaty of 1783 had provided for the surrender of the Northwest, England retained her hold on Detroit and other strategic trading posts until 1796. For thirteen years, therefore, there was the anomalous political situation of British garrisons within American territory, even though from 1788 an American government was established in the same area. Jay's Treaty ended this singular state of affairs, and when British troops and officials withdrew from Detroit and the other posts which had been occupied a chapter in North American history was closed. There was no longer reasonable ground for the hope, hitherto held by Simcoe, that some turn of fortune might undo the treaty of 1783 and re-establish British rule south of the Lakes.

The first serious attempt at settlements in the new Province of Upper Canada was at Niagara. The corps of Loyalists known as Butler's Rangers, named after the commander, Lieutenant-Colonel John Butler, wintered at Niagara between 1778 and

1783 and their presence and protection attracted Loyalist refugees and other newcomers. The necessity of supplying both garrison and refugees with food, as well as the need of some definite policy with respect to settlement, was forced upon the administration at Quebec. In the summer of 1780 it was decided that settlers should hold their lands free of rental, that they should be provisioned for a year, and that they should receive necessary seed and implements. Surplus produce over and above their own needs was to be sold to the garrison at prices which the commander would fix. By the end of the year settlement on this basis had begun and a return made in August, 1782, showed sixteen families, numbering sixty-eight persons. When peace came in 1783 and the Rangers were disbanded, a majority of them elected to remain at Niagara so that in the summer of 1784 there were two hundred and fifty families, a number which increased considerably during the next few months as expelled Loyalists continued to arrive from New York and Pennsylvania. A much larger number of Loyalists, however, was placed at this time on lands set aside for them along the St. Lawrence River and the Bay of Quinte.

Apart from the regulations above mentioned the government took no further immediate interest in the unsettled western section of the province beyond the appointment of a few officials. It was of more pressing importance to care for the large Loyalist migration now arriving in the eastern portion of the province. A few individuals made their own way into the wilderness lying between the Detroit and the Niagara rivers, and the Indian population was largely increased when the Six Nations, who had retained their allegiance to the King, were settled on lands along the Grand River.

Lieutenant-Governor Simcoe, early in his term of office, manifested a particular interest in the peninsula which today is known as Western Ontario. When the Upper Canada Assembly had concluded its first session and the business incident thereto had been cleared away, Simcoe journeyed westward to the Detroit River. Travelling in the winter months involved hardships but he was eager and enthusiastic. Leaving Niagara on February 4, 1793, he and his party arrived at Detroit two weeks later and were again at Niagara by March 10. Major E. B. Littlehales, Simcoe's military secretary, kept a journal in which incidents of the journey and some of the Governor's observations and opinions were recorded.[1] The country through which the party passed was, for the most part, uninhabited. Along the north shore of Lake Erie there were individual settlers, but inland was still a thick and tangled forest through which Indian trails formed the only means of travel. Detroit, founded more than ninety years earlier, retained much of its French character and was still an important link in the fur trade. On the Thames River, seventy-five miles east of Detroit, were Moravian missionaries with their Indian charges, exiles from the new Republic.

Simcoe's interest during this journey centred not chiefly upon Detroit but upon the River La Tranche (Thames) beside or upon whose waters he travelled for some distance during both stages of the journey. While at Montreal, prior to entering his new province, the Governor had been interested in noting the course of this river upon the maps which he consulted. Its branches, uniting in a single stream at the very centre of the peninsula, stretched far inland in two directions. No decision had yet been made as to a site for the provincial capital, and even before he saw the river itself Simcoe had come to the conclusion that the forks, where the branches united, would be an excellent situation for the seat of government. It was nearly thirty miles inland from Lake Erie, which, although a handicap to communications, would be of military advantage in the event of an American invasion. The branches of the river, leading off to remote districts, would facilitate the extension of the Indian trade, while the main stream, flowing into Lake St. Clair, would be navigable for small boats for a considerable distance from its mouth. Major Littlehales records the marked satisfaction with which Simcoe found his preconceived views of the river's advantages confirmed by actual inspection.[2]

Simcoe's plans embraced more than the location of the provincial capital. He fixed upon "the head of the carrying place between Lake Ontario and the Thames" (the site of the present city of Woodstock) for a town which would bear the name Oxford. Near the mouth of the Thames he planned to establish a second town, Chatham, a sort of sub-capital and to serve also as a naval and ship-building centre. A town plot was later surveyed at Chatham, lots granted to several persons of unquestioned loyalty, and work begun on several small gunboats.

[1] *Simcoe Papers*, I, 288-93.
[2] *Ibid.*, I, 292-3.

Chatham must have been a busy little place for a year or two, but when Simcoe left the province it was soon abandoned and tradition says that some of the wooden boats which were left in an unfinished state were burned by pioneer settlers in order to salvage the iron. More than a generation passed before there was further activity at either Chatham or the Forks.

Simcoe remained in Canada but four years, yet in that brief period he placed his impress sharply upon the province and its institutions. To his credit may be placed the setting up of the new government, the promotion of much useful legislation, the initiation of road building, and, at all times, a deep concern for the general welfare of the inhabitants. His ardent imperialism and his reverence for the British constitution were such that at times he became almost lyrical in his correspondence. Upper Canada, as he pictured it, was to be a modern British province and its people model colonists. Fate seemed to have been kind in providing him with such hand-picked Britishers as the Loyalists. With this nucleus, setting the tone and temper, the future seemed assured. What Simcoe did not perceive was that his infant colony was set down in the very heart of American population movements and political developments which would exercise continuous and pervading influence upon its future growth. Even before he left the province in 1796 these influences were apparent. International boundaries were no obstacles to people who had crossed mountains and forded rivers seeking a better land in which to live. By 1796 the proportion of Loyalists to the whole population was decreasing, ten years later they were in a minority. Along the St. Lawrence River they were influential but in the western district, in the peninsula which Simcoe regarded so highly, the Loyalist element was scarcely noticeable amidst the diversity of people who came in to take up land or engage in trade. Travellers who visited both sides of the boundary waters saw little difference between the two peoples.

Simcoe realized that in the working out of his plans for a steady accession of population the United States must be the main source from which to draw. There was little prospect of early immigration from the British Isles apart from half-pay officers and some disbanded soldiers, since the common folk, even if minded to go out to the wilderness of Upper Canada, could not do so without public or private assistance. Though England's population was growing at a greater rate after 1790 than in the preceding decade, emigration was not thought of as an outlet for the surplus, poor rates being still considered the remedy for pauperism. Moreover, by the time Simcoe had entered upon his Canadian duties wars had begun in Europe that were to last for more than twenty years, an era in which the home government had no wish to see its population diminished by emigration. The United States became, therefore, the main source from which people might be drawn, and the movement of American settlers into the province which began in Simcoe's time continued unabated until the outbreak of war in 1812.

Even before Simcoe's arrival in Upper Canada there had been indications that in the westward movement following the Revolutionary War Upper Canada would share with the Ohio River valley in additions of population. As early as 1789 the provincial Land Boards reported that people were coming in from the United States to apply for lands "without any intention to settle them, but merely to make money by the sale of them."[3] The Land Boards exercised their own judgment, however, in admitting Americans. The minutes of the Niagara Board show that examination was made into the loyalty and more particularly into the character of all such persons as appeared before them. Those approved were required to take the oath of allegiance. Probably few immigrants had any scruples in this matter for consciousness of American nationality was weak in the early years after the Revolution.

The anonymous writer of "Canadian Letters,"[4] describing a tour through Upper and Lower Canada in 1792-3, says that in the summer of 1793 great numbers of people emigrated to Upper Canada, principally from Vermont, Massachusetts, and the neighbourhood of the Mohawk River: "A proclamation of the Governor's was their inducement to come in. It can not be supposed that all these people were satisfied with the proffers that were made them. Many were discontented. The Governor was aware that had he granted lands in the proportions required, it would have rendered these persons not settlers, but

---

[3] C. E. Cartwright (ed.), *Life and Letters of the Late Hon. Richard Cartwright . . .* (Toronto, 1876), p. 86. Cartwright describes the confusion in the land regulations, pp. 86-8.

[4] "Canadian Letters: Description of a Tour thro' the Provinces of Lower and Upper Canada in the Course of the Years 1792 and '93," *Canadian Antiquarian and Numismatic Journal*, ser. 3, IX, nos. 3-4 (July-October, 1912). The writer of this work appears to have been on friendly terms with the merchant class and defends their interests as against Simcoe.

mere land jobbers, a description of men that he very properly took every opportunity of reprobating."[5]

Isaac Weld, writing in 1796 concerning these non-Loyalist American immigrants, thought that the self-interest which led them originally to come into Canada operated in favour of their remaining there. It was the prospect of getting land on advantageous terms which had induced them to emigrate; land was still a cheaper article in Canada than in the United States; and as there was so much more waste land in the former than in the latter country, in proportion to the number of inhabitants, it would probably continue so for a length of time to come. Weld, describing the rapid growth of the town of Niagara, attributed it in part to "the wonderful emigrations, into the neighbourhood, of people from the States. . . . So sudden and so great has the influx of people, into the town of Niagara and its vicinity, been, that town lots, horses, provisions, and every necessary of life have risen, within the last three years, nearly fifty per cent in value."[6]

Writing to Lieutenant-Governor Hunter in 1799, Richard Cartwright reviewed the character of both Loyalist and non-Loyalist migrations into Canada, pointing out that Simcoe, in his keen desire to secure population, had seen fit to supersede the earlier regulations governing the distribution of waste lands and by proclamation had invited Americans to enter the province. Thereupon, speculators had flocked in from the United States promising to bring in settlers, and the Loyalists heard with astonishment and indignation, "persons spoken of as proprietors of townships whom they had encountered under the banners of the rebellion, or who had been otherwise notoriously active in promoting the American revolution." So little was done by these speculators that in 1797 the government felt quite free to cancel such grants. Cartwright questioned the wisdom of allowing so many Americans to enter the province, pointing out that the majority of the population westward from the Bay of Quinte was of American stock. He did not impute hostile or treacherous sentiments to these people, but he did think that it was a mistake to suppose that they had come to the province because of any preference for the form of government. They

[5] *Ibid.*, pp. 53-4.
[6] Isaac Weld, *Travels through the States of North America and the Provinces of Upper and Lower Canada in 1795-1797*, 4th ed. (London, 1800), pp. 286, 359.

had come with no other purpose than to better their circumstances by acquiring land upon easy terms.[7]

Cartwright did not overlook the value of the American immigrants to the country. "It must be admitted," he wrote to Hunter, "that the Americans understand the mode of agriculture proper for a new country better than any other people, and being, from necessity, in the habit of providing with their own hands many things which in other countries the artizan is always at hand to supply, they possess resources in themselves which other people are generally strangers to." Similar testimony to the enterprise and skill of the American farmers in Upper Canada was given by Hugh Gray who, writing in 1807, said of them:

There are no people who so well understand the business of clearing a new country, and making it productive. They are active, industrious, hardy, and enterprising, to a degree that is scarcely to be credited till ocular demonstration convinces you of the fact. In these points the Canadians are not to be compared to them; nor are any of the emigrants from Europe by any means so valuable. In short, the American, when he makes a "pitch" (as they term it, when they make an establishment in the woods) is quite at home, and following the profession he has been habituated to from his infancy. The emigrant from Europe has everything to learn; and besides that, he has to unlearn all his European habits.[8]

To counteract the effects of the American immigration Cartwright suggested the settlement among them of "men of tried loyalty and who have been bred up in habits of subordination, in sufficient numbers to discountenance that affectation of equality so discernible in the manner of those who come to us from the American republic."[9] With this sentiment Simcoe would have agreed, finding in the half-pay officers a nucleus of gentry to maintain aristocratic ideas. The difficulty lay in the fact that the gentry were few in numbers and slow in coming while the Americans were numerous and pushing their way into the province. Simcoe found to his dismay also that Englishmen were quite

---

[7] Cartwright, *Life and Letters*, pp. 93-6.
[8] Hugh Gray, *Letters from Canada, Written during a Residence There in the Years 1806, 1807, and 1808 . . .* (London, 1809), p. 364. The reference to Canadians probably means French Canadians.
[9] Cartwright, *Life and Letters*, p. 97.

ready to look for good investments in the new Republic, even buying land in New York State in preference to Upper Canada and offering it for sale to his settlers. "I consider such an application of the product of British Capital injurious to Great Britain," he wrote in 1794, "and under present circumstance, disloyal in its effects."[10]

There are no accurate records of this early immigration from the United States but its extent may be conjectured from the observations of travellers and from the visible effects upon social conditions. We lack also any records of those who left Upper Canada for the United States in this period, for even some of the British half-pay officers crossed the border and became American citizens. Boundary lines meant no more to them than to the land-hungry American farmers; each was seeking what Simcoe would term "private emolument."

Before 1800 several settlements distinctively American in their population had developed. Yonge Street, north from York, was peopled chiefly by Quakers and German Mennonites, newcomers who had responded to Simcoe's invitation. Westward from the Niagara River there were numerous American settlers whose presence was noted by Patrick Campbell when he journeyed as far as the Grand River in 1792. Meeting a man with a sleigh and a team of oxen, Campbell asked him if he had come from the head of the lake: "He answered in a twang peculiar to the New Englanders, 'I viow nieu you may depen I's just-a-comin'; 'And what distance may it be from hence?' said I; 'I viow nieu I guess I do'no – I guess nieu I do'no – I swear nieu I guess it is three miles'; he swore, vowed and guessed alternately, and was never like to come to the point, though he had but that instant come from it." Campbell's companion damned the man "for an old Yankee rascal, that never gave a direct answer in his lifetime, and was sure he had only come from New England but that or the preceding year at the farthest."[11]

Robert Hamilton wrote from Fort Erie in October, 1799: "The number of Emigrants to this part of the Province this summer surpasses anything we have formerly known or could have suspected. On the way to this place I yesterday passed

[10] Simcoe to Lord Dorchester, York, March 16, 1794, *Simcoe Papers*, III, 190. He had the satisfaction, however, of seeing some settlers leave the English-owned Pulteney lands in New York State and come to Upper Canada.

[11] Patrick Campbell, *Travels in the Interior Inhabited Parts of North America in the Years 1791 and 1792* (Toronto, 1937), p. 157.

Eleven Covered Waggons, mostly drawn by four stout horses and carrying families, who had crossed the ferry at this place the day before. These people seem determined to remain and as Government has now stopped giving away Lands, they must purchase wherever they can find Land to suit them."[12]

The Whisky Rebellion in Pennsylvania, so rigorously suppressed by Washington and Hamilton, resulted in some emigration from that state to Upper Canada. John Maude, an English traveller, encountered families in 1800 near Bath, New York, coming from the disaffected area in Pennsylvania. "We fought seven years to get rid of taxation and now we are taxed more than ever," they told Maude, who learned from them that many more were removing to Upper Canada.[13]

American immigration continued unabated during the decade after 1800. Christian Schultz, visiting Niagara in 1807, found the greater part of the inhabitants were Americans who had lost little of their former nationality. "They never seek to disguise their sentiments in public," he wrote, "but express themselves with as much freedom as you would do at the Theatre or Tontine Coffee-House."[14]

Upper Canada on the eve of the War of 1812 was described by Michael Smith, an American, who had been resident in the province for some years as a schoolmaster and Baptist preacher. He was a man of intelligence and had prepared his description of the province for publication, but the coming of the war delayed its printing until 1813. He left the province in December, 1812, after he had appeared before the Board of Examiners at Kingston. There he admitted that he had never taken the oath of allegiance. Smith shows intimate acquaintance with the conditions of the province. His estimate of the population in 1812 was 136,000, not including Indians. Four-fifths of these, he said, were of American origin and only one-fifth of British origin.

---

[12] Robert Hamilton to John Askin, Detroit, Fort Erie, October 20, 1799, Ontario Historical Society, *Papers and Records*, XX (1923), 47.

[13] John Maude, *A Visit to the Falls of Niagara in 1800* (London, 1826), p. 60. Maude doubted whether such immigrants would be useful to Upper Canada: "They will form a nest of vipers in the bosom that now so incautiously fosters them, and in which they will infix their deadly fangs the moment they can do it with impunity. This consequence I do not hesitate to predict; for I never saw a bad subject make a good citizen, so neither do I believe a bad citizen can make a good subject.

[14] Christian Schultz, *Travels on an Inland Voyage . . . Performed in the Years 1807 and 1808 . . .* (New York, 1810), II, 55.

Of the American element only one in four was Loyalist or of Loyalist descent. "Within the term of twelve years," he wrote, "the inhabitants of Upper Canada have increased beyond conjecture, as the means of obtaining land have been extremely easy."[15]

As Smith noted, and as others noted also, the striking characteristic of the population was the preponderance of people from the United States. Had the process of Americanization not been checked by the war, Upper Canada would soon have been virtually an American colony. The tens of thousands who were turning their backs upon the older states and moving westward seemed almost unconscious of international boundaries, and change of allegiance from republic to monarchy, or from monarchy to republic, was made with apparent unconcern. These non-Loyalist migrations into Canada present a transition stage in the development of American nationalism. Though many of these people had been on the colonial side during the War of Independence they were not necessarily enthusiastic over the separation and might, indeed, be disillusioned, as in Pennsylvania, with the advent of new governments. In any case, they seemed to find no difficulty in again coming under monarchical institutions in Upper Canada.

To assume, as officials and Loyalists so often did, that these people were at heart disloyal was quite unjust. For the most part they were less interested in the form of government under which they lived than in the regulations with regard to land. It mattered little to them whether their Governor was Peter Hunter or Arthur St. Clair, whether there was an Assembly or a trio of judges, whether the basis of government was the Northwest Ordinance of Congress or the Canada Act of the imperial Parliament. The really important question before them was the possibility of bettering their condition. To describe them as "republicans," with all the reproach that might be understood by that word prior to 1812, and even later, was unfair and unmerited. They were not as a group republicans, they were merely thorough-going democrats, differing in no respect from

[15] Michael Smith, *A Geographical View of the Province of Upper Canada, and Promiscuous Remarks upon the Government* . . . (Hartford, 1813), pp. 62-3. Of this book five other editions subsequently appeared. Smith's estimate of the total population of Upper Canada is too high but his estimate of its composition is probably near the mark.

the people who in the same period were taking up land and forming new communities in the region of the Ohio River.[16]

[16] M. L. Hansen, *The Mingling of the Canadian and American Peoples* (New Haven, 1940), is the most intensive study of population movements between Canada and the United States that has yet appeared. The migration of non-Loyalist Americans to Upper Canada in the period before the War of 1812 is examined in chapter IV. Hansen died before the completion of his study and it was prepared for publication by J. B. Brebner. Working in a field which had not hitherto been explored, Hansen has made a most important contribution to the record of Canadian-American relations. See also A. L. Burt, *The United States, Great Britain and British North America from the Revolution to the Establishment of Peace after the War of 1812* (New Haven, 1940), pp. 178-84. Burt's study leads him to agreement with the analysis of Upper Canada's population made by Michael Smith in 1812.

3: The War of 1812-1814

I trust I shall not be presumptuous when I state that I verily believe that the militia of Kentucky are alone competent to place Montreal and Upper Canada at your feet.

—HENRY CLAY (1810)

I tender you the invaluable blessings of Civil, Political and Religious Liberty. . . . You will be emancipated from Tyranny and Oppression and restored to the dignified station of Freemen.

—GENERAL WILLIAM HULL (1812)

A country defended by Free Men, enthusiastically devoted to the cause of their King and Constitution, can never be conquered.

—GENERAL ISAAC BROCK (1812)

In the year 1812 the people of Upper Canada found themselves involved in a war with the United States for which they had as little responsibility as the people of minor European states who in that same period were trodden underfoot by the armies of Napoleon. As a British colony they necessarily had to accept the consequences of British foreign policy, but as a community living in North America they could conceive of no grievance against the people of the United States which might bring war nor did they see where the United States in turn could have any real grievance against them. These Upper Canadians were chiefly of American origin, linked to the Republic in many cases by family ties, and after the heat of the revolutionary period had cooled down there had been considerable intercourse between the province and the states. W. H. Merritt, principal promoter of the Welland Canal and himself a veteran of the War of 1812, recalled at a later date the "twenty-four years passed in mutual services and friendly intercourse [which] had nearly obliterated the old feelings engendered by the revolution." The settlers, he says, frequently visited the western counties of New York; "going back to the colony" they called it.[1] There was probably a more friendly feeling towards the United States on the part of the people living west of the Niagara River than was true of those in the eastern part of the province where Loyalist anti-American sentiment lived on, a state of mind easily explainable in view of the losses which many of these people

[1] J. P. Merritt, *Biography of the Hon. W. H. Merritt . . .* (St. Catharines, 1875), p. 15.

had sustained during the period of the Revolution. Isaac Weld, who was in Upper Canada before 1800, contrasted the disappearance of anti-American feeling in England with the attitude of the Upper Canada Loyalists, of whom he said: "It is there common to hear, even from the children of the refugees, the most gross invectives poured out against the people of the states, and the people of the frontier states, in their turn, are as violent against the refugees and their posterity."[2] Time would probably have moderated the anti-American feeling even among the Loyalists had not the countries, for a second time, become involved in war. The effect of this second struggle was to turn the prejudice into a cult, to be perpetuated through the years and nourished by writings and organization.[3]

The bulk of the common people of Upper Canada could know but little of the affairs of Europe. An American newspaper might be passed about in a community or a traveller from Montreal or the seaboard might bring news that was already months old. All else was largely rumour. Even the officials were sometimes ignorant of what was transpiring in Europe. Mails being subject to the perils of war, letters which were intended for the government of Canada might receive their first reading at the hands of curious and deeply interested persons in Paris or in some other European capital. But British officials, ill-informed though they might sometimes be, realized the elements of danger in the position of the United States as a neutral in the struggle with Napoleon and knew that in case of a war between England and the Republic Canada would probably be the battleground. It was necessary, therefore, to be prepared, and as early as 1807 schemes of defence were receiving consideration.

The year 1807 might easily have brought war. In the *Chesapeake* incident the administration at Washington had a *casus belli* with which even New England would have found it hard to disagree. But the government under the leadership of Jefferson "wooed peace with unwearied enthusiasm." The reverberations of the *Chesapeake* affair extended far inland to Upper Canada where sentiments were expressed that might well have shocked the authorities had they come to their notice. In a public house at Niagara where the attack upon the *Chesapeake* was the topic

[2] Isaac Weld, *Travels through the States of North America and the Provinces of Upper and Lower Canada in 1795-1797* (London, 1800), p. 415.

[3] Sir Wilfrid Laurier attributed his defeat in the federal election of 1911 in part to United Empire Loyalist antipathy to any interference with, or control of, Canadian affairs by the United States.

of conversation Christian Schultz heard men say: "If Congress will only send us a flag, and a proclamation declaring that whoever is found in arms against the United States shall forfeit his land we will fight ourselves free without any expense to them." Travelling towards York, the provincial capital, he met a group of farmers who had just heard the news of the *Chesapeake*. They inquired from him whether he thought it would lead to war. Schultz replied that he did not believe the British government would sanction such an unwarranted proceeding as the attack upon the American warship and would be ready to make amends to the United States. The group expressed their disappointment "as they hoped that it would end in a rupture in which event they expected to become a part of the United States." At Queenston the sole topic of conversation appeared to be war, and Schultz found there, as at Niagara and Fort Erie, "a determined partiality towards the United States and a decided and almost avowed hostility to the British government." At Newark, where there was a garrison of about two hundred men, preparations for defence had been actively under way ever since the arrival of news of the attack on the *Chesapeake*.[4] At Detroit the affair of the *Leopard* and *Chesapeake* occasioned "much ferment," the Governor immediately calling upon all the inhabitants living within a distance of thirty miles to assist in erecting defence works.[5]

Jefferson's embargo following the *Chesapeake* incident gave considerable impetus to trade along the Canadian border, the large profits obtained from smuggling being sufficient temptation to turn almost whole communities into law-breakers. Along the Niagara River and from ports on Lake Erie goods were brought into the province. The Rev. William Case, a Methodist preacher, arriving at Black Rock in 1808 from the New York conference which had just assigned him to Canada, found that the embargo would prohibit the transport of his property across the border. The preacher went to a hay-loft and made his difficulties a matter of prayer. Returning to his lodgings, a stranger said to him: "I should not wonder if the missionary should jump into the boat, take his horse by the bridle, and swim round the embargo." Case did so.[6]

[4] Christian Schultz, *Travels on an Inland Voyage . . . Performed in the Years 1807 and 1808 . . .* (New York, 1810), II, 50, 55, 96-7.

[5] *Michigan Historical Collections*, XV (1909), 42.

[6] William Case, *Jubilee Sermon Delivered . . . at London, C.W., June 6th, 1855* (Toronto, 1855), pp. 58-9.

In Upper Canada the war excitement quieted during 1809 and 1810, though in those years the Indian question was becoming more and more an irritant to the people of the American West. Rightly or wrongly, many Westerners believed that British policy was responsible for the troubles with the Indians and voices were heard declaring that the solution for the Indian problem lay in the expulsion of the British from Canada. John Thomas, a resident of Upper Canada, on a trip to Tennessee in 1809, found difficulty in doing business because of the prevailing war spirit. Writing from Hopkins Court House on December 11 of that year, he said: "I am afraid of a war with the United States as the people are much exasperated at the conduct of the English in general. . . . Should this be the case, business done or not, you may expect my immediate return before any stroke can be made on either side . . . business begins to slacken and merchants are distrustful of a war and its consequences."[7]

One group within the Canadian provinces viewed the possibility of war not only with equanimity but even with a measure of enthusiasm. The merchant class, with headquarters at Montreal but with fur-trading agencies and interests extending over half the continent, saw in a war with the United States the possibility of recovering sway over the great Northwest Territory which had been removed from their control by the Jay Treaty. In a memorial which they presented in 1812 their point of view was plainly set forth. "Posterity will hardly believe," they declared, "although history must attest the melancholy and mortifying truth, that in acceding to the Independence of the Thirteen Colonies as States, their Territory was not merely allowed to them, but an extent of Country, then a portion of the province of Quebec, nearly of equal magnitude to the said Thirteen Colonies or States, was ceded, notwithstanding not a foot of the Country so ceded was at the time occupied by an American in Arms, nor could have been, had the war continued."[8]

Simcoe had dreamed of recovering Britain's lost American colonies by peaceful methods, but these merchants were quite prepared in 1812 to fight for the recovery of the area in which their fortunes might be advanced. They did not even wait for a

7 Ontario Historical Society, *Papers and Records*, XII (1914), 66.
8 Public Archives of Canada, Series Q, CXXX-CXXXI, 117-18. See D. G. Creighton, *The Commercial Empire of the St. Lawrence, 1760-1850* (Toronto, 1937), chapter VII, for an excellent statement of the position of the merchant class in relation to the War of 1812.

declaration of war to offer their services. Captain Gray, the Deputy Quartermaster-General at Montreal, was able to assure Prevost of their co-operation and help six months before the United States began hostilities.

The Heads of the Companies [he wrote] *are exceedingly grateful to Your Excellency for taking an interest in the protection of their Trade, . . . they will enter with zeal into any measure of Defence, or even offence, that may be proposed to them. . . . They express every wish to be useful in the common cause. . . . They have tendered all their vessels for the service of the Govt. if the Exigencies of the War should make it necessary to call for them. In short they are full of Loyalty and Zeal, and manifests a degree of public spirit highly honorable to them. By means of these Companies, we might let loose the Indians upon them throughout the whole Extent of their Western frontier, as they have a most Commanding inflence over them.*[9]

The merchant groups were even ready with war plans for the authorities. They suggested as a first step the capture of the American post at Michilimackinac and removal of the garrison from St. Joseph Island to the falls of St. Mary's. They themselves were prepared to take the offensive on Lake Superior, "acting in concert with the force at the Straits of St. Mary's." The outcome of such operations, they believed, would be "to dislodge the enemy from any position he may take upon the Lake and in short exclude him entirely from any participation in the navigation or Commerce of Lakes Superior, Huron and Michigan."[10]

This became, in part, the plan of operation eventually adopted. Michilimackinac fell to the British in the first month of the war, but in 1813 the defeat of Barclay on the water and Procter on land so endangered its security that immediate action was necessary. A cairn and tablet erected in 1938 by the Canadian government near the forks of the Nottawasaga River mark the place where Lieutenant-Colonel Robert McDouall built the little flotilla of boats which left Nottawasaga Bay in the early spring of 1814 and fighting its way through ice and storms effected the relief of the British garrison in May. Whatever

---

[9] Gray to Prevost, Montreal, January 13, 1812, *Michigan Historical Collections*, XV (1909), 70-2. Sir George Prevost was Governor of Canada and Commander of the forces in British North America.
[10] *Ibid.*, p. 71.

might befall other parts of the country, no effort was too great to retain those distant posts which were the keys to trade and commerce. The war ended with the British in control of the Upper Lakes and the upper Mississippi Valley. There was bitter disappointment, therefore, among the merchant class when in the peace negotiations at Ghent that for which they had chiefly contended was completely lost.

The zeal of "big business" interests in Canada for war with the United States had its counterpart in the attitude of producers and merchants in the western states, who in the years immediately preceding the war found themselves thwarted in their efforts to find satisfactory markets. Prices in the Mississippi Valley fell to lower and lower levels after 1805 with no corresponding decrease in costs of production or in the prices of imported goods.[11] These disturbing business conditions contributed to the war-like attitude of the western farmers. Their economic distress they considered due to British interference with the country's commerce, and when Jefferson's more peaceful measures did not prove effective they were ready for war.[12]

Isaac Brock was the outstanding British figure in the War of 1812. His energy, foresight, and military skill were worth battalions in the summer and early autumn of 1812, and without

[11] See G. R. Taylor, "Prices in the Mississippi Valley preceding the War of 1812," *Journal of Economic and Business History*, III (November, 1930), and also his study of "Agrarian Discontent in the Mississippi Valley preceding the War of 1812," *Journal of Political Economy*, XXXIX (August, 1931).

[12] The several theses which have been advanced as to the reasons for war in 1812 are surveyed by W. H. Goodman, "The Origins of the War of 1812: A Survey of Changing Interpretations," *Mississippi Valley Historical Review*, XXVIII (September, 1941). Goodman is of the opinion that while nineteenth-century historians over-estimated the significance of maritime matters "contemporary historians are perhaps committing an equally serious error in the opposite direction." A. L. Burt has made an intensive and useful study of the origins of the war in his *The United States, Great Britain and North America from the Revolution to the Establishment of Peace after the War of 1812* (New Haven, 1940). Burt gives first place to maritime issues; doubts whether the Indian menace, so much played up by the Republican press, had any appreciable influence in bringing on war; and considers the possible conquest of Canada as having had little weight. J. W. Pratt in his *Expansionists of 1812* (New York, 1925) says (p. 14) . . . "without them [the maritime issues], it is safe to say, there would have been no war, just as the writer feels safe in saying that without the peculiar grievances and ambitions of the West there would have been no war." The latter part of this thesis is rejected completely by Burt.

his presence and leadership at that time much of Upper Canada would probably have been in the hands of the enemy before the close of the year. Though he fell within less than four months after the declaration of hostilities, he is very properly regarded as the saviour of British Canada in its darkest hour of peril.

Brock faced four serious difficulties at the opening of the war: an Assembly hesitant of adopting war measures, a population largely of alien origin, a militia in the western districts that had little stomach for real fighting, and Indian allies vacillating and difficult to control. To this list of difficulties might be added a fifth in the over-cautious Prevost, his superior at Quebec. It required courage and determination to overcome these handicaps in the face of an advancing enemy, but Brock was resolute. "Most of the people have lost all confidence," he wrote at the end of July, "I, however, speak loud and look big."

Brock's difficulties with the Upper Canada Assembly were not unlike those which occur in any democratic country in time of war when there is conflict between the point of view of the professional soldier and that of the civil administration. Without waiting for the expected declaration of war, Brock desired the Assembly to pass legislation suspending habeas corpus and requiring everyone to take an oath of allegiance. Both measures were defeated, the latter by the casting vote of the Speaker. Brock attributed the Assembly's attitude to the "truly alarming" influence exercised over its members by the vast number of settlers from the United States.

The Assembly's hesitancy with respect to a surrender of its civil liberties is not surprising. War had not yet been declared and any such action would have aroused criticism. The Assembly did, however, pass legislation for the apprehension of deserters from the regular military forces and appropriated £5,000 for training the militia. This, however, was as far as the members would go, and Brock had to accept their decision. When the Assembly came together again in July, with war now a reality, he expected to find a better spirit but was again disappointed. His plea for even a temporary suspension of habeus corpus was refused and seeing that there was nothing to be gained by prolonging the session, the Assembly was dismissed. "The truth is," he wrote at the time, "that, with of course few exceptions, every body considers the fate of the country is already decided, and is afraid to appear conspicuous in the promotion of measures in the least calculated to retard the catastrophe."[13]

Brock's address to the Assembly on July 27 showed his determination to "speak loud and look big." It was probably intended, as such documents so often are, for propaganda purposes and was replete with compliments to the loyalty of the militia and the co-operation of the Assembly with the military authorities. But even while he was addressing the Assembly some of the militia were openly showing their lack of enthusiasm for service, and a few days later the Assembly itself rejected the measures which he had suggested. Such were the conditions facing Brock when he wrote to Baynes, the Adjutant-General:

My situation is most critical, not from anything the enemy can do, but from the disposition of the people. . . . The population, believe me, is essentially bad. . . . A full belief possess them all that this Province must inevitably succumb. . . . This prepossession is fatal to every exertion. . . . Legislators, Magistrates, Militia Officers, all, have imbibed the idea, and are so sluggish and indifferent in all their respective offices that the artful and active scoundrel is allowed to parade the Country without interruption, and commit all imaginable mischief. . . . They are so alarmed of offending that they rather encourage than repress disorders or other proper [sic] acts. I really believe it is with some cause they dread the vengeance of the democratic party, they are such a set of unrelenting villains.[14]

Through Brock's correspondence during the whole summer of 1812 there runs this note of disappointment and indignation over the apathy of so many of the people in the face of invasion. He had not at any time believed that the whole population was loyal, though in December, 1811, he had expressed confidence that a large majority would prove faithful.[15] Six months later he was quite disillusioned. From Fort George he wrote to Prevost at the middle of July:

There can be no doubt that a large portion of the population in this neighbourhood are sincere in their professions to defend

---

[13] Brock to Baynes, York, August 4, 1812, William Wood (ed.), *Select British Documents of the Canadian War of 1812* (Toronto, 1920-8), I, 408. Hereafter referred to as Wood, *Documents*.

[14] Brock to Baynes, York, July 29, 1812, Wood, *Documents*, I, 396.

[15] Brock to Prevost, York, December 2, 1811, Wood, *Documents*, I. 272.

the country, but it appears likewise evident to me that the greater part are either indifferent to what is passing, or so completely American as to rejoice in the prospects of a change of Governments. Many who now consider our means inadequate would readily take an active part were the regular troops encreased – these cool calculators are numerous in all societies.[16]

The London District was even more marked by disaffection than the Niagara District which so worried Brock. In the London District there was a preponderance of American settlers, among them several notorious characters who had received grants of land. When General Hull was on Canadian soil in July, 1812, his cavalry penetrated as far as the village of Delaware, more than one hundred miles east of Detroit, and was welcomed by some of the people thereabouts. Brock reported this to Prevost as another example of the disloyalty with which he had to contend.

During the summer months of 1812 public confidence was probably never lower than on the July day when Brock addressed the Assembly, closing his speech with the ringing challenge: "A country defended by Free Men, enthusiastically devoted to the cause of their King and Constitution, can never be conquered." From Oxford on that day Colonel Thomas Talbot wrote an account of his futile efforts to raise a detachment of Norfolk militia for service under Captain Chambers in the Detroit region. "When I reached the ground from whence the Detachment was to march," Talbot said, "I found a large assembly of the Farmers with their Women, who upon my approach addressed me, by declaring that their Men should not March, upon this I enquired if there were any Magistrates present, the answer was, several, I required one to come forward, on which Mr. Bemer appeared. I asked him how he as a Magistrate could permit such proceedings, he offered no excuse, but said that he conceived the measure of withdrawing any of the Militia from Long Point was highly improper." In the concluding portion of the letter, after detailing this and other discouraging experiences, Colonel Talbot, with an eye open to his own interests, suggested to Brock, "If you should be forced to send to Genl. Hull, do let me know as those in promise of land on performing their settlement duties should be included in such conditions as may be entered into and something relative to myself."[17]

Brock reported the Norfolk situation to Prevost with these comments:

> *I conceived the Long Point Militia the most likely to show the best disposition of any in this part of the Country, and their refusal to join Captain Chambers indicates the little reliance that ought to be placed in any of them. My situation is getting each day more critical. . . . The population, though I had no great confidence in the Majority, is worse than I expected to find it – And all Magistrates &c &c appear quite confounded, and decline acting – the consequence is the most improper conduct is tolerated – The officers of Militia exert no authority, everything shews as if a certainty existed of a change taking place soon.*[18]

It would be but tedious to repeat all of Brock's caustic references to Assembly, people, and militia at this time. For the most part they relate to that section of the province lying between York and Detroit. Disaffection was not confined to this area; it was, however, much more marked in the area west of Niagara than elsewhere. Brock, in his last official letter, written on the day before his death, told Prevost that "were it not for the number of Americans in our ranks we might defy all their efforts against this part of the province."[19]

Non-Loyalist Americans in Upper Canada at the opening of hostilities were in a difficult position. Few of those who had entered the province from the close of the Revolutionary War down to 1810 expected that they would encounter a second war between England and the people of the United States. For many of them it had been but a chance whether they came into Upper Canada or found homes to the south of Lake Erie. Many had family connections with western New York State or elsewhere so that the struggle took on some of the characteristics of a civil

---

[17] Colonel Thomas Talbot to Brock, Oxford, July 27, 1812, Wood, *Documents*, I, 382-4. It can scarcely be doubted that Talbot's personal unpopularity with the settlers was one reason for the attitude of the Norfolk militia as at a later date and under other leadership they gave good service.

[18] Brock to Prevost, York, July 28, 1812, Wood, *Documents*, I, 386.

[19] Brock to Prevost, Fort George, October 12, 1812, Wood, *Documents*, I, 604.

war, relatives on opposite sides of the border being enrolled in their respective militias.

Michael Smith, who remained in the province until the close of 1812, has left us an account of the reaction of these people to the declaration of hostilities. At first, he says, they were panic-stricken, ceased from business, and sometimes even neglected to prepare food. Only after a time did they resume their usual activities.[20] When the flank companies of the militia were called to St. George and were told that after getting their equipment they might return to their homes, they obeyed cheerfully, not knowing that war had been declared. "Had they known of the declaration of war," he adds, "and that they were to be detained for that purpose. I am of opinion that but few would have complied with the orders, though most of them were under obligations so to do, having taken an oath to that effect. . . . Upon the declaration of war, the governor issued a proclamation, making it treason for anyone to attempt to cross the line. Had not this been done, one half of the people would have left the province."[21]

Smith analyses the American settler's point of view when caught between the obligation of British military service and the possibility that in the event of an American victory he might be treated as a traitor. Hull's bombastic proclamation, threatening vengeance upon the people of Upper Canada if they were found fighting in the company of the Indians, placed the American settler in sore plight since he could be quite sure that some of the Indian tribes would be allies of the British in the war. When the militia were assembling at Fort George, Smith had an opportunity to converse with many who passed his home. He found that nearly all were of the same mind, that if Hull threatened Fort George and they were ordered to march against him they

[20] Michael Smith, *A Geographical View of the Province of Upper Canada* . . . (Hartford, 1813), p. 106.

[21] *Ibid.*, pp. 87-8. Tilly Buttrick Jr., an American, who was on the Canadian side when war was declared and was detained for a time, says that at the outbreak of hostilities "waggons were daily coming in from the backwoods loaded with men, women and children, many of whom were in a very distressed state; they begged for permission to cross to the United States, many of whom were formerly from there; but instead of this request being granted, many of the men were made soldiers and their horses taken and employed in the service of government" (Tilly Buttrick, *Voyages, Travels and Discoveries of Tilly Butrick Jr.*, Boston, 1831, p. 47). Buttrick's narrative was reprinted in Reuben Gold Thwaites (ed.), *Early Western Travels, 1748-1846* (Cleveland, 1904), VIII.

would refuse to do so, "but not a man would have joined him and fought against the King." Hull's proclamation really strengthened the British cause among these people. The American settlers as a group had no desire to fight either for or against Hull and his declaration that he came to free them from tyranny was, as Smith frankly says, "mere notion – for if they had been under any, they could at any time have crossed the line to the United States."[22]

The slight advantage which was given to the Upper Canada authorities by the reaction to Hull's proclamation was followed by further gains in public respect when Michilimackinac was captured and Brock was victorious at Detroit. Of the effects of this latter victory Smith says:

> *The surrender of the fort of Detroit, and all the Michigan Territory, were events which the people of Canada could scarcely believe, even after they were known to be true. Indeed, when I saw the officers and soldiers returning to Fort George, with the spoils of my countrymen, I could scarcely believe my own eyes. . . . After this event, the people of Canada became fearful of disobeying the government—some that had fled to the wilderness returned home – and the friends of the United States were discouraged, and those of the King encouraged. . . . The army now became respectable, and a dread fell on those who had opposed the government. The people now saw that it was as much as their property and lives were worth to disobey orders, and now what they had been compelled to do, after a while they did from choice.*[23]

The Upper Canada authorities took advantage of their increased prestige at this time to arrest some of the malcontents in the western section of the province. A militia party captured Ebenezer Allan and Andrew Westbrook, two leaders of the disloyal element in the London District. A third troublemaker, Simon Zelotes Watson, who was with Hull at Detroit, managed to evade capture and in 1813 was holding the rank of major in the United States army. Several other residents of the London and Western districts were made prisoners when Hull surrendered, having previously gone over to the enemy. Some were

[22] Smith, *A Geographical View*, p. 89.
[23] *Ibid.*, p. 92.

paroled but four were indicted for treason at Sandwich in September, 1812.[24]

A further stage in the change of opinion showed itself after the Battle of Queenston Heights had brought added prestige to British arms. There was still some measure of resistance to military service but many of those who had shared in the fighting now felt that the others should bear their share of hardships and dangers. "Not only the officers of the army and the Indians were engaged to compel obedience," says Smith, "but all the militia that had been in the service; they thought it hard and unreasonable that they must bear all the burden and dangers of the war; therefore a number of them were zealously engaged to bring forward the disobedient, although their neighbours and relations."[25] One result of these raids in search of shirkers was the formation of gangs which went off to the woods to avoid service. These later turned into marauding bands, committing serious depredations upon the property of loyal inhabitants.

After the Battle of Queenston Heights, where Brock fell, there was bitter resentment against the United States, even among some who had formerly been secretly favourable to the American cause. By this time it had been demonstrated that the war was to be no walkover for the American armies; a continued stiff resistance might, therefore, bring an early peace. As Smith put it, "They [the militia] feel it their duty to kill all they can while they are coming over, that they may discourage any more from invading the province, that the government may give up the idea of conquering it, and withdraw their forces, that they may go home also; for they are greatly distressed in leaving their families so long, many of whom are in a suffering condition."[26]

In October the Executive Council decided that the time had come to expel from the province those who refused to take the

---

[24] Brock wrote to Baynes on August 4, 1812, informing him that a petition had gone forward to Hull signed by many inhabitants of Westminster inviting him to advance and promising to join him. This was the section in which Allan and Westbrook were prominent. "What in the name of heaven can be done with such a vile population," was Brock's comment. See Wood, *Documents*, I, 409.

[25] Smith, *A Geographical View*, p. 96.

[26] *Ibid.*, p. 100. Prevost writing to Bathurst on August 24, 1812, remarked that the inability of the United States to overrun the country "was become so manifest that His Majesty's subjects in both provinces are beginning to feel an increased confidence in the Government protecting them" (Wood, *Documents*, I, 491-2).

oath of allegiance, a measure which Brock had advocated as early as the beginning of 1812. General Sheaffe, Brock's successor as civil administrator of the province, accordingly issued a proclamation ordering all who claimed exemption from military service on the ground of American citizenship to report before military boards sitting at Kingston, York, and Niagara and to apply for passports to cross the border. Provision was made for a modified form of oath or security for good conduct in cases where serious hardships would result from expulsion.[27]

The difficulties with which Brock had contended were in turn encountered by his successor. Sheaffe wrote to Prevost from Fort George at the end of the year: "It mortifies me extremely to have to report . . . that both sickness and desertion increased among the militia after the date of my last despatch." Sheaffe recognized, however, that the desertions were in large part due to the distress in the settlers' homes through sickness, lack of food, and other hardships.[28] From Niagara Colonel Claus issued a circular to the effect that desertions from the First Regiment of Lincoln Militia had become so great that he felt it necessary to inform every officer.[29] General Vincent, writing to Prevost six months later, was also disheartened: "With respect to the militia," he wrote, "it is with regret that I can neither report favorably of their numbers nor of their willing co-operation. Every exertion has been used and every expedient resorted to, to bring them forward and unite their efforts to those of His Majesty's Forces with but little effect and desertion beyond all conception continues to mark their indifference to the important cause in which we are now engaged."[30]

As late as March, 1814, General Drummond, writing to Lord Bathurst, drew attention to the legislation of the recent session of the Assembly authorizing the suspension of habeas corpus, declaring certain persons aliens and vesting their estates in the Crown. Of this legislation Drummond said:

That there are many whom it will be found necessary to detain in custody under the provisions of the former, there is

[27] Public Archives of Canada, Series C, 688 B, 127, 154-6; Wood, *Documents*, I, 643-4.

[28] Sheaffe to Prevost, Fort George, December 16, 1812, Wood, *Documents*, I, 662.

[29] E. A. Cruikshank, *Documentary History of the Campaign upon the Niagara Frontier in the Year 1812* (Welland, n.d.), p. 275.

[30] Vincent to Prevost, Fort George, May 18, 1813, Wood, *Documents*, II, 100.

*too much reason to apprehend, and not a few will experience the
effects of the two latter. Having said so much with respect to the
disaffected spirit evinced by some, it is at the same time but
justice to say that the greater part of the inhabitants are well
disposed, and many have on various occasions manifested their
loyalty and devotion to the service by their actions in the field.
Those chiefly who have shewn the opposite disposition, it is
satisfactory to know, are such as have from time to time crept
into the Province from the neighboring States and settled on
lands which they purchased from individuals. This practice will,
I trust, be effectually guarded against in future.*[31]

Disloyalty extended, however, even to the ranks of the
Assembly of the province. During the course of the war two of
its members and also one former member went over to the
enemy. These three were Benajah Mallory and Abraham Marcle,
both of American origin, and Joseph Willcocks, a British citizen
by ancestry and birth who had come directly to Upper Canada.
Mallory represented the counties of the London District from
1804 to 1812 but failed of re-election in the latter year. He went
over to the enemy early in the war. Marcle was suspected of
disloyalty and was under arrest for a time in the summer of
1813. He was permitted to return to his home near Ancaster
but soon after crossed the border and was active in raids which
were made upon the province. The actions of these two men
may be attributed to their natural sympathies but the case of
Willcocks is more puzzling. He was employed by Brock in 1812
in a confidential mission to the Six Nations Indians and is
believed to have fought at Queenston Heights. A year later,
however, he was busily engaged in organizing a mounted force
(calling themselves Canadian Volunteers) with which he ravaged the Canadian frontier until killed at Fort Erie on September 4, 1814. Both Marcle and Willcocks were formally expelled
from the Assembly on February 19, 1814.[32]

In June, 1814, came the most vigorous effort thus far made
to stamp out disloyalty. At the famous "bloody assize" held at
Ancaster, three judges tried nineteen prisoners charged with
high treason. One pleaded guilty, fourteen were found guilty on
the evidence presented, and four were acquitted. When sentences

[31] Drummond to Bathurst, March 20, 1814, Ontario Historical Society,
Papers and Records, XIX (1922), 39.
[32] See A. H. U. Colquhoun, "The Career of Joseph Willcocks," *Canadian
Historical Review*, VII (December, 1926).

of death were pronounced on June 21, petitions at once poured in on behalf of the accused men, and the Executive Council, the three judges, and the Attorney-General faced the duty of deciding whether all fifteen should die. In the end seven were granted reprieves but eight were hanged at Burlington Heights on July 20, 1814. That was just five days before the Battle of Lundy's Lane.[33]

The Grand Jury at Ancaster, while dealing with the nineteen prisoners, also recommended indictments for high treason against a number of others who had not yet been apprehended. Judgments of outlawry were proclaimed against nearly thirty persons, whose lands thereby became forfeit to the Crown. Among those indicted was Abraham Marcle, former member of the Assembly, and the notorious Andrew Westbrook who had terrorized the inhabitants of the London District by his marauding raids.

Three years of war greatly affected the social and economic conditions of Upper Canada. In the first few weeks of hostilities, the period when it remained to be seen whether there would continue to be a British Province of Upper Canada, there was confusion and almost complete cessation of business. This condition was of short duration, however, for almost immediately the government began to make purchases with promissory legal-tender "Army Bills," which, though depreciated slightly at times, had the merit of being uniform and in convenient denominations.[34]

American restrictions on trade with Canada had become ever more severe in character as the difficulties between the United States and Britain approached the breaking point and enforcement of the regulations was finally so strict that smuggling became a risky business. Brock noted in a letter to Prevost in April, 1812, that along the Niagara River "armed Men in Coloured Clothes are continually patrolling the shore." The embargo had serious consequences for Upper Canada, however,

[33] See W. R. Riddell, "The Ancaster Bloody Assize of 1814," *Ontario Historical Society, Papers and Records*, XX (1923). See also Wood, *Documents*, III, part I, 282-4.

[34] This type of currency, coming into use in July, 1812, amounted in March, 1815, to £1,249,996 but was reduced to less than £200,000 by May, 1816, the office of issue being finally closed in December, 1820. The contraction of this currency probably hastened the coming of banks. See *Journal of the Canadian Bankers Association*, II (1894-5), 113-14.

for by the early spring of 1812 flour had risen to eight dollars and a half a barrel and Brock estimated that forty thousand barrels which would have gone to Montreal from south of the lake would be kept from that market.[35] Salt was another commodity whch soon began to rise in price, little of this needed article being produced in the province. In February, 1813, it was selling for fifteen dollars a barrel at Niagara, and Charles Askin, writing at that time, predicted that it would be twenty dollars or more by the spring of the year.

Throughout the whole period of the war, one of the chief administrative problems was how to save the crops as they came to maturity. The mobilization of the militia in June, 1812, seriously affected the harvests of that year despite the fact that many men were allowed to return home for brief periods. A report on the crops in the Western District at the end of August indicated that wheat was less than half and corn not one-quarter of the usual yield. As soon as snow came in the winter of 1812-13 the high prices offered by the British authorities for flour and pork brought large supplies from the United States. In the months of December and January hundreds of sleighs were almost constantly on the road from Montreal and other places in the lower province, carrying provisions and military stores to Kingston, York, Niagara, and other points in Upper Canada.[36]

In the summer of 1814 the order for a levy *en masse* of the militia of the London, Niagara, and Home Districts brought a sharp protest from the farmers of York County who declared that unless sufficient men were left to secure the harvest there would be neither supplies for the commissariat nor food for the inhabitants. As a result of this petition two officers were sent through the country urging that every effort be made to thresh the grain earlier than usual. In the Detroit River region at that time the American forces were demanding the delivery of all available flour, wheat, and oats, promising to pay twelve dollars per barrel for flour, a dollar and a half a bushel for wheat, and seventy-five cents for oats. Penalties were threatened should any farmer fail to deliver his surplus crop.[37]

Shortage of grain and the necessity of conserving supplies led to the enactment in March, 1813, of the first prohibitory liquor legislation in Canadian history. The Upper Canada

[35] Wood, *Documents*, I, 186, 191.
[36] Smith, *A Geographical View*, pp. 100-2.
[37] Wood, *Documents*, III, part I, 296-7.

Assembly first authorized the administrator of the province to forbid distillation of whisky, but as this would have closed the distilleries all over the province and deprived soldiers of their accustomed drink there was some anxiety in official circles. A proclamation was then issued withdrawing the general prohibition, but by November the high prices being offered by distillers made it advisable to enforce the legislation in order to keep the price of flour within reasonable limits. However, before this second prohibition was announced, an ample supply of hard liquor had been laid in for the troops.[38]

There was no public relief organization in Upper Canada when the war opened but need suggested the idea and there came into being the Loyal and Patriotic Society of Upper Canada, founded at York in December, 1812. Its aims were to aid the families of the militia while the men were on duty, to care for wounded and sick soldiers, and to reward valour. This was the first humanitarian organization in the history of the province. Five years after the war, when a hospital was constructed at York, a large part of the cost was subscribed by the Loyal and Patriotic Society from its considerable unexpended funds. The Society was severely criticized for its failure to do more for the soldiers.

The difficulty so frequently experienced in moving troops and supplies, because of the state of the roads, or lack of roads, resulted in considerable expenditure for this purpose even during the course of the war. Drummond informed Bathurst in March, 1814, that a large portion of the revenue of the province had been appropriated for road building and repair. Interest in the subject did not cease with the close of the war, the Assembly in February, 1815, setting aside £20,000 for roads and bridges. A year later the appropriations for such purposes amounted to £21,000. These large votes of money were made necessary by the destruction of the war years and by the general need of improving communications. Tilly Buttrick, who journeyed over the western districts in 1816, wrote: "I was sensibly struck with the devastation which had been made by the late war: beautiful farms, formerly in high cultivation, now laid waste; houses entirely evacuated and forsaken; provisions of all kinds very

---

[38] The original act, passed in 1813, was renewed in 1814 and finally expired March 15, 1815. See W. R. Riddell, "The First Canadian Prohibition Measure," *Canadian Historical Review*, I (1920), 187-90.

scarce; and where once peace and plenty abounded, poverty and destruction now stalked the land."[39]

The war naturally left in its wake strong feelings of resentment against the American government and people. Few incidents created more lasting bitterness than the raids during 1813 and 1814 upon the settlements between Niagara and Detroit. Procter's defeat at Moraviantown in October, 1813, so alarmed Prevost that he was prepared to abandon the province as far east as Kingston and to disband the militia in the western districts. Fortunately there were men nearer the scene who had greater confidence, and a stand was made at Burlington. The situation, however, made it possible for a band of marauders from Buffalo, who were joined by some of the disloyal element in the Long Point country, to plunder the loyal inhabitants in that area. At the same time raiders under the leadership of Benajah Mallory, former member of the Assembly, appeared in the Grand River country. Lieutenant-Colonel Henry Bostwick, of the Oxford militia, led an expedition of forty-five volunteers which surprised the invaders, killing three and capturing eighteen, four of whom were subsequently executed. In May, 1814, the little port of Dover on Lake Erie was raided and burned. Abraham Marcle, another former member of the Assembly, participated in this raid, acting as a guide for the invaders. An affidavit made at the time stated that twenty dwellings, three flour-mills, three distilleries, twelve barns, and other buildings were destroyed. The chief sufferer was Colonel Robert Nichol who lost property valued at £5,000. There was some uneasiness at Washington over this wholesale destruction of private property and the conduct of Colonel Campbell who led the expedition was the subject of an official inquiry.[40]

A vivid description of the manner in which this raid affected one homestead was written by Mrs. John Harris who, as a young girl, lived in the Long Point settlement.

On the 15th [of May, she wrote], *as my mother and myself were sitting at breakfast, the dogs kept up a very unusual barking. I went to the door to discover the cause; when I looked up, I saw the hill-side and fields, as far as the eye could reach, covered with American soldiers. They had marched from Port Dover to*

[39] Tilly Buttrick Jr., *Voyages, Travels and Discoveries*, p. 82.
[40] See E. A. Cruikshank, "The County of Norfolk in the War of 1812," Ontario Historical Society, *Papers and Records*, XX (1923).

Ryerse. Two men stepped from the ranks, selected some large chips, and came into the room where we were standing, and took coals from the hearth without speaking a word. My mother knew instinctively what they were going to do. She went out and asked to see the commanding officer. A gentleman rode up to her and said he was the person she asked for. She entreated him to spare her property, and said she was a widow with a young family. He answered her civilly and respectfully, and expressed his regrets that his orders were to burn, but that he would spare the house, which he did; and he said, as a sort of justification of his burning, that the buildings were used as a barrack, and the mill furnished flour for British troops. Very soon we saw columns of dark smoke arise from every building, and of what at early morn had been a prosperous homestead, at noon there remained only smouldering ruins. . . . My father had been dead less than two years. Little remained of all his labours excepting the orchard and cultivated fields.[41]

Remembrance of such incidents as the above burned deeply into the hearts of many of the inhabitants of the province, creating an anti-American prejudice that lasted through their own lives and was passed on to their children. In the case of the Dover raid the depredations were authorized by commissioned officers, placing the responsibility upon the United States government. Certain other offences, however, could be attributed to the malice of former inhabitants, an example being the deliberate murder of Captain William Francis of the Norfolk militia who was called to a window and shot dead when he appeared. Other occupants of the house were forced to leave, after which the place was burned and the body of the murdered officer consumed. In later years this murder quite easily became a part of the general tradition of American excesses.

In the London and Western Districts outrages were frequent during 1814, former residents of these areas acting as guides to parties which destroyed property and captured officers of the militia. At the end of January a party led by Andrew Westbrook captured Captain Daniel Springer and twelve Middlesex militia who were occupying Westbrook's own house in Delaware Township. The raiders set fire to the house and barns, destroying everything. Three weeks later Westbrook raided Point aux Pins

[41] Egerton Ryerson, *The Loyalists of America and Their Times, from 1620 to 1816* (Toronto, 1880), II, 256.

and in April, at Oxford village, he captured Major Sykes Touseley. In May, and again in July, raids were made upon Port Talbot, the home of Colonel Thomas Talbot, houses being plundered and crops destroyed. At the end of August Oxford was visited for a second time and in September Port Talbot again suffered, mills and dwellings being burned. These raids were so frequent in number and so marked by personal animosity on the part of Westbrook that an appeal was eventually made to Brigadier-General McArthur at Detroit by some of the leading inhabitants of the district. Westbrook's repeated raids upon Port Talbot were no doubt the result of animosity towards Colonel Talbot with whom he had collided in the days before the war. He probably hoped to capture his enemy but in this he failed. He did, however, capture Colonel Mahlon Burwell who was closely associated with Talbot's enterprises.

From the close of the War of 1812 may be dated that strong feeling of British allegiance which is so characteristic of the province of Ontario. With the departure during the war of many former residents holding pronounced American sentiments, the British tone was at once strengthened and within a few years was solidified by the arrival of tens of thousands of British immigrants. Americans were soon re-entering the province also, but never again would they set the pattern of social life as before 1812. The war itself became a valued tradition and to the close of the century, at least, the texts used in the schools of the province reflected the deeply Loyalist point of view of the war. Indeed, the history texts, commonly in use in this period, presented but two facts of contact between the United States and Canada – the coming of the Loyalists at the close of the Revolution and the fighting of the War of 1812, both being utilized to strengthen the sense of British allegiance. The losses and sufferings of the Loyalists at the hands of the Americans received special emphasis. The story of the war dwelt particularly upon the victories.[42] Moreover, the Canadian song best known to all school-children, "The Maple Leaf," echoed this sentiment:

[42] Dr. James T. Shotwell, in a letter to the author, has recalled that in his school-days in a Western Ontario town the Battle of Queenston Heights stood out as the one great military event. "We boys," he says, "used to divide up in the school yard and fight that battle between ourselves – that is, if we could get anyone who was willing to take the American side."

At Queenston Heights and Lundy's Lane,
Our brave fathers, side by side,
For freedom, homes, and loved ones dear,
Firmly stood and nobly died;
And those dear rights which they maintained,
We swear to yield them never.
Our watchword ever more shall be,
The Maple Leaf forever.[43]

A sentiment of hostility to the United States, based upon the traditions of the Loyalists and of the events of the War of 1812, was thus nurtured long beyond the pioneer society in which it first originated.

[43] The first two lines of this verse have been modified in recent years to read:

On many hard-fought battle fields
Our brave fathers, side by side, etc.

4: American Immigrants After 1815

The inhabitants of Upper Canada consist of British and Americans, with several families of German, and some of French extraction. From this mixture arises a great diversity of manners and customs in the province. But as the emigrants from the United States form by far the greater moiety of the people, the rest are, in some measure, compelled to conform to their habits and usages.

"A Few Plain Directions . . . by an English
farmer settled in Upper Canada" (1820)

The British government in January, 1815, authorized the Lieutenant-Governor of Upper Canada to refuse grants of land to persons of American nationality and to prevent them from even entering the province. With this policy of exclusion, the governing group in the province, strongly anti-American in sentiment, was in entire agreement. Upper Canada was to be peopled henceforth only by those of sound British views, of which class a nucleus would be found in the soldiers soon to be discharged from the regiments in America, a certain number of whom were to receive grants of land. Furthermore, the troopships on their westward voyages were to bring out bodies of Scottish and Irish emigrants to be settled preferably in Upper Canada. It was in connection with these plans that the admonition was given: "You will not in any case grant land to Subjects of the United States and use your best endeavours to prevent their settling in the Canadas until you shall hear from me."[1]

This official prohibition of American immigration came at a time when there was under way in the United States one of the largest migrations of people that the Republic has ever known. "Old America seems to be breaking up and moving westward," wrote Morris Birkbeck, an English visitor, in 1817, as he found himself in the stream of people headed for the West.[2] People in central New York declared that they had never seen such a procession of home-seekers as journeyed by in the winter of 1814. The roads westward were thronged with "flitting families from the Eastern States." At Zanesville fifty waggons crossed the Muskingum in one day and from many other places came like

[1] Bathurst to Drummond, London, January 10, 1815, Wood, *Documents*, III, part I, 508-9.
[2] Morris Birkbeck, *Notes on a Journey in America*, . . . (Philadelphia, 1818), p. 31.

reports of the trek then under way.[3] In the period between 1812 and 1820 six new western states were admitted to the Union, in each of which there continued to be rapid growth. The embargo, the war, and the post-war depression combined to disturb older communities, to send thousands westward, and to create new communities towards and eventually beyond the Mississippi.

The policy of exclusion of Americans from Upper Canada was soon challenged from within the province itself. Businessmen were not interested in assisted emigration of British paupers, to be placed on bush farms. Such people would not add much to the trade of the province; indeed, they were likely to pass quickly into the United States. To the merchants, and more particularly to those holding lands for speculative purposes, it seemed a wiser policy to divert to Upper Canada some portion of the stream of home-seekers from the eastern states who, in addition to their experience and acquaintance with North American conditions, were also more likely to buy their land.

This businessman's point of view found expression in the provincial Assembly in April, 1817, when Robert Nichol, who had been Quartermaster-General of the militia during the war, presented a series of eleven searching resolutions intended to establish the wisdom of allowing Americans again to enter the province. Furthermore, the extensive Crown and clergy land reserves were declared to be impediments to the development of the province. Nichol had in the past been a miller, merchant, and land-owner, and was related to or associated with several of the large land-holding families in the Niagara District. His sentiments on the land and immigration questions could be regarded, therefore, as substantially those of an influential element within the province.

Lieutenant-Governor Gore, thoroughly alarmed by the action of the Assembly in approving several of the resolutions, forestalled further action by a hurried prorogation, "rather," as he said, "than to wait until such dangerous Resolutions, reported and adopted, should be promulgated to the Public, through the medium of the press." At this time also, a prominent land-owner and magistrate, William Dickson, who had been selling land to Americans, was dismissed from office. Gore, writing to Lord Bathurst in 1817, explained that the interruption of immigration from the United States was particularly offensive

[3] See J. B. McMaster, *History of the People of the United States* (New York, 1900), IV, 383-4.

to land speculators who had become possessed of vast tracts in the loose era of the pre-war days. These speculators were dependant chiefly upon immigration from the United States to realize a profit upon their investments.

This was the beginning of an agitation, in which business interests were always prominent, that led in the end to the virtual abandonment of the prohibition of American immigration. Running concurrently with this agitation, and forming an essential part of it, was a controversy lasting until 1828 over the general question of naturalization of aliens. Under Bathurst's instructions of 1815 magistrates had been forbidden to administer the oath of allegiance to Americans, except by special permission. When the Assembly protested in 1817, Bathurst at once pointed out that the naturalization requirements actually applying to Upper Canada were those dating from the reign of George II which required seven years' residence and subscription to various oaths and declarations. These conditions, he announced, would henceforth be enforced.

The agitation was renewed in 1821 when Barnabas Bidwell, a native of Massachusetts, was elected to the Assembly from Lennox and Addington. The administration declared him ineligible because he had not taken the required oaths, charging also that he was a convicted criminal. When his son, Marshall Spring Bidwell, was elected in his place, he also was declared to be an alien and his opponent was awarded the seat. The Assembly, indignant at this action, voided the decision. Both Bidwells had taken the oath of allegiance but not the oaths prescribed by Bathurst; nor, indeed, had anyone else. Accordingly, probably a majority of the people in Upper Canada were legally disqualified from holding any public office and had no valid title to their property. Such a state of affairs was intolerable, and appeals for remedial legislation were made to the British government by both the Lieutenant-Governor and the Assembly. Bathurst suggested that the Upper Canada Assembly pass legislation conferring the rights of citizenship on the Americans then residing in the province. The insinuation contained in this suggestion that Americans, however long resident, were foreigners, even though they might have fought in defence of the province, aroused a storm of indignation. For two years the issue was tossed back and forth, between the two branches of the Legislature and between the Legislature and the imperial Parliament. In the end, with the approval of the British authorities, a bill was introduced in the Assembly (by Marshall Spring Bidwell) providing that all persons who had received grants of land, held public office, or had taken the oath of allegiance and had been settled in the province in or before 1820 were to be recognized as British citizens without qualification of any kind. Others might be admitted to citizenship at the end of seven years' residence.

This legislation was retroactive and proposed no policy for the future. It was, however, a rebuff to the reactionary, anti-American element whose prejudices were provoking strife and retarding progress. Lieutenant-Governor Maitland, who had opposed every step leading towards relaxation of the exclusion policies, and had insinuated that Americans were disloyal, declared that he was "mortified" by this triumph of "an unworthy and falling faction." Bathurst may have felt equally mortified but in the difficult situation he had to make some concessions. The Upper Canada officials remained unfriendly towards American immigration but it was difficult to dam back the tide of people in search of land. As late as 1831 Sir John Colborne wrote in alarm over the influx of American land seekers, but Goderich, from the Colonial Office in London, had no suggestion to offer other than that the Attorney-General might take a few test cases to the courts and that a proclamation might be issued warning aliens against acquiring land before becoming naturalized.[4] After 1825 the bulk of the newcomers to the province were from the British Isles, but there continued to be a considerable American element as well. Many of the American immigrants after 1820 were people with capital, and, what was of equal importance, with technical experience which was turned to the development of industries. Their enterprises provided employment in lines other than agriculture and added new sources of wealth. This can best be illustrated by presenting a few examples of such activities.

The presence of considerable deposits of bog iron within the province early attracted the attention of Upper Canada authorities. In the year 1800, Wallis Sunderlin, from Vermont, established himself in Leeds County in the eastern part of the

---

[4] The Bidwell cases which gave early prominence to the question of naturalization are dealt with by W. R. Riddell, "The Bidwell Elections," Ontario Historical Society, *Papers and Records*, XXI (1924). W. H. Merritt, of Welland Canal fame, appearing before a select committee of the provincial Assembly in 1828 pointed out that the exclusion of Americans had chiefly benefited Ohio at the expense of Upper Canada.

province and a year later was turning out some bar iron and also pots and kettles for the use of the settlers. Some time after 1815 an Englishman, John Mason, erected a small furnace on Potter's Creek in the Long Point country where bog iron was accessible in large quantities. In 1820, after Mason's death, the enterprise was taken over by a group of young Americans from the State of New York, among them being Joseph Van Orman, Hiram Capron, and George Tillson. Their energy and skill developed an extensive manufacturing business and provided employment for many people. Capron and Tillson retired from the firm during the later 1820's in order to embark upon other enterprises in neighbouring counties and Benjamin Van Orman came from the United States to join his brother. In 1829 Elijah Leonard came also, from Syracuse, as superintendent of the works. He was one of a family which since the middle of the seventeenth century had been engaged in iron manufacture in America.[5] In 1834 Leonard established a foundry in St. Thomas which in 1838 was removed to London where it has since been in continuous operation.

The separation of Capron and Tillson from the Van Ormans in 1825 was of lasting importance to other communities. Tillson first opened a forge on Otter Creek at what is now the site of the town of Tillsonburg, but soon embarked in other ventures, particularly milling, thereby laying the foundation of the town's growth. Capron made an extensive purchase of land at the forks of the Grand River in which there were enormous deposits of gypsum which he developed.[6] The settlers looked up to Capron from the first weeks of his association with its community enterprises, and he was soon "King Capron" to all the countryside. From the gypsum beds which he first opened there developed an industry of large proportions with properties in several counties in Western Ontario and plants at half a dozen places.

The Van Ormans continued in business at Normandale until about 1850 when the supply of bog iron began to give out and when they also began to feel the competition of manufac-

---

[5] See W. J. Patterson, "The Long Point Furnace," *Canadian Mining Journal*, LX (September, 1939), 544-9.

[6] The presence of these gypsum deposits had been known before the War of 1812. Michael Smith speaks of the discovery of this valuable resource in his *A Geographical View of the Province of Upper Canada* (Hartford, 1813), p. 32, and notes that "no soil can be better adapted to the use of plaster than that of the district of London."

tures imported from England and the United States. During their period of greatest activity they found time, nevertheless, for various business ventures aside from the manufacture of iron. They undertook several road-building contracts for the provincial government and also the dredging of a channel through the Long Point peninsula to facilitate navigation. During their years of manufacturing activity the Van Ormans turned out cook stoves, box stoves for heating purposes, pots, kettles, mill castings, and many other articles. These they sometimes peddled up and down the lake shore, putting in at the little ports and selling to the local merchants who in turn disposed of the articles to the settlers.[7]

In Gosfield Township near the Detroit River another extensive deposit of bog iron was opened and developed by two Ohio iron-makers, Eleakim Field and B. P. Cahoon, their enterprise being known as the Colbourne Furnaces. They commenced operations in the autumn of 1831 and by March of 1832 were turning out from four to five tons of pig iron every twenty-four hours and employing from sixty to seventy men. Their products included stoves, pots, kettles, mill and plough irons, fire dogs, and potash cauldrons. The *Canadian Emigrant*, published at Sandwich, was able to testify to the excellence of their product when it said: "The present number of the *Emigrant* is printed in a pair of Imperial chases, cast at the iron works of Messrs. Field and Cahoon, Gosfield. They are perfect matches and as soft as wrought iron. Both chases weigh about 50 lb. and only cost three dollars: a pair of wrought iron of the same dimensions would cost twenty-four."[8]

Tanning, an industry closely related to an agricultural community, was developed by the skill and enterprise of Americans in various places in Upper Canada. Simeon Morrill operated a tannery and made shoes in London as early as the 1830's. When London was incorporated as a town in 1847 he became its first mayor. He was the first large employer of labour in the place and was noted for paying his wages in cash, a practice somewhat

---

[7] See F. E. Leonard, "The Normandale Furnace." Ontario Historical Society, *Papers and Records*, XX (1923), 92-3. See also the Simcoe *Reformer*, September 24, 1931. In the *Courier of Upper Canada*, April 21, 1832, J. B. Van Norman advertises pig and scrap iron at £7 10s. per ton. The name Van Orman, originally used, later became Van Norman as above.

[8] *Canadian Emigrant* (Sandwich), September 29, 1832. In the issue of March 1, 1832, there is a description of the iron works in Gosfield.

unusual at that time. His tanneries were twice destroyed by fire but in each case he quickly rebuilt the plant and sought to avoid similar disaster by organizing the town's first volunteer fire brigade. He was a stockholder and prominent in the organization of the London and Port Stanley Railway and the London Savings Bank, as well as one of the founders of the Board of Trade. He was interested in all educational developments and when the first large school was built in London in 1849 he presented it with a bell costing £100 and also offered the interest on £1,000 annually towards the support of the school. Ellis Walton Hyman, a native of Pennsylvania, was another American tanner who established himself in London (1834). He soon placed his business on a wider basis by securing contracts from the military authorities for boots for the British regiments then in garrison in London. He established a packing plant and was associated with other manufacturing and financial enterprises. The tanning industry which he founded has had more than a century of continuous operation.

James M. Williams, born in Camden, New Jersey, was a man of varied activities. On his arrival in London in 1845 he engaged in the carriage-making business but soon removed to Hamilton where he began the manufacture of railway cars. During the 1850's he became interested in the oil deposits near the St. Clair River, dug the first oil well at Oil Springs and established one of the first oil refineries in Canada. Later he manufactured pressed tinware, being a pioneer also in this line of business. He was interested in the promotion of railways, a director of several financial companies and from 1867 to 1875 was Hamilton's representative in the Ontario Legislature. Edward Campbell, also an American, was engaged in glass making in the Grand River region as early as 1834. In that year the provincial Assembly was asked to give incorporation to the Upper Canada Glass Factory and it was stated by Campbell that a larger factory was proposed to be built in Cayuga Township.

Hamilton owed much of its earlier industrial development to the American businessmen who settled there. Edward and Charles Gurney, of Oneida County, New York, began the manufacture of stoves about 1843 and developed an industry of large proportions. They were interested in many other enterprises apart from their foundry. Edward Jackson, born in Connecticut, began business as a tinsmith at Niagara in 1826, but later established his business in Hamilton and was interested in other enterprises elsewhere in Canada. He was one of the earliest directors of the Gore Bank and a supporter of railway schemes planned to contribute to the trade of Hamilton. Jacob Winer, coming to the same city from the United States, established a drug business in 1830 which he carried on successfully until his retirement in 1884. He was a member of the City Council for several years and one of the founders of the Hamilton Board of Trade in 1845.

American capital also played an important part in the development of transportation facilities within the province. When the Welland Canal project was proposed by W. H. Merritt, whose name is so closely connected with that enterprise, it was J. B. Yates, of Chittenango, New York, who was most prominent in financing operations. His family had fought on the revolutionary side but they were connected with the Butlers at Niagara, Loyalists of Loyalists, and through his visits to them he had become acquainted with the canal scheme and gave it his support. He grasped the magnitude of the work and its importance to the province. The biographer of W. H. Merritt says: "It is unnecessary to be invidious, yet we think that were it not for the assistance of Mr. Yates, the success of the canal at this time would hardly be accomplished."[9]

Samuel Zimmerman, who came from Pennsylvania in 1844, was railway promoter, railway lobbyist, and railway contractor at one and the same time. He began his career in Canada by undertaking a contract on the Welland Canal, then branched off into transportation projects which at the time were springing up like mushrooms. He was associated with the construction of the Great Western Railway and the Suspension Bridge at Niagara, the Erie and Ontario, Woodstock and Lake Erie, Port Hope and Lindsay, Cobourg and Peterboro railways, the Sarnia branch of the Great Western, and the proposed construction of the Great Southern Railway to run in a direct course from the Detroit to the Niagara River. He was proprietor of foundries and docks on the Niagara River, founder of the Zimmerman Bank, had large real estate holdings in the principal cities and elsewhere, and at Niagara was in control of such utilities as the gas and water supplies.[10] In the promotion of his enterprises he was said by his

[9] J. P. Merritt, *Biography of the Hon. W. H. Merritt . . .* (St. Catharines, 1875), p. 162.
[10] See *Canadian Merchants' Magazine and Commercial Review* (Toronto), I, 177-81.

critics to have used methods which, in the words of one writer, "virtually made him ruler of the province for several years." His influence in political circles was strong and was used for the advancement of his numerous schemes. His operations were so extensive that many places became dependent upon him for their prosperity and numerous individuals found their interests involved with his in such a way that they ceased to be free agents. He was one of the type of "practical men" who had built railways and canals in New York and Pennsylvania and who now found Canada a field ready for harvesting. Zimmerman was killed in 1857 when a train went through an open drawbridge over the Desjardins Canal near Hamilton.[11]

Contributions of American skill and enterprise such as have been mentioned in connection with London, Hamilton, and Niagara might be presented from a score of other places. J. H. Fairbank, coming from New York State, became one of the outstanding figures in the oil developments in Lambton County. Hiram Walker, a native of Massachusetts, founded the extensive distilleries which bear his name. Several successful manufacturing industries established in Guelph in the 1850's were under American management. George J. Goodhue, who came from Vermont to St. Thomas in 1822, was a representative of the shrewd speculating type, and at his death in 1870 was credited with being the wealthiest individual in the western part of the province. Though not an active politician, he was a member of the Legislative Council of Canada from 1841 to 1867. Jacob Hespeler was representative of yet another group, those of European birth but of American experience. He left his home in Würtemberg at an early age and spent some years in the United States before coming to Waterloo County. He was merchant, miller, distiller, and manufacturer. He developed water-powers and applied them to the use of his mills. The prosperous community which grew up around his enterprises bears his name today in recognition of the contribution which he made to its upbuilding and progress.

Patrick Shirreff, when touring Upper Canada in 1833, observed that most of the active business people in the province at that time had come from the United States. Shirreff observed

---

[11] T. C. Keefer, outstanding Canadian engineer, severely condemned the business methods of Zimmerman in his article on "Travel and Transportation" contributed to *Eighty Years Progress of British North America* (Toronto, 1863). See pages 221-4.

also that nine out of ten of the hotel-keepers and stage-drivers whom he encountered were Americans. He might have added, as others noted, that in almost every community there were American mechanics whose practical knowledge and skill caused their presence to be valued by the community. The Rev. William Proudfoot recorded in November, 1833, that he had met "Mr. Sheppard, the axe-maker, who has come to reside in London. . . . He is a keen enterprising American." American axes were so superior to all others that the arrival of a skilled axe-maker in a community might well deserve record. The same could be said of the printers who came and went between western New York and Upper Canada. Milton W. Hamilton's description of the craft in New York State[12] would apply to conditions in Upper Canada in almost every particular. Joseph K. Averill, Chauncey Beach, James Beardslee, Ezra S. Ely, Bartimus Ferguson, Samuel Heron, Hiram Leavenworth, Silvester Tiffany, Samuel Hall Wilcocke, and William W. Wyman were among the New York State men who played a part in early printing in Upper Canada.

In its earlier years Upper Canada offered limited scope for professional men, and save in the field of medicine few American names appear before 1840. In medicine, however, the American contribution was noteworthy. A striking number of the men who practised this profession in the province were graduates of American medical schools, chiefly of the Fairfield Medical School in Herkimer County, New York. Beginning in 1822 the names of students from Upper Canada appear year by year in its records, as many as twelve being there at one time, though not all proceeded to a degree. Elijah Duncombe attended lectures in 1830 and then wrote the examinations of the Upper Canada Medical Council. Being unsuccessful he returned to Fairfield for another year of study after which he was admitted to practice in the province. David Duncombe, who enrolled in 1824, and whose name did not again appear in the lists, was admitted in 1828. John Crumbie, on the other hand, attended during four successive years, ending with 1830, when he received his degree. He was at once admitted to practice in Upper Canada and spent all of his later life in Peel County.

In the *Colonial Advocate* of August 19, 1824, appeared the

[12] See M. W. Hamilton, *The Country Printer, New York State, 1785-1830* (New York, 1936).

announcement of a medical school to be opened at St. Thomas under the joint direction of Dr. Charles Duncombe and Dr. John Rolph. A letter addressed by Dr. Rolph to Colonel Thomas Talbot, seeking his patronage, proposed that in addition to the instruction in medicine there should be a dispensary at which medical advice would be given freely to those needing it. There is no record that the St. Thomas school was ever opened, perhaps because no students appeared, but the idea found realization in Rolph's own school of medicine which he established at Toronto in 1843 after an exile of six years following the Rebellion of 1837. It was incorporated in 1853 as the Toronto School of Medicine and later became the medical department of Victoria University.

Standards of the profession improved after 1817 when the Upper Canada Medical Board was instituted as an examining body before whom applicants for licence to practise were required to appear. The number of medical men in the province possessing some qualifications at this time did not greatly exceed forty, though there were many others professing to have healing knowledge and preying upon the weakness or credulity of the people. Some of these quack doctors could neither read nor write so as to be understood. The Kingston *Gazette* of June 2, 1812, copied an account sent to a Mrs. Gould by one of these self-taught physicians: "To Dr. for medsin and attendants whene he was chokd with a large peas of Butter no of meat £3."

The first physician to appear before the new Medical Board was an American, Dr. John Gilchrist, a native of Bedford, New Hampshire, and a graduate of Yale Medical School. In 1822 he became surgeon to the Northumberland militia regiment and was later a member of the provincial Assembly. He was arrested as a rebel during the troubles of 1837-8 but was soon released, nothing being found against him except his American origin. Other men came forward year by year with diplomas and certificates and testimonials asking to be allowed to practise in the province, and the Medical Board scrutinized them all with care. During its first year of office the number admitted was eight, among them being Dr. Charles Duncombe, later prominent in the troubles of 1837. In January, 1820, six candidates were rejected with a recommendation to further study and "attendance on a course of lectures at New York." During the second year only four applicants were licensed, while eight were rejected, four of them for a second time. Two Fairfield graduates appeared in April, 1832, and were accepted, but in April, 1834, a Fairfield product was rejected because of his inability to define either of the words physiology and pathology though he displayed "tickets from his college of two courses of lectures and a doctor's degree after four years of study."

The distribution of medical men was uneven at this time but the standard of the profession was higher than might have been expected under the conditions then existing. As early as 1832 the doctors in the London District organized the London District Medical Society, adopting a constitution, electing officers, and naming a committee to secure the adherence to the rules of the Society of all those practising in the district. During the 1830's disciples of Samuel Thompson, of Vermont, who taught a botanic method of treatment, entered the province. An edition of Thompson's *New Guide to Health* was published at Hamilton in 1832 and the cult soon found followers. The Thompsonians carried on their practice without a licence and in defiance of the law for a number of years. They were later known as Eclectics and ultimately became absorbed in the general profession.[13]

The legitimate practitioners had not only to combat the activities of charlatans of all kinds but also had to meet a credulity which was spread by religious bodies. At the height of the cholera outbreak of 1834, the *Christian Guardian*, organ of the Methodist Church, published an editorial under the heading "Remarks on the Cholera, its Moral Causes and Remedies," which viewed the plague as a punishment for moral evil.[14] Similar sentiments were expressed in a sermon delivered by the Rev. John Bethune, a leading minister of the Church of England in the province.

The devotion of the physicians to their duties during the cholera outbreaks of 1832 and 1834 forms a noble chapter in the history of medicine in the province, several losing their lives in attendance upon the victims of the plague. Among the American-born practitioners in Upper Canada at the time of the outbreaks was Dr. Elam Stimson who deserves remembrance not alone for his services to the sick but also as an original investigator who made a contribution to medical literature. He was born in Connecticut in 1792 and after serving with the

---

[13] William Canniff, *The Medical Profession in Upper Canada, 1783-1850* (Toronto, 1894), pp. 69-75.
[14] *Christian Guardian*, August 20 and September 3, 1834.

American forces during the War of 1812 studied medicine at Yale and Dartmouth, graduating in 1819. He came to Upper Canada in 1823, locating first at St. Catharines but removing to Galt a year later and to London in 1828. He was at the latter place during the cholera outbreak of 1832, his wife and one of his children being victims. After their deaths he removed to St. George where he continued to reside until his death in 1869. In 1835, following the second outbreak, he published a pamphlet, *The Cholera Beacon*, in which he embodied his observations of the nature of the disease and also his ideas of correct treatment. This was probably the first original medical treatise ever published in Upper Canada and even today it has value because of its detailed description of the symptoms and character of the disease as the author witnessed it in the western part of the province.[15]

In the realm of religion the American contribution bulked large, as will be shown in other chapters of this volume. With the exception of the Church of England and the Roman Catholic Church, almost every religious body was first introduced into the province from the United States and drew heavily upon the United States for its leaders and teachers.

Travellers in the province during the 1830's invariably noted the large number of Americans whom they encountered. Many recorded the prevalence of American customs and characteristics or the American ways of doing business. The civil and military authorities continued to have the bogey of American influences ever before them and in 1833 Sir John Colborne appears to have had in mind a possible division of the province, with London as the capital of the more westerly section. By sending large numbers of British settlers to this region he hoped to counteract "the influence of Yankeeism so prevalent about St. Thomas and along the lake shore." Such at least were the sentiments which he expressed to the Rev. Benjamin Cronyn,

---

[15] *The Cholera Beacon, Being a Treatise on the Epidemic Cholera: as It Appeared in Upper Canada, in 1832-4: with a Plain and Practical Description of the First Grade, or Premonitory Symptoms, and the Various Forms of Attack, by which the Disease May Be Detected in Its Curable Stage; together with Directions for Successful Treatment. Designed for Popular Instruction* (Dundas, 1835). A copy of the pamphlet is in the library of the Surgeon-General's Department at Washington. It was reprinted in full in the University of Western Ontario *Medical Journal*, VII (December, 1936 and February, 1937) and also in the *Transactions* of the London and Middlesex Historical Society as part XV (1937).

Anglican rector at London. The completion of Mr. Cronyn's church building in London with funds contributed by the government was a part of the crusade against "republicanism."[16]

The feelings of the inhabitants towards Americans were of a mixed character. Patrick Shirreff encountered much anti-American prejudice in 1833, chiefly among persons lately come from Britain, though it was remarked that no class of people absorbed the worst American characteristics so easily as some of the British immigrants. Edward Allen Talbot, Irish immigrant and author, expressed his surprise that though the inhabitants of Upper Canada were made up of almost every race the tendency was towards assimilation to a single type – American. "I shall renounce all pretensions to discernment if many of the inhabitants of Upper Canada are not the most accomplished Yankees on the other side of the Atlantic,"[17] was Shirreff's opinion in 1833. "In Upper Canada the feeling is totally Yankee and the inhabitants care not a fig for the institutions of Great Britain," was the more extreme view expressed by John MacTaggart who spent three years in the country during the later 1820's.[18]

A more thoughtful opinion was that expressed by John R. Godley in 1842 when he wrote:

The Canadians are neither British nor American: the local circumstances and situation of the country (which are among the most powerful influences which form national character) tend towards the latter; and the tendency is increased by the vicinity of, and intercourse with the States: on the other hand, early habits and associations, communication with their friends in the old country, political and ecclesiastical institutions, and the antipathy produced by rivalry and collision with their American neighbours, unite them to Great Britain. I think they are more American than they believe themselves to be, or would

[16] See the diary of the Rev. William Proudfoot, March 8, 1833. This diary, extending from June, 1832, to September, 1848, has been published in ten parts. The first three parts, covering the period June, 1832, to March 16, 1833, were published in nos. VI, VIII, and XI of the *Transactions* of the London and Middlesex Historical Society; the remaining seven parts are printed in the Ontario Historical Society's *Papers and Records*, XXVI-XXXII (1930-6). Hereafter referred to as *Proudfoot Diary*.

[17] Patrick Shirreff, *A Tour through North America; together with a Comprehensive View of the Canadas and United States as Adapted for Agricultural Emigration* (Edinburgh, 1835), pp. 408-9.

[18] John MacTaggart, *Three Years in Canada; an Account of the Actual State of the Country in 1826-7-8* . . . (London, 1829), I, 207-8.

like to be considered; and in the ordinary course of things, as the emigrants cease to be so large a proportion as they do now to those born in the province, they must become more so; still it is very important to recollect that here is a national character in process of formation, and that now is the time to infuse into it, as far as possible, those elements which we are accustomed to consider valuable in our own.[19]

The general situation was quaintly put by Adam Fergusson's Yankee guide at Kingston who asked him if he thought that another war between England and the United States was likely to occur. Fergusson thought such a tragedy unlikely, to which the guide replied: "Well, sir, I guess, if we don't fight for a year or two, we won't fight at all, for we are marrying so fast, sir, that a man won't be sure but he may shoot his father or his brother-in-law."[20]

[19] John R. Godley, *Letters from America* (London, 1844), I, 200-2.
[20] Adam Fergusson, *Practical Notes Made during a Tour in Canada and a Portion of the United States in* MDCCCXXXI . . . 2nd ed. (Edinburgh, 1834), pp. 147-8.

5: Schools and the State

Such education as may be necessary for people in the lower degrees of life, necessarily requiring but little expense, may at present be provided for by their connections and relations.

—JOHN GRAVES SIMCOE (1792)

What made our revolution a foregone conclusion was the act of the general court, passed in May, 1647, which established the system of common schools. . . . But it was in making education not only common to all, but in some sense, compulsory on all, that the destiny of the free republics of America was practically settled.

—JAMES RUSSELL LOWELL

In the quarter-century after 1815, public education in Upper Canada had to contend with restrictions and inequalities handed down from the past and embodied not only in habits of mind but in laws. The vital question was whether common-school education should be under clerical control and restricted in scope as in England or should follow the more democratic example of the newer American states. Agitation over this question was a fruitful source of unrest before the Rebellion of 1837, being one phase of the general struggle for equal rights. Clerical control of education was zealously championed by the Rev. John Strachan, Rector of York and later Bishop of Toronto. Strachan fought hard to obtain for his church in Canada privileges which even at that time were tending to disappear in England, and his tactics long frustrated those who favoured a democratic system of schools free from clerical control.

Education was a matter of government concern from the very foundation of the province. Lieutenant-Governor Simcoe planned the establishment of a university at his proposed capital in the western section of the province. When, more than seventy years later, a divinity college was founded in this locality, members of the Simcoe family sent his portrait to be placed in its halls, recalling thereby his early and intense interest in higher education. Simcoe had also favoured the establishment of grammar schools to which the sons of officials and of the better-class inhabitants might be sent, but of common schools there is little if any mention in all the Governor's voluminous correspondence. The subject gave him no concern. What was needed, in his opinion, was educational opportunity for those who would comprise the professional and administrative classes in the province. He repeatedly pressed upon the home government the need of setting aside lands as an endowment for this purpose and the grants made in 1797 were in answer to his plea.

Not until ten years later, however, were the first district grammar schools established, and it was soon realized that this step was in the wrong direction. The grammar schools were accessible to but a few, their courses of study were unsuited to the conditions and needs of the province, and they were under considerable clerical influence. In the Assembly there was outspoken criticism, and a sharp division of opinion arose between the two branches of the Legislature, members of the Council defending the aristocratic system while the Assembly steadily voiced a demand for common schools. On the eve of the War of 1812 petitions were presented from several districts protesting against the limited school facilities. Inhabitants of the Midland District recited in their petition that "a few wealthy inhabitants and those of the Town of Kingston reap exclusively the benefits of it [the grammar school] in this District. The institution, instead of aiding the middling and poorer class of His Majesty's subjects, casts money into the lap of the rich, who are sufficiently able, without public assistance, to support a school in every respect equal to the one established by law." A similar petition from the Newcastle District declared that the school legislation of 1807 was "entirely useless to the inhabitants."[1]

Those inhabitants of Upper Canada who were of American origin had brought with them the idea of the common school, though there was as yet little in the newer western states that might serve as an educational example. Not until 1825 did Ohio, the oldest of the states carved out of the Northwest Territory, establish a system of common schools supported by taxation. Indiana recorded its first attempt at a common-school system in 1816, with legislation permitting electors in a township, if they saw fit, to establish schools; but since no money was provided few came into existence. This state had a struggling university and numerous academies before it could report any common schools. Illinois in its legislation of 1825 went only so far as to make permissive the establishment of schools which would be maintained by taxation. It was not upon the example

---

[1] *Ontario Bureau of Archives, 9th Report* (Toronto, 1912), 16. Both of the petitions quoted were received by the Assembly on February 11, 1812.

of these newer western states that Upper Canada was to model its legislation. Nor did the suggestion come from contemporary New England practice since, during the first forty years of Upper Canada's history, public-school sentiment was at a low ebb in Massachusetts and the East, with decentralizing tendencies at their height. American influence upon school legislation in Upper Canada can be traced more directly to the State of New York where a system of state schools had been established in 1812, with a Superintendent of Education in charge. The New York State law provided that electors in each township should choose three commissioners to mark out as many school districts as seemed proper. In each district three elected trustees were to manage the local school. Support was to come from state and people, each township being required to raise by taxation as much as it received from the state treasury. At first some of the municipal areas refused to tax themselves, and to meet this situation the tax was made compulsory. By 1821, 300,000 children were enrolled in 6,300 school districts.[2]

Common schools in Upper Canada were few in number in the year in which New York State enacted its legislation. Michael Smith, himself a teacher, wrote in 1812: "The greater part of the inhabitants of Canada are not well educated for as they were poor when they came to the province, and the country being but thinly settled for a number of years, they had but little chance for the benefit of schools." Three privately supported schools were favourably mentioned by Smith, that at York taught by the Anglican rector, one on the Bay of Quinte taught by an American, and a third in the village of Niagara taught by one Reva Burns. He suggested that teachers settling in other parts of the province, particularly in the London District, would receive support.[3]

Addressing the Legislature at the opening of the session of 1816, on his first appearance since before the war, Lieutenant-Governor Sir Francis Gore suggested changes in the school system of the province. His address embodied a frank admission that the grammar schools did not meet public needs and that what was required was a system of township schools, accessible to the children of the settlers. From these elementary schools,

[2] See A. D. Mayo, *The American Common School in New York, New Jersey and Pennsylvania. Report, U.S. Commissioner of Education, 1895-6*, chapter VI.

[3] Michael Smith, *A Geographical View of the Province of Upper Canada* (Hartford, 1813), pp. 63-4.

it was expected that a few children of superior ability would enter the grammar schools and from the latter a few would go on to a provincial seminary or university.

The Assembly was evidently expecting such a recommendation for the Select Committee appointed to consider the matter quickly presented not only a report but also a bill, which was passed during the session. While the report emphasized the need of a university to check the tendency to send youths to the United States for their higher education, it stressed even more the fact that nothing had yet been done to provide education for the humbler inhabitants. The bill introduced in February, 1816, which in due time became the Common School Act of that year, was the first of the series of measures determining the nature of common-school education in the province. It bore marked resemblance to the New York State legislation of 1812. In each of the ten districts into which the province was divided there was to be a board of education which should prescribe the courses of study, specify the textbooks, and make all necessary rules for the government of the schools. Within the district any community which could furnish at least twenty children might be formed into a school section and elect three trustees. These trustees were to provide a school and could both appoint and dismiss teachers, who must, however, be British subjects or have taken the oath of allegiance. The Legislature voted a sum equivalent to $24,000 annually to be apportioned among the districts on the basis of population. The district boards were to distribute this among the schools and whatever additional sum was required by any individual school had to be met by fees or subscriptions.

The Committee appointed by the Legislature spent only three weeks in drawing up its report. The legislation was too hastily prepared and the defects which appeared were quickly seized upon by opponents of the measure. If the framers of the bill believed that their legislation would provide the province with adequate common-school facilities, they must soon have been disillusioned. School-houses could not appear as by magic, properly trained teachers were not available, trustees had little conception of their duties, and abuses of various kinds developed, tending to discredit the system.

A school system suited to the needs of the province might have done much at this time to restore a war-stricken people. In the Province of Nova Scotia in the same period there was a literary renaissance inspired by strong local patriotism. It is true that Nova Scotia had not suffered as had Upper Canada; indeed, it had emerged from the struggle with money profit and with an atmosphere of optimism and high hopes. Although education in the province suffered much in later years as a result of sectarian rivalries and jealousies, the leaders in the period immediately after the war were convinced of its value, and the practical aspects of education were particularly emphasized.[4] In Upper Canada, on the other hand, the question of education, instead of being a unifying and cementing influence, provoked dissension and unrest. Between 1816 and 1820 little real advance was made. In 1819 supporters of the grammar schools offered to increase the number of such institutions and have them serve in part the function of common schools. The offer was rejected and in 1820 the Common School Act of 1816 was renewed, some strengthening amendments being included. Finally, in 1824, the act was made permanent, grants being conditioned upon the character and efficiency of the teachers as shown by the examinations of the district boards.

In the period between 1820 and 1824 an unsuccessful effort was made to introduce in Upper Canada the English system of Lancastrian schools which had already been tried out in New York City as early as 1808 and ten years later in Philadelphia. The system, as it was proposed to introduce it in Upper Canada, included religious instruction according to the doctrines of the Church of England. The Lancastrian plan was advocated chiefly by the Rev. John Strachan who laid his ideas before the Home Office and received its approval in 1822. A year later the Lieutenant-Governor, on his own authority, created a provincial Board of Education to have control over all schools receiving state aid and to have charge also of all the lands and funds set aside for educational purposes. The Act of 1824 recognized this supervising body as a part of the school system of the province.

Through the next thirteen years there may be traced an ever-growing uneasiness with regard to the measure of clerical control exercised or sought to be exercised over the schools. Strachan, who became chairman of the Board of Education, had large powers over all the educational activities of the province,

---

[4] See *Journal of Education for Nova Scotia*, September, 1936; also D. C. Harvey's article on "The Intellectual Awakening of Nova Scotia," *Dalhousie Review*, XIII (April, 1933), and reprinted in *Historical Essays on the Atlantic Provinces* (Carleton Library, 1967).

and when in 1827 a royal charter was granted for a university it was found that the document gave the Church of England a pre-eminent place in its constitution and government. This particular question was joined with other educational grievances as a part of the general indictment of the administration in 1837.

It would be tedious to recount the many details of the controversy between 1824 and 1837. There was continuous difficulty in finding the money with which to carry out the provisions of the law. In the Assembly's session of 1832 it was pointed out that provincial grants did not exceed a shilling per pupil and that therefore not more than ten dollars a year was provided towards the teacher's salary. Local taxation for school purposes was as yet unknown, though in 1833 the Legislature conditioned its grants upon the raising by the trustees of any school of an amount twice as great as was received. Commissions were appointed to inquire into the question of public education, the most noteworthy being that headed by Dr. Charles Duncombe, member for Oxford, which reported in 1836. This report emphasized the need of practical education, therein being in harmony with Nova Scotian ideas of an earlier date. Its recommendations included local taxation for school purposes, elective school boards, inspection of schools, training of teachers, and prescribed textbooks. The presentation of this document, so obviously reflecting American influences,[5] and the refusal of the Legislative Council to make any radical change in the existing system, were among the closing developments of the period. In 1837 came the armed uprising under Mackenzie and when the smoke of battle had cleared away educational reform became a part of the general reconstruction of the 1840's.

It is difficult to estimate the extent of the earlier popular demand for common schools. While there was much discussion of the subject in the Assembly, it may be questioned if the majority of the pioneer farmers, intent on the clearing of land and securing a livelihood, desired anything beyond provision for the most elementary education. Here and there throughout the province clergymen and others opened small academies and boarded their pupils. In the larger villages young women conducted private schools for the smaller children. The farmers in

---

[5] The Legislative Council rejected the report as being "nearly, if not altogether, a transcript of the school law now in operation in the neighboring state of New York" (J. G. Hodgins, *Historical Educational Papers and Documents Illustrative of the Educational System of Ontario, 1792-1853*, Toronto 1911-12, I, 62).

the townships could usually find some old soldier or an itinerant American to give a scanty measure of training to their children. As a rule, however, this would be in the winter months when there was less demand for the labour which even children could contribute to the tasks of pioneer life. It is no pleasing picture that has come down to us of many of the teachers at this period. The *Canadian Christian Examiner* stated in 1838 that "it is painful to have to record that a great proportion of our teachers are men of intemperate habits." The same journal referred to "the degraded state" into which the profession of teaching had fallen in the province.[6] On the other hand there were men like Jonathan Huston Clendennan, a native of Pennsylvania, who for twenty-five years taught the school in St. Catharines and exerted an influence for good in the whole community.[7]

Apart from the more general influence of neighbouring American states upon the school system of Upper Canada, there were two minor influences which from time to time occasioned concern. These were the American teacher and the American textbook. As early as 1802 a Major William Graham, living on Yonge Street north of the town of York, complained to the authorities of the activities of two American schoolmasters in his neighbourhood. He wrote:

> *They use all their efforts to poison the minds of the youth by teaching them in republican books, and in particular the third part of Webster's History. Nothing would give me more pleasure than for you and other officers of the Government to look on pages 113 to 149 of the third part of Webster's History. Youths educated in such books will by and by have the privilege of voting members for our Assembly and filling the House with their own kind, and when that is the case what may the Governor and Council expect but trouble.*[8]

Major Graham may have been prejudiced against these men simply because they were Americans; on the other hand, there probably was considerable American bias to teaching in communities where the population was predominantly of alien

---

[6] *Canadian Christian Examiner*, II (1838), 355, 359.

[7] His death in 1836 at the age of 51 was recorded in the St. Catharines *Journal* of May 5, 1836, high tribute being paid to his character and services.

[8] Major William Graham to the Hon. D. W. Smith, March 29, 1802. See Ontario Educational Association, *Proceedings* (1900), pp. 273-4.

origin. The War of 1812, during which most of the schools were closed, eliminated the more offensive type of teacher and the Common School Act of 1816 stipulated that teachers must be British subjects or take the oath of allegiance. Nevertheless, when American immigration was resumed after the war, many teachers entered the province, some of good repute and some of ill, if we may judge by the records that have come down. Dr. John Rolph, writing in the 1830's, said it was melancholy to find in many of the common schools "a herd of children, instructed by some anti-British adventurer instilling into the young and tender mind sentiments hostile to the parent state . . . teaching them an anti-British dialect, and idiom; although living in a Province and being subjects of the British crown."

A letter appearing in 1832 in the *Canadian Emigrant*, asked the editor for his answer to the following question: "Do you imagine that the Board of Education for the Western District will grant money out of the District Treasury to a teacher of a common school, an American, who is opposed to Sir John Colborne and the present administration, who refused to sign an address to His Majesty, who supports Mr. Mackenzie's grievance petition and who reads and recommends the *Colonial Advocate*?" The editor was non-committal in his reply; he did not know how the Board would act, probably they would consider themselves governed by the statutes.[9] The Toronto *Patriot*, one of the extremely anti-American newspapers, objected to any but British subjects being employed to teach Canadian children, its argument being: "If an American educates the child, the child will grow up with a strong American bias, – an American, that is filthy in his habits, – an American, that is with a nasal twang in his pronunciation, – an American, that is a free-thinker, or fanatic, in religion – and an American, that is an inveterate hater of the British government in his political opinions."[10]

These ill-natured remarks indicate political prejudice rather than considered judgment. The American teachers were probably neither better nor worse than the average of other races, either in scholarship or in character. Mrs. Anna Jameson, an Englishwoman of culture who visited the province in the 1830's, described Upper Canada schoolmasters as "ill-fed, ill-clothed, ill paid or not paid at all, always either Scotch or American and totally unfit for the office they had undertaken." Judged by the standards in England this might be true, but without these ill-fed, ill-clothed, and ill paid teachers schools could not have existed in any but the more populous communities. There were ignoramuses and there were occasional knaves among the American school-teachers, but there were others who came into the remote settlements, not only giving to the children the only instruction they would ever receive but also bringing some intellectual interests, however small, into communities where such interests were but few. It was commonly the practice in Upper Canada, as in the United States, that the teacher should "board around" in the homes of the children attending school, shifting his quarters weekly or at a longer interval. The custom was not without value in making the teacher acquainted with the parents as well as the children. The presence of the teacher in the home, particularly if he were from another land, must also have brought interest to people living in a narrowing environment. Sometimes the teacher was also a preacher as in the case of a Scot living near Guelph, who wrote: "I taught school last winter, and received £10 besides my board, and intend to do the same next winter. I preach every Lord's Day and am also paid for my ministry."[11]

The use of American textbooks naturally aroused the ire of those who saw therein an insidious influence operating upon the minds of the children. Texts in history and geography were particularly under suspicion. We have already noticed the complaint made by Major Graham in 1802 with regard to the anti-British sentiment of Webster's *History*. Similar complaint was sometimes made of Olney's *Geography*. Captain J. E. Alexander, a British officer, wrote after a visit to an Indian mission on the Credit:

> I went into the school room, where I saw American school-books in which Great Britain was not spoken of in the most respectful terms. I also saw American maps in which we were altogether excluded from the shores of the Pacific, the American and Russian territory joining in the northwest; also the boundary of the northeast brought up to the St. Lawrence. Now all this is unbearable among Indians under the protection of the

[11] *Counsel for Emigrants, and Interesting Information from Numerous Sources Concerning British America* . . . 3rd ed. (Aberdeen, 1838), p. 69.

Canadian government, and who would, I fear, be of little use to us in the event of another war.[12]

It was chiefly because they were available and because they were suited to the common needs that American school books were in use. In many a backwoods district there were few texts of any kind other than those which were the teacher's own property. The Hon. David Mills, veteran parliamentarian and Minister of Justice of Canada after 1897, has related that when he first attended school in Kent County in the early 1830's the only book which he possessed was Cobb's *Spelling Book*, published at Erie, Pennsylvania.[13] There were but two geographies for the whole class, one copy each of the American texts by Olney and Woodbridge. Despite this meagre equipment, Mills acquired during his common-school days an interest in geography that continued through life and that was put to practical use when he acted as chairman of the Commission to determine the boundaries between the provinces of Ontario and Manitoba.[14]

There was probably more criticism of the use of American texts than was justified by the facts. The settlers were poor and textbooks passed from father to son or from pupil to pupil until they were worn to tatters. An American teacher coming into Canada would naturally bring his own books with him, as did a teacher named Forsyth who taught near Brantford immediately after the War of 1812. It is recorded that he used Mavor's *Spelling Book*, which was of old-country origin, an American reader, Morse's *Geography*, and Dobell's *Arithmetic*, the latter two being American books.[15] When feelings against the United States were aroused, the textbooks of American origin could be

[12] J. E. Alexander, *Transatlantic Sketches or Visits to the Most Interesting Scenes in North and South America and the West Indies, with Notes on Slavery and Canadian Emigration* (London, 1833), II, 164.

[13] Cobb's *Juvenile Readers* were advertised in the *British American Journal* (St. Catharines) throughout 1834, with commendations from American sources. The Public Archives of Canada has a copy of *Juvenile Reader No. 3* reprinted at Brockville, Canada West, in 1844. It has a frontispiece "The Indian and the British Officer" which has no relation to any of the contents and was evidently intended to give a good British appearance. The contents, while American in tone, were not in any way obnoxious.

[14] Mr. Mills, late in life, wrote a reminiscent account of his boyhood days in Kent County, the manuscript of which is in the possession of the author. He recalls one teacher who, in the absence of anything better, drew large maps and placed them on the walls of the log school-house.

[15] Ontario Historical Society, *Papers and Records*, XII (1914), 68-9.

pictured even as morally unsound. The Toronto *Commercial Herald* expressed such views in its pious wish "that the trash of infidels and the wild theories of republicans may no longer corrupt the susceptible mind of childhood."[16]

A resident of the London District, writing in 1832, said of the schoolmasters and the schools:

> *As there is a want of clergymen, so, I believe, there is of schoolmasters. Those settled in townships generally receive two dollars per quarter for each pupil badly paid, and may have, perhaps, thirty pupils during the winter months. They complain greatly, I am told, of being too dependent on the whims and caprices of a few leading persons around them. . . . In a country where the labor of children is valuable to the colonist, it can not be expected that they will be left at school beyond the age of ten or twelve years; it is, therefore, of supreme importance, that, previous to this period, they should have all the advantages which sound and uninterrupted education can confer.*[17]

The writer of this letter, a cultured Irishman, saw nothing disproportionate, however, in the generous provision made for Upper Canada College at York, of which he said: "Future generations will bless the memory of Sir John Colborne, who, to the many advantages derived from the equity and wisdom of his government, has added that of a magnificent foundation for the purpose of literary instruction. The lowest salary of any of the professors of this institution is £300 per annum, with the accommodation of a noble brick house and the privilege of taking boarders at £50 per annum."[18]

In a neighbouring township of the County of Middlesex, Robert Davis, a farmer, wrote at this time: "My children are without education, and must remain so, unless I shift my quarters . . . the aristocracy dread the common people getting education, well knowing that knowledge is power, and that power which always destroys toryism." Davis wrote this after a visit to Ohio where he was impressed by the provision in the Ohio constitution for the setting aside of one section in each township for school purposes. A year later his sense of injustice

---

[16] Quoted in the *Western Herald* (Sandwich), November 9, 1838.
[17] T. W. Magrath, *Authentic Letters from Upper Canada* . . . (Dublin, 1833), p. 204.
[18] *Ibid.*, p. 205.

made him a participant in the uprising in Upper Canada and he died from wounds received at Amherstburg.[19]

The contrast between the agitated mind of Davis, as revealed in the few sentences quoted, and the complacency, almost eighteenth century in character, of his fellow-Irishman, more happily situated in life, reveals the conflict of opinions in the province. Had Davis known more of the use and abuse of the school lands in the United States, he would have been less sure that Ohio and its neighbours had found the solution for common-school support. Provincial lands in Upper Canada were not readily salable, and the Assembly was not prepared to impose local taxation for school purposes. As late as 1835 it rejected without discussion a bill in which local taxation was put forward as a minor source of revenue. On the other hand, the grants for common-school support were pitifully small when compared with the generous support given to institutions such as Upper Canada College which served only the sons of the well-to-do. The question was more deeply embittered by its religious phase, the Church of England seeking a control over education which the other religious bodies resented and opposed.[20]

[19] Davis was the author of a booklet, printed at Buffalo in 1837, bearing the title: *The Canadian Farmer's Travels in the United States of America in which Remarks are Made on the Arbitrary Policy Practiced in Canada, and the Free and Equal Rights and Happy Effect of the Liberal Institutions and Astonishing Enterprise of the United States.*

[20] The Rev. John Strachan's ambitions to control public education in the province are clearly set forth in a letter which he wrote to the Bishop of Quebec, November 10, 1817, and from which the following is taken: "It was my intention had the bill I proposed last winter to appropriate a Sum of money annually to assist Students in divinity passed into a law to point out the propriety of a General Inspector of Education to whom all returns shall be made such a Person the Govt might have appointed without any Salary in the first Instance to avoid Expence. This office I should have undertaken and it might have been carried into a Precedent that the Minister of York should be Inspector. By this means . . . the established religion would have had a permanent influence over the Education of the people and the whole indirectly placed under the Control of the Bishop who could have advised with and instructed the Inspecter" (*Canadian Historical Review,* XIX (1938), 399-400).

6: Methodism and Its Conflicts

Mr. Donaldson from the 10th concession told me that the Methodists and Baptists have exceedingly increased in the township. God only knows, I hope in His Mercy so to bless my labor that they and all who hold errors will not increase.

—THE REV. WILLIAM PROUDFOOT (1833)

A charge to keep I have,
A God to glorify,
A never-dying soul to save,
And fit it for the sky.

—CHARLES WESLEY

The early religious history of Upper Canada bears many resemblances to that of the American Northwest in the same period but has also some striking points of difference. It was a mission territory, as was the Northwest, and into it came representatives of many religious bodies, following up their adherents, seeking converts from among the indifferent, and at times proselytizing from other groups. American influences upon the religious life and denominational characteristics of Upper Canada were widespread and their effects were often permanent in character. The two most distinctively evangelistic sects, the Methodists and the Baptists, first entered the province from the United States, and though each increased its membership at a later date through immigration from the British Isles the American characteristics persisted for a long time. Indeed, the Methodism of Upper Canada maintained full connection with its parent organization in the United States until 1828, the bond being sufficient to endure even the strains of war. The notable success which attended early Methodist and Baptist effort in Upper Canada indicated that these bodies were best suited to deal with a scattered pioneer population, too few in number and too poor in resources to support settled church establishments but by no means indifferent to religion.

That which chiefly differentiated Upper Canada from the neighbouring American territory, so far as religion was concerned, was the effort that was made to impose upon the Canadian community an ancient church establishment and to give to this particular establishment rights, privileges, and public financial support which were withheld from other religious bodies. Directly or indirectly this condition of affairs affected adversely a majority of the inhabitants and eventually it became one of the chief political issues. It was often clouded by irrelevant argument and there was much misconception in England both as to the nature of the grievances and as to the character of the religious bodies which were outside the bounds of official favour. When the *Quarterly Review* as late as 1820 could describe the Upper Canada Methodists as "for the most part gross and ignorant enthusiasts" it was not likely that its readers would have any real understanding of the state of religion in the province overseas.

The legal basis for the special privileges with which the Church of England in Canada was endowed is found in the Canada Act of 1791 which brought the province into existence. The sections of the Act which relate to religion leave little room for doubt that it was the intention of the British government to establish the Church of England in Upper Canada. The onus of making legal provision for establishment was, however, thrown upon the local Legislature, and though no such provision was ever made in Upper Canada the authorities both in England and in the province itself acted as if the establishment were a part of the constitution. Various practices, such as the precedence always given to the clergy of the Church of England, tended to strengthen this idea.

Any examination of the terms of the Canada Act, in so far as religion is concerned, should be made from the point of view of its framers in 1791 and not from that of the disputants of some later day. The British Parliament in 1791 ordained that lands equal in amount to one-seventh of the Crown grants should be set apart for the support of a Protestant clergy. In later years there was almost endless discussion of the meaning of the word Protestant as used in the bill, but there can be little doubt that Parliament meant the established Church of England. Though it was argued that the Church of Scotland was also an established body within the realm and should, therefore, be entitled to share in the provision for public support, no move was ever voluntarily made by the British authorities to aid the Church of Scotland in Upper Canada. Only one church was thought of in 1791 as entitled to state aid, that being the Church of England.

The first challenge to this ecclesiastical monopoly came from the Presbyterians, but it was the Methodists who in the end made the most determined assaults upon the privileged Anglican position. More specifically, it was that branch of the Methodist Church in Upper Canada which was of American origin which contended for greater democracy in the relations of church and state, maintaining that the clergy reserves ought to be used for the support of all Protestant bodies. This argument, however, was based on conditions existing in the province long after the passing of the Canada Act rather than on any interpretation of the word Protestant as used in the legislation of 1791.

Canadian Methodism has often emphasized the fact that its doctrines were first preached in Canada by British military officers, Tuffey at Quebec and Neal in the Niagara District, but it is no less true that the first regular Methodist preacher in Upper Canada was William Losee, a probationer of the New York Conference, who was authorized by Freeborn Garretson, his presiding elder, to visit Canada and did so in 1790. When he returned to the United States he carried a request from the people in Upper Canada that a preacher be sent to them, and in answer to this request he himself was sent in 1791 to Kingston and the Bay of Quinte country, being succeeded in 1792 by an ordained minister, Darius Dunham.[1]

The western section of the province had at first only the services of a layman, Major George Neal, and one of his converts, Christian Warner, who had also been a soldier. These men prepared the way for the coming of Darius Dunham in 1795 when the country bordering on the Niagara River was organized into a circuit. Year by year, in the annals of the New York Conference to 1810, and thereafter in the annals of the Genesee Conference to 1824, is recorded the work of the missionaries of the American Methodist Episcopal Church in Upper Canada. Had it not been for the labours of these Methodist preachers and of the early Baptist missionaries, the majority of the inhabitants of Upper Canada would have lived in a state of religious destitution, for the Church of England had but a handful of men in its service and had not yet caught the missionary spirit which later led it also to make use of itinerant preachers.

Adaptability to whatever conditions they encountered made the work of the early Methodist preachers highly effective. Their mobility, their simple ritual, their hearty singing, their simplicity

[1] J. E. Sanderson, *The First Century of Methodism in Canada* (Toronto, 1908), I, 27.

of utterance, and their understanding of the mind and heart of common folk enabled them to wield an influence unequalled by any other group. The period from 1800 to 1840 was an heroic era in Methodist missions in Upper Canada. A presiding elder would travel one thousand miles every quarter, or four thousand miles a year, through forests, by rude trails, facing rain or snow, having no settled home as a rule, and receiving for himself $80; for his wife, if he were married, $60 and what provisions he would need for his family; in all an entire allowance of less than $300.[2] Nathan Bangs, who first came to Canada in 1802, has recorded that in riding from one appointment to another the preachers sometimes had to pass through forest wildernesses of from ten to sixty miles, camping in the woods when overtaken by night or finding shelter in an Indian's hut where the curling smoke of the fire ascended through an opening in the roof. Mrs. Amelia Harris, a pioneer of the Long Point country and a member of the Church of England, wrote long after of the Methodist preachers as she remembered them from her girlhood days:

Their sermons and prayers were very loud, forcible and energetic, and if they had been printed verbatim would have looked a sad jumble of words. They encouraged an open demonstration of feeling among their hearers – the louder the more satisfactory. But notwithstanding the criticism cast upon these early preachers, were they not the class of men who suited their hearers? They shared their poverty and entered into all their feelings; and although unlearned, they taught the one true doctrine – to serve God in spirit and in truth – and their lives bore testimony to their sincerity. In this world they looked forward to neither preferment nor reward; all they expected or could hope for was a miserable subsistence.[3]

A taunt frequently thrown at the Methodist itinerants was that they were "unlearned." It was quite true that among these missionary preachers there were men of little education, but the Methodist Church from the days of Wesley had placed emphasis upon education, and candidates for the ministry, even when engaged in the most remote fields of work, were required to

[2] George F. Playter, *The History of Methodism in Canada* . . . (Toronto, 1862), p. 100.

[3] Mrs. Amelia Harris, "Historical Memoranda," Egerton Ryerson, *The Loyalists of America and Their Times* (Toronto, 1880), II, 252-3.

carry on definite courses of reading. The Rev. Alvin Torry, an early missionary to the Six Nations Indians, has recorded that during the first year of his itinerancy in the United States he read portions of Dr. Coke's works and also Wesley's notes on the New Testament. In 1825 he wrote that his field of labour had then become so extensive that no time was allowed for rest and no time for study except when on horseback or before light in the morning. "From the first year of my itinerancy," he said, "I had endeavoured to follow Mr. Wesley's rule for preachers: Rise at four in the morning. This gave me time for reading, meditation and prayer before most of families would be out of their beds."[4] Though Torry received only $100 a year, half of which went for the support of his mother, he purchased a set of Clarke's *Commentaries* in 1820 which cost him $60 in all, paying for the work in small instalments.

When the Canada Conference was organized in 1824 one of its first actions was to examine into the educational preparations of its preachers. Playter, in his *History of Methodism in Canada,* lists the books an acquaintance with which was regarded as "indispensably necessary" for admission into the ministry, and also those which were recommended to the candidates to peruse as "useful and ornamental" study. A survey of the two lists indicates a course of reading which had both depth and variety and which would constitute no mean educational equipment if mastered.[5]

The growth of Methodism in Western New York and in Upper Canada brought about the formation in 1810 of the Genesee Conference of which the Methodists in Upper Canada were a part. There was at that time no reason to doubt the continuance of the amicable relations hitherto existing with the New York Conference, but within two years war came and until 1816 all religious effort was much disturbed. In the Ancaster, Niagara, and Long Point circuits there were in 1812 about 1,100 Methodists, of whom one-quarter were soon called into the militia or otherwise employed in the service. Several of the preachers who had been appointed to Upper Canada made their way into the country despite the state of war and continued their work. Soon, however, the effect upon the societies was notice-

---

[4] The Rev. William Hosmer (ed.), *Autobiography of Rev. Alvin Torry, First Missionary to the Six Nations and the Northwestern Tribes of British North America* (Auburn, 1864), pp. 93, 131.

[5] Playter, *History of Methodism in Canada,* p. 260.

able, the able-bodied men being called into the militia while older men were engaged in the transport of supplies and materials of war. Religious meetings were eventually attended only by old men, women, and children.[6] No preacher from Upper Canada was present at the meeting of the Genesee Conference of 1813, nor at that of 1814, but in each year the preachers within the province came together and arranged for the carrying on of their ministry. Playter records that despite the destruction of property around Ancaster, Niagara, and Long Point the collecting hat would sometimes be filled with bank bills and silver when passed about at a quarterly meeting. The war made money more plentiful than at any previous time.

The Genesee Conference which met in June of 1815 resolved that the war being over it would go on with its work in Canada but would be careful in its choice of preachers, "that offence, as far as possible, might be prevented." The men sent into Canada were mostly of British birth while the two or three Americans who were appointed were described as "of moderate politics and prudent in conduct." For the first time in three years a report was received from the Upper Canada churches. It showed a membership of 1,435, the Ancaster circuit having 459 and the Niagara circuit 220. No report was received from Detroit.[7] A year later the membership had increased to 1,777. There were then five Methodist meeting-houses in the region westward from Niagara, the most distant being in the Township of Woodhouse in the Long Point country. The war years had sadly interfered with the carrying on of religious work of any kind and had brought the usual lowering of morals and confusion of mind. By 1816, however, congregations were coming back to a normal state and by the use of revival methods there were gratifying increases in membership during the next few years. It was at this time that four sons of Colonel Joseph Ryerson, an Anglican resident of the Long Point country, came under Methodist influence and experienced "conversion." One of the four was Egerton, a boy of but twelve years of age, who in later years was to be a most eminent figure in Canadian Methodism and the most stalwart defender of its rights in the struggle over the pretensions and claims of the Church of England. Six years after his conversion he gave in his name for membership with the Methodists and was promptly ordered to

[6] *Ibid.*, p. 118.
[7] *Ibid.*, pp. 143-4.

leave his father's house, which he did for the space of two years.[8]

The War of 1812 gave opportunity for critics and opponents of Methodism to question the loyalty of its preachers and members because of the American background of the church. Some of its members left the country at the outbreak of war, or were later ordered to leave. Nevertheless, it was probably true that there were as many Methodists in the Upper Canada Militia between 1812 and 1815 as members of any other single religious body and there is nothing to indicate that Methodists were less ardent in their support of the war than other religious groups. In the end, however, the war years brought striking changes in the relationship of Upper Canada Methodism to its parent body in New York State. The disturbed conditions of this period, during which the preachers in Canada were prevented from attending the American conferences, laid the foundation for the separation that came a decade later. The disloyalty cry did not cease with the close of the war but, being found an effective means of propaganda against Methodism, continued in increased degree. The situation was further aggravated in 1816 by the arrival of representatives of the British Wesleyan Church. From Quebec, where they were the outstanding Methodist group, they came into Upper Canada and friction soon developed. The rivalry between the two Methodist groups continued until 1820 when an agreement was reached by which the Wesleyans withdrew from Upper Canada (except at Kingston) and the Methodist Episcopal Church no longer interested itself in Lower Canada. In that year the Genesee Conference met at Lundy's Lane, on Canadian soil, but even this effort to emphasize international amity was used to discredit the Canadian body. Within the church itself the feeling was growing that the American connection created prejudices which even piety and good living could not efface. The crisis came in 1824 when at the general conference of the Methodist Episcopal Church held in Baltimore demands were made by a few non-accredited and disgruntled Canadian delegates for separation, while the accredited delegates, though opposing separation, also favoured some change. Out of this situation came the creation of a Canada Conference within the American church, but the controversy having begun, could not be quieted. Henry Ryan, the presiding elder who in the past had stoutly defended the interests of the Methodist

[8] C. B. Sissons, *Egerton Ryerson, His Life and Letters* (Toronto, 1937), I, 5-6.

Episcopal Church, now began a vigorous propaganda against the American connection and what he termed "the tyranny of Yankee bishops."[9] At the first meeting of the new Canada Conference it was evident that complete separation was inevitable. However kindly the memories of the past might be, it was realized that Canadian Methodism could survive only by freeing itself from all connection with the United States. This was done in 1828.

The Canada Conference was but in its infant stage when it found itself projected into a struggle with the authorities of the Church of England, a struggle which in the end sounded the death knell of ecclesiastical privilege in the province. Notwithstanding the fact that the Methodists were the largest individual religious body in Upper Canada, they were still under legal disabilities in the matter of holding property and their ministers were not allowed to solemnize marriage. Moreover, they were frequently subject to scornful allusions on the part of high Anglican clerics and government officials. Jacob Mountain, Bishop of Quebec, for example, had once described the Methodist preachers as "itinerant and mendicant . . . a set of ignorant enthusiasts whose preaching is calculated only to perplex the understanding and corrupt the morals; to relax the nerve of industry and dissolve the bonds of society."

The death of Bishop Mountain in 1825 became the occasion for a furious blast by Archdeacon Strachan of Toronto, delivered in the course of a funeral sermon for his superior. After presenting the claims of the Church of England to be the established church of the colony and entitled to exclusive enjoyment of the clergy reserves, Strachan proceeded to make disparaging references to the other religious bodies. They were represented as ignorant, incapable, idle, disloyal, and imbued with "republican" opinions. The province was pictured as being in a state of utter moral and religious destitution. With the exception of some ministers of the Church of Scotland, the religious teachers of the other denominations, according to Strachan, came "almost universally from the Republican States of America, where they gather their knowledge and form their sentiments." He proceeded to warn the British government that if it did not imme-

---

[9] Ryan broke with the Canada Conference in 1828 and with a few other disaffected ministers organized a Canadian Wesleyan Methodist Church which in 1841 united with the Methodist New Connexion Church. It had less than two thousand members at that time. Ryan died on September 2, 1833.

diately provide efficient help the mass of the population would be nurtured and instructed in "hostility to our parent Church; nor will it be long till they imbibe opinions anything but favourable to the political institutions of England."

For the first time in its history, Upper Canada Methodism fought back. A champion appeared in the person of Egerton Ryerson, born in an Anglican home, a convert to Methodism, and at this time the junior preacher on the Yonge Street and York circuit. It was an indication of the growing sense of strength of the Methodist Church that it refused longer to tolerate abuse even from the most powerful of its critics. Ryerson's reply, which was written in a few days and in the intervals of regular duty, was a devastating document, publication of which produced a sensation in the little provincial capital and later throughout the province. No portion of Strachan's attack was left unanswered. To the charge that the Methodist preachers were of American origin and republican in their sympathies, Ryerson's reply was brief and to the point: "The assertion is false. They are not republicans; neither are they infected with republican principles, nor have they come 'almost universally from the republican states of America'." Of all the Methodist ministers in Upper Canada there were but eight who had not been born and educated in British dominions and all but two of these had become naturalized subjects.

Methodism in Upper Canada became a political force with the publication of Ryerson's pamphlet. In some respects this was unfortunate, but it was inevitable so long as the claims put forward by Archdeacon Strachan received the approbation and support of government. On the one hand stood the embryo establishment, proposing to make itself almost a department of state within the province; opposing stood the dissenting groups, Methodism in particular, demanding separation of church and state and public education free from clerical control.

Methodist history in Upper Canada at this time, as in England in the same period, has significance and importance in the struggle between democratic and non-democratic elements within the state. Between 1815 and 1840 Europe witnessed the struggle of peoples in various countries to achieve freedom, a state of affairs from which England was not exempted. There the Industrial Revolution had sent masses of people into manufacturing centres where long hours and bad housing and intolerable social conditions bred unrest and disease and degradation.

Parliament could see no remedy for this but that suggested by the established church, namely, to build more churches, and so in 1818 it voted one million pounds to the new Church Building Society on the ground pleaded by Lord Liverpool that religion was useful for the preservation of order. It might have been argued that so also was the penal code with its more than two hundred crimes for which the death penalty could be imposed. But even church building did not prevent the spread of a radicalism that was strongly tinged with atheism. Methodism could not pass through this period unaffected by the changes that were taking place. The Wesleyan movement had begun with a bias towards established order and authority in government. Wesley warned his followers against party politics; their business was to save souls. Jabez Bunting, who long dominated the movement, declared that "Methodism hates democracy as much as it hates sin." But however conservative the leaders might be, they were not always followed. As early as 1796 the clerical conferences, with their tendency to become autocratic, were being faced by a growing liberalism which resulted in that year in the revolt of Alexander Kilham and the founding of the Methodist New Connexion, to be followed in 1810, 1827, 1835, and 1849 by other secessions. "The radical agitation filling the general political life of the nation continued to be faithfully represented in the Methodist Societies."[10] The Methodist Episcopal Church was the voice of this new liberalism in Upper Canada in the 1820's. It corresponded to the lesser Methodist groups in England, whereas Wesleyan Methodism, which had entered the province at the close of the War of 1812, resembled the more conservative element in the homeland.

Archdeacon Strachan apparently learned nothing from his first encounter with Ryerson. In 1827 he again made insinuations concerning the other religious bodies, particularly against the Methodists, in a document submitted to the British government as a basis for increased grants for church support and for the charter and endowment of a university. After making exceptions of two ministers of the Church of Scotland, four congregational ministers, and "a very respectable English missionary who presides over a Methodist meeting in Kingston" (a Wesleyan), he described the rest as "for the most part, from the United States, where they gather their knowledge and form their

---

[10] See H. Watkin-Jones, "Methodist Thought in Contact with Modern History," *Hibbert Journal*, XXXVI (October, 1937), 56-68.

sentiments." "Indeed," he added, "the Methodist teachers are subject to the orders of the conference of the United States of America; and it is manifest that the Colonial Government neither has nor can have any more control over them, or prevent them from gradually rendering a large portion of the population, by their influence and instructions, hostile to our institutions, civil and religious, than by increasing the number of the established clergy." This was bad enough, but even worse was an accompanying "Ecclesiastical Chart" in which the number of clergy of the Church of England was exaggerated while the number of those of other denominations was much diminished. As the minutes of the Methodist conferences were published annually, and contained from year to year the names and stations of all ministers, there was no possible excuse for such misrepresentation as appeared in the chart. Strachan suggested that the number of Methodist ministers in the province was between twenty and thirty. Ryerson in his evidence before a committee of the Assembly stated that the correct figures were 71 local or settled clergy and 46 itinerants, or a total of 117. As to the other denominations, of whom Strachan had stated that they had "very few teachers and those seemingly very ignorant," Ryerson stated that there were actually 45 Baptist clergymen in the province, and added: "Although they may be ignorant of political intrigues, they are as well acquainted with the truth, doctrine and duties of the Bible as the clergymen of the Church of England."

The year 1827 may be regarded as the zenith of Strachan's power and influence. He had over-reached himself and from that time on, though still powerful, he was placed on the defensive. He sought to vindicate his position in a speech which he made before the Legislative Council on March 6, 1828, and which was later published in pamphlet form. William Ryerson, after reading it, wrote to his brother Egerton suggesting that he answer it in "a candid, mild and sweet stile." This was done in a series of eight letters which appeared simultaneously in the *Upper Canada Herald* and *Colonial Advocate*. In general the discussion was calm and judicial, though strong feeling was visible in those portions of the letters which dealt with Strachan's aspersions on the Methodists as a body. With regard to the Church of England Ryerson's conclusion was that it was not established in Canada, nor should it be established in the best interests of the church itself.

Though Methodism in Upper Canada had freed itself from the "entangling alliances" of the United States, in part in 1824 and completely in 1828, it continued to face difficulties arising out of the presence in the country of representatives of the British Wesleyan Church, to whom the authorities tended to extend favours not offered to the more distinctly Canadian branch. This was a continuance of the old anti-American prejudice but was also intended to weaken Methodism by dividing its forces. We can see today that the American type of Methodism in Upper Canada had little in common with the British Wesleyan group. George Ryerson, who attended the Wesleyan Conference in England in 1831, confirms this in the impressions of the gathering which he wrote for the eye of his brother Egerton:

> *Perhaps I do not use too strong terms when I say that I detest their politics and I much dislike their blind veneration for the writings of Mr. Wesley (excellent in themselves, but not inspired, and containing much of human infirmity and the prejudices of a High Church education); their exalted opinion of themselves and their system, their servile reverence for great men and great names and their servile clinging to the skirts of a corrupt, secularized and anti-Christian Church. They are very generally either anti-Reformers or half-hearted, lukewarm, hesitating reformers . . . altogether I fear that the Wesleyan Conference is an obstacle to the extension of civil and religious liberty.*

George Ryerson regarded the Wesleyan system as unsuited to Canada and saw serious objections to a suggestion which had been made that a general superintendent for the new Canadian Methodist Episcopal Church should be chosen from the British Wesleyan Conference. "I think it will be far better for you to look to the U.S. for a Gen. Superintendent," he advised. "Better to bear the temporary censure of enemies in Canada, than the permanent evil and annoyance of having a Church and State Tory Superintendent from this country."[11] Canadian Methodism did what Ryerson suggested, appointing an American-born preacher, William Case, as President *pro tempore*,[12] thereby recognizing also his part in the building up of the work in

---

[11] Sissons, *Egerton Ryerson*, pp. 137-9.

[12] William Case was born in 1780 and had come to Canada in 1805 as junior itinerant with Henry Ryan. After 1833 he served as a missionary to the Indians.

Canada. Less is known of the personality of Case than of many other early figures in the church, but the impression which he made upon his contemporaries has been well recorded by John Carroll, the historian of early Methodism in Upper Canada.

This new phase of Canadian Methodist history lasted only five years but it was notable for the inauguration in November, 1829, of a church paper, the *Christian Guardian,* with Egerton Ryerson as its first editor. His pen soon placed it in the forefront of Canadian journalism, even though he was always under more or less restraint. The tug between what he wished to say and what his conference associates would permit him to say was often in evidence.

Of equal importance in this period was the decision made by the Conference of 1830 to establish a college. This was Methodism's answer to the attempt of Archdeacon Strachan to gain for the Church of England full control of secondary and higher education within the province. In 1827 Strachan had secured from the British government a charter for King's College, the proposed provincial university, the provisions of which placed it completely within the control of the Church of England. So great was the outcry against the charter that nothing came of it at the time. When Sir John Colborne became Lieutenant-Governor in 1828, he received an intimation that it would be well to leave the business of founding a university in abeyance. He then came forward with the more modest plan of establishing an institution for secondary education. This resulted in the foundation of Upper Canada College, a school of traditional English type, its curriculum strictly classical and its pupils drawn from the well-to-do families. It was no solution, however, for the problem of public education in the province at large, though its support came from public funds. For this reason the Methodists set themselves to the task of establishing a school to which ambitious youths from poorer homes of whatever denomination might come for training. Upper Canada Academy, as this new institution was named, was established at the town of Cobourg. Since no government aid could be obtained, Egerton Ryerson went to England in 1835 to secure subscriptions and while there he also secured a royal charter, the first charter ever granted to a college not under state church control. Upper Canada Academy was the first of several denominational colleges which arose in the next few years and which in two instances developed into universities.

The agreement of 1820 between the British Wesleyans and the American Methodist Episcopal Conference had left the Upper Canada field to the latter body while the British group confined its activities to Lower Canada. But this arrangement was by no means acceptable to Sir Peregrine Maitland, Lieutenant-Governor of Upper Canada, nor to the Colonial Office in London. Lord Bathurst was soon in communication with the Wesleyan Missionary Committee and in a letter to Maitland, written in May, 1821, expressed his hope that the agreement would be reconsidered. He also intimated that additional grants would be sought for support of an enlarged Church of England establishment in Upper Canada as "an effectual way of counteracting the plan which seems to be on foot of establishing an American influence by the means of a Methodist clergy connected with the United States."[13]

Bathurst returned to the subject two months later, making mention of conversations with the Wesleyan authorities in England, in whom, he said, he had always found "a readiness to promote the views of government." He was prepared to acquit them of having acted otherwise than in ignorance of the "evil consequences" likely to result from their policy in Upper Canada but he could not "be insensible of the danger of leaving the instruction of the Colonial population in the hands of missionaries who are by Birth and education more or less bound to promote the Political interests of a Foreign state." To this he added: "The only effectual remedy appears to be a considerable addition to the number of the clergymen of the Church of England resident in the Province and as the only obstacle to this increase hitherto has been the want of funds for their support I shall think it my duty to submit to Parliament in the next Session such an augmentation to the sum heretofore voted to the Society for the Propagation of the Gospel as shall enable them to add very considerably to the number of their Missionaries in the Province."[14]

Knowing as they did the attitude of the Colonial Office towards their work in Canada, the Wesleyan Missionary Committee was ready to reverse its policy if opportunity were afforded. This was made possible in 1828 when the Canada Conference withdrew from all its American connections. The

[13] Bathurst to Maitland, London, May 21, 1821, Public Archives of Canada, Series G, supplemental volume.
[14] Bathurst to Maitland, London, July 24, 1821, *ibid.*

Wesleyans at once interpreted this as freeing them from earlier restrictions and laid plans for placing preachers in the upper province. In the spring of 1832 a party of missionaries set sail, accompanied by the Rev. Robert Alder, a secretary of the Missionary Committee. The situation was viewed with consternation by the Canada Conference since it meant rivalry and dissipation of effort. A dramatic step was taken. Alder arrived in Upper Canada to find that the leaders of the Canada Conference were prepared to unite with the Wesleyans and would make important concessions to achieve this end. Thus union was brought about in the autumn of 1833. The name of the church in Upper Canada was changed from Methodist Episcopal to Wesleyan Methodist, an annual presidency was substituted for the Episcopacy, ordination of local preachers was discontinued, and Indian missions were placed under the British Wesleyan Missionary Society. The American-born branch of Methodism seemed to have been completely swallowed up by the British body; its history might have been regarded as at an end. But such was not the case; fifty years later there was still a strong and vigorous Methodist Episcopal body which, when it finally did enter a larger union, brought with it a distinct contribution of men, of property, and of energy.

The marriage in 1833 between American-born Episcopal Methodism and British-born Wesleyanism turned out unhappily. The union was based upon expediency rather than love and it came to grief chiefly over the rights and privileges of a mother-in-law. There was an incompatibility from the first which handicapped growth and gave critics opportunity for sneers. The inauguration of the union was also the signal for a schism which, while not at first of large proportions, showed nevertheless the lack of unity.

The British Wesleyan Conference had mixed motives in its decision to re-enter the province which, by the agreement of 1820, had been left as the field of the Methodist Episcopal body. The decade of the thirties brought many Wesleyan Methodists to Canada, people whom that church would wish to follow up. Moreover, the missionary spirit in England at the time furnished ample funds to carry on work in the colonies or elsewhere. Added to these factors, however, was the widespread impression in both church and government circles that the brand of Methodism in Upper Canada was, if not disloyal, at least openly opposed to the government, and that something must be done to preserve the good name of Methodism in general. A plausible excuse for re-entering Upper Canada was found in the needs of the Indian missions. The Canada Conference might reasonably have expected that it would be approached in the matter but no such courtesy was observed, the Conference being merely informed in 1832 that a group of Wesleyan missionaries would shortly arrive in the province and be assigned to stations. It was this announcement which precipitated the hasty decision to propose union, a move for which the Ryersons were chiefly responsible.

The Rev. Robert Alder who accompanied the missionaries sent out in 1832 was a typical representative of the conservative Wesleyan element, deeply respectful towards the Church of England. He was recalled by his contemporaries as a man of medium height and sturdy build with a large head crowned by curly locks, bearing a rather striking resemblance to King George IV. In Toronto, Alder and his associates received courtesies from Archdeacon Strachan which were in marked contrast to the treatment long meted out to Canadian Methodists. Doors that had been closed to the Ryersons and their colleagues were opened to the newcomers from the British Isles. Alder even presented an address to Sir John Colborne on behalf of the Wesleyan missionaries in which he stated that they were "prompted no less from a sense of duty than from inclination to abstain from all political disputes." It did not add to the comfort of the Ryersons to see this address first published in the *Courier*, a paper bitterly hostile to their cause.

Alder carried on his negotiations in two quarters. He met officially with the Canada Conference to discuss the basis of union but he also conversed and corresponded with Sir John Colborne, arriving at certain understandings as to the course which the new Methodist body would pursue. The Conference was not informed, for example, that the government would henceforth make an annual grant of £900 towards the Indian missions. Had that been known there would doubtless have been misgivings. The Conference might have had further misgivings had it known that Alder, writing privately to Colborne, had expressed his desire to put an end to camp meetings and to make the *Christian Guardian* "an exclusively religious journal."[15] He

[15] Thomas Webster, *Life of Rev. James Richardson* (Toronto, 1876), p. 263.

even inquired privately from Colborne whether his own appointment as the first President of the new united church would be viewed with acceptance in official circles. The Lieutenant-Governor must have been greatly reassured as to the future character of Methodism in Upper Canada after conversing with this ambassador from the British Wesleyan Conference but there were many Methodists who felt uneasy in mind even while the preliminary negotiations were under way. Mutterings were already being heard in district meetings and in lesser courts of the church over the fact that they had not been consulted before such far-reaching changes were made in the character of Methodism in the province. This discontent suggests one of the differences between the British and American points of view. British Methodism, ruled by its preachers, regarded union as a concern of the preachers alone. Canadian Methodism, more democratic in character, felt that the humblest member of the body, through the circuit quarterly meetings and the district meetings, should be able to influence decisions.

Egerton Ryerson represented the new Canadian church at the Wesleyan Conference of 1833 in Manchester where the terms of union were accepted. Upper Canada Methodism which had hitherto operated under an episcopal system was to have an appointed President sent out each year by the British Conference. Some of the old-time Methodist preachers, veterans of the Methodist "cavalry," must have been astonished when in 1833 they saw the Rev. George Marsden presiding over the new Wesleyan Methodist Church in Canada. Small in stature and venerable in appearance, he would have attracted attention in any North American community by his dress: round-breasted coat, knee breeches, black silk stockings, with silver knee and shoe buckles. Accompanying Marsden, whose stay in Canada was only temporary, was the Rev. Joseph Stinson, the superintendent of missions, for whose work the English Conference had promised an annual grant of £1,000. His was to be a permanent office and likely to be of considerable importance and influence within the church.

Weaknesses in the new Wesleyan Methodist Church of Canada soon appeared. From the point of view of the official group at York, the essential difference between the two uniting bodies was that one was of American origin and the other British. It was expected that in union all the distinctly American characteristics would disappear and that the straight British type

would survive. But while the union itself was viewed with satisfaction, it was difficult to lay by at once prejudices long maintained. After sneering at Methodists and questioning their
loyalty for forty years, it was not easy to accept them in their
new state, even with a President from England whose carriage
and dress reflected the utmost respectability and conservatism.
Thus, during the decade of the thirties, we find the old loyalty
issue raised again and again, particularly in the troubled days of
1833. The baton of American origin could not be erased from
the Methodist shield even by marriage into the best British
Wesleyan circles.

On the part of some of the British Wesleyan missionaries
there was also an attitude of superiority towards the Canadian
brethren that did not make for amity. The British Wesleyans
were out to control the new church and to take no nonsense
from colonials. A question that arose immediately after union
produced a marked difference of opinion. Methodist practice in
North America gave a form of ordination to local preachers,
even though the latter devoted a considerable part of their time
to farming or other secular pursuits. It was a system that had
given much power to Methodism in America since in the intervals between the visits of the itinerants it was the local preachers
who held the Methodist groups together and through the class
meeting and other religious exercises nurtured their spiritual
life. To the British missionaries, unaccustomed to ordination of
local preachers, the American practice seemed offensive and was
stoutly opposed.

There were other indications of lack of harmony. In some
larger places where both Wesleyan and former Episcopal congregations existed, the British Wesleyan preachers would have
nothing to do with their Canadian colleagues. Newspapers
critical of Methodism seized gleefully upon such signs of disunion, as also upon the fact that not all of the former Episcopal
group had entered into union. The continuing body after 1833
clung to the old name and by its secession was partially responsible for the decrease of 1,109 members reported in 1834. The
united front of the Church of England contrasted sharply with
the divisions in Methodism, divisions which became even more
noticeable with the coming of representatives of such English
secessions as the Primitive Methodist Church, the Bible Christian Church, and the New Connexion Methodist Church. One
of the unhappy fruits of division was an unwholesome rivalry

for members and adherents. The little village of Wyoming, in Lambton County, for example, had no less than three Methodist churches prior to the union of 1883 and had churches of other denominations as well.

Whatever might be the extent of such difficulties as have already been mentioned, the rock upon which the new Methodist body came to grief lay in the Wesleyan attitude towards the established church. The British Wesleyans could not rid their minds of a belief that the Church of England had of right a position in Upper Canada that was shared by no other religious body. This point of view, creeping constantly into correspondence, gave great irritation to men who had spent their best years in combating such ideas. An example of the Wesleyan attitude may be found in a letter addressed to Egerton Ryerson in 1838 by the Rev. Joseph Stinson, the superintendent of missions. Discussing Ryerson's editorial policies in the *Christian Guardian* he wrote: "I think as Wesleyan Methodists we ought openly and fearlessly to advocate the righteous claims of our own church, but we ought to do it without detracting from the merits or opposing the interests of other churches, particularly that church which is so closely connected with our Government as is the Church of England, opposed as a dominant church, but not as an establishment."[16]

The Ryersons and the Canadian Methodists in general would ask why in a North American community one church should by right be more closely connected with the civil government than any other. Over this question, raised long before 1833, controversy could not be stilled. But whereas before 1833 Methodism had presented a united front, after 1833 its ranks were divided. To the Wesleyan element there was something akin to abuse of one's own mother in speaking ill of the Church of England. Those, however, who had come out of the old American-born branch would feel that the Church of England ought to stand on its own feet in Upper Canada, maintaining itself without special aid or privilege. This was an issue that would not down. With its two constituent elements pulling in opposite directions Methodism in Upper Canada was in an unhappy situation during all of the years between 1833 and 1840. The break-up of the union in the latter year came chiefly over this issue.

[16] Joseph Stinson to Egerton Ryerson, November 2, 1838, Sissons, *Egerton Ryerson*, I, 491.

Methodism as such played no part in the Rebellion of 1837. For four years there had been a complete estrangement between Egerton Ryerson, the chief figure in Methodism, and the leader of the extreme reform group, William Lyon Mackenzie. Indeed Mackenzie denounced Ryerson during this period with much the same vehemence that he expended upon members of the Family Compact. Infiltration of British Wesleyan missionaries after 1833 and the influence of Egerton Ryerson tended to make the church more conservative in those troubled times but did not preserve it from the reproach of being connected with the final outbreak of violence. The same insinuation was made against all other denominations which had American origin or any American connection in the past, notably the Baptists, Quakers, and Universalists. Little restraint had been shown by critics of these religious bodies in the period before the uprising; when it was quelled they gave free rein to their bigotry, placing the blame for the troubles of the province upon the lack of sound religious teaching, meaning thereby their own particular brand of religious teaching.

The revengeful activities of provincial officials after the Rebellion form one of the saddest features of the period. Men of all classes were shocked by the executions at York of Lount and Matthews. Egerton Ryerson came publicly to the defence of Marshall Spring Bidwell who had been deceived by Sir Francis Bond Head into leaving the province and was then charged with fleeing from justice. In striking contrast to Ryerson's action was the tone of the pastoral letter issued by the Rev. William Harvard, the British President of the Conference. In the columns of the *Christian Guardian* he called upon the preachers to examine each individual name in their societies "in order to be fully satisfied of the Christian loyalty of all who may be returned as members of our church to the ensuing conference," instructing further that if any person ill-affected towards the Crown applied for church membership he was to be "kindly but firmly told . . . that he has applied at the wrong door."[17]

Events in the Conference of 1838 showed a revival of

---

[17] The Rev. John Carroll was of the opinion that the rift in Methodism leading to the separation of 1840 was begun when the President of the Conference ordered the superintendents of circuits to institute an inquiry in all their societies for any who had compromised their character for loyalty. This was resented by the church membership. See John Carroll, *"Father Corson"; or the Old Style Canadian Itinerant* . . . (Toronto, 1879), pp. 95-6.

liberalism in Methodist ranks. Egerton Ryerson was given a clean bill of health over his defence of Bidwell and was restored to the editorship of the *Guardian*. Immediately the paper reflected the change, the clergy reserves question being again discussed freely and frankly. Sir George Arthur's repressive policies were criticized, as was also a snap verdict in the Assembly on the question of reinvesting control of the clergy reserve lands in the imperial Parliament. The papers of Sir George Arthur, when examined, may yet reveal his relations with the British Wesleyans. He probably protested against the editorial policies of the *Guardian* for in the spring of 1838 the Toronto *Patriot* published a letter signed by four secretaries of the Wesleyan Missionary Society, stating that the attitude of the *Guardian* would be a subject of discussion at the next British and Canadian conferences and that the Rev. Robert Alder would visit Canada to deal with the matter. It was indeed ironic that an announcement of British Wesleyan policy should be made, not through the official organ of Methodism in the province but through the columns of a newspaper bitterly hostile to that church body. Ryerson in his reply stated plainly that the affairs of the Wesleyan Methodist Church in Canada (missionary appropriations excepted) were under the sole direction of the Canadian Conference – a plain intimation that the British Wesleyan Conference was exceeding its jurisdiction. Relations between the Canadian and British bodies were now approaching a crisis. The real issue was as between a Canadian church and a colonial branch of a British church. When the Conference met Alder was again present and was given a respectful hearing, but Egerton Ryerson was re-elected editor of the *Guardian* – this time by a vote of 60 to 13. "Colonial and Canadian ideas had met on the floor of the conference and the latter had prevailed."[18]

There was a general air of depression in the Conference, however. The report on membership showed that in the six years of union there had been a decrease of 849, though the four years of independence prior to 1833 had seen a 60 per cent gain. There was also a marked tendency for Methodist preachers of a certain type to drift off to the ministry of the Church of England. Three such secessions were reported in 1839. On the part of the friends of Alder there was a disposition to assume that they alone spoke for the church, even though others might

[18] Sissons, *Egerton Ryerson*, I, 510.

be members of a committee. Stinson, the President of the Conference, and Richey, superintendent of the Toronto District, both Alder men, consulted privately with both Arthur and Lord Sydenham, ignoring Ryerson. It was later revealed that Stinson and Richey had written to Sydenham in 1840 that "the Church of England being in our estimation, the Established Church of all the British Colonies, we entertain no objection to the distinct recognition of her as such." This admission was contained in a letter asking that any appropriations which might be made to Methodists in a settlement of the clergy reserves should be given to "the Wesleyan Methodists who are now and who may be hereafter connected with the British Wesleyan Conference." Egerton Ryerson, when consulted by Sydenham, contended that grants should be made to the Conference of the Wesleyan Methodist Church in Canada. The Governor in the end favoured Ryerson's contention and so expressed himself in communications to the Colonial Secretary. An attempt made at the Conference of 1840 to repudiate the position taken by Ryerson was defeated by a vote of 59 to 8.

From the minutes of the Conference it is apparent that many ministers were dissatisfied with the workings of the union. Yet most of the dissatisfied group would have hesitated to urge dissolution. At the Conference of 1840 Egerton and William Ryerson were instructed to proceed to England and consult with the British Conference. Stinson was later added as a delegate, and in the end he was accompanied by his associate, Richey, of Toronto. In England the Ryersons were received coldly, none of the ordinary courtesies of Conference being accorded to them. A week went by before their business was brought up and it was then referred to a committee. Egerton Ryerson protested and the rump of the Conference, most of its members having gone home, almost without debate rescinded the union of 1833. At Toronto in October the Canadian Conference heard officially of the British decision. Fifteen of its ministers decided that they could no longer travel with the Canadian body, one of these being the venerable missionary, the Rev. William Case. So ended seven years' effort to impose upon a North American system the policies of a church body nurtured amid the conservatism of England.

The seven years of union were followed by seven years of separation during which there was marked progress, and then by a second union in 1847. But by this time the character of

Canadian Methodism had become more definitely established and Wesleyan influence upon its future had been rendered less effective by the presence in the field of English secessionist bodies, the Primitive Methodist Church, the Methodist New Connexion, and the Bible Christian Church. These branches, more akin to the Canadian type of Methodism than to British Wesleyanism, at a later date also came into the body of Canadian Methodism and by their coming helped to shape the character of the church.

Some further account needs to be given of the continuing Methodist Episcopal Church after 1833. Unions of churches in Canada have seldom been marked by a complete unanimity. This was the case in the coming together in 1833 of the Canadian Methodists and the British Wesleyans. A small group of ministers and laymen, opposed to so complete a change of polity and viewing it as an outright surrender to the British body, determined to continue both the name and organization of the Methodist Episcopal branch. When they assembled in their first Conference in 1834 there were but eleven ministers to carry on the work. They were without churches or parsonages and no one knew definitely how large a following might exist. At the second Conference in 1835 the membership was reported to be 1,243 with ministers numbering twenty-one. Substantial gains in membership were recorded in both 1836 and 1837 but only a small gain in 1838. For this the troubles of the preceding year may be blamed. The Methodist Episcopal Church, by reason of its American origin, was peculiarly open to the innuendos of critics and opponents and a considerable number of its members removed to the United States in 1838. From that time, however, gains in membership were reported regularly, reaching a total of 8,880 in 1845. In that year the church went outside of its own constituency to call the Rev. J. Alley of the Black River Conference in the United States to the office of bishop, succeeding the Rev. John Reynolds who had been elected in 1835. In that year also appeared the first number of the *Canada Christian Advocate* which soon became the organ of the body and continued so for almost forty years. Education also became a concern of the Methodist Episcopal Church, resulting in the establishment of Belleville Seminary in 1857. Nine years later this institution advanced to the status of a university empowered to grant degrees, but after its charter was amalgamated with that of Victoria University in 1884 it continued only as a collegiate institution.

Through the third quarter of the century the Methodist Episcopal Church was an active and influential body. Men of outstanding character and ability occupied its chief office of bishop, the Rev. Philander Smith from 1847 to 1870, the Rev. James Richardson to 1874, and in the last decade of separate existence the Rev. Albert Carman. The year 1874 witnessed an important union of Methodist bodies in Canada, the Conference of the Maritime Provinces joining with the Wesleyan Methodist Conference of Ontario and Quebec and the New Connexion Conference to form the new Methodist Church of Canada. Nine years later, in a new wave of union sentiment, the Methodist Episcopal body, together with the Primitive Methodists and the Bible Christian Church, joined the earlier united body. In the deliberations preceding this union there was no more outstanding figure than Bishop Carman, and as the completely unified church entered upon its new day he was elected as one of its two general superintendents. At the union of 1883-4 the Methodist Episcopal Church had 228 ministers, 25,671 members, and church property valued at more than a million and a half dollars.

7: The Baptists and Presbyterians

The Baptists here are more numerous than the Methodists, both sects are unco' good, or rigidly righteous. I have seen young men and maids pray and groan with tears in their eyes. The people who are of the Kirk of Scotland and the Secession Church are accounted lukewarm and unconverted.

—WILLIAM BOSTON, writing from Lobo Township (1830)

The township is entirely settled with Highlanders, chiefly from Sutherlandshire. They are mostly serious and well-disposed people, accustomed to regular attendance on public ordinances, and very desirous of having a clergyman among them. . . . They hold meetings every Sabbath for prayers, praise and reading devotional books.

—THE REV. GEORGE ROMANES, writing from Zorra Township (1833)

American emigrants to Upper Canada, whether Loyalists or mere land-seekers, brought with them principles of democracy and the idea of religious liberty. But religious liberty in America meant something more than the mere right of a group of Christian believers to worship in their own manner without interference of any kind. It meant also the liberty of the individual to change from one church body to another at any time and for any reason that might appear good in his eyes. This looseness of church connection was much noticed by British travellers who in their own land were accustomed to life-long adherence to one particular belief. Whatever the Loyalists may have been before they migrated to Upper Canada, a subject upon which there is little information, they were soon swept in large numbers into the Methodist ranks. In the same way other groups of immigrants, forsaking previous religious affiliations, became Baptists, Presbyterians, or Anglicans for no other reason than that one of these religious bodies was active in the community in which they made their new home.

Baptist missionaries from the United States entered Upper Canada both in the east and the west in 1803. Joseph Cornell, sent by the Massachusetts Domestic Missionary Society, crossed the St. Lawrence at the end of January, 1803, to "Cataraqua," and thence riding a circuit of two hundred miles found people who had been in the province as long as fourteen years without religious ministrations, and children who, he said, did not know what a Bible was when it was shown to them. Before returning to the United States Cornell organized a church of fourteen members at Stephentown.[1] In the same year, 1803, Lemuel Covell entered Upper Canada at Niagara and journeying westward to the Long Point country assisted in establishing a congregation in Charlotteville Township. This was not the first Baptist church in the western part of the province for at least as early as 1796 there was a little congregation at Beamsville, in Clinton Township, which had probably been organized by emigrants from the United States. Its origins, however, are obscure. In 1804 Caleb Blood, while journeying and preaching about the head of Lake Ontario, received word from Long Point that there was "a work of Divine Grace" in that place and that thirty or forty persons were ready for baptism. He was unable to visit them, but in 1805 Peter Roots went among them and later in the same year Elder Covell made a second visit, of which he says: "There are now two churches of our order near Long Point . . . the one consisted when I left them of forty-two and the other of twenty-four members, where three years since there was no church and only a few scattered brethren." The Charlotteville church had a minister at this time, Titus Finch, ordained in the fall of 1804,[2] and when David Irish visited Long Point in 1806 he was privileged to attend the meeting of the second (Townsend) church at which the members agreed to the ordination of Peter Fairchild, one of their number.[3] While engaged in this journey through the Long Point country, David Irish was informed that Elder Covell was sick in Clinton Township and hastened to his bedside, but arriving found him dead. He was buried in Upper Canada.[4] Irish later journeyed as far west as the Oxford settlement on the Thames River and preached there. The missionary journeys of these four men, Covell, Blood, Roots, and Irish, aided in the establishment of the first Baptist churches but it was more particularly the labours of men like Finch, Fairchild, and others who were residents of

---

[1] *Massachusetts Baptist Missionary Magazine*, I, 13. This periodical was published irregularly, the first number of volume I being dated September, 1803. while the twelfth number is dated January, 1808.

[2] The name of Titus Finch appears in the minutes of the Court of Quarter Sessions of the London District for June 9, 1807, when he was granted a licence to solemnize marriage (Ontario Bureau of Archives, *Report*, 1933, p. 97).

[3] *Massachusetts Baptist Missionary Magazine*, I, 204, 260. Fairchild was a native of New Jersey and one of the earliest settlers in Norfolk County.

[4] The Rev. Lemuel Covell died October 19, 1806. His obituary appears in *ibid.*, I, 286-8 and an elegy on his death in the same volume, 380-2.

Canada which spread Baptist beliefs through the western section of the province.

Frontier conditions, such as have been described, prevailed down to the period of the war with the United States. As the population moved westward within the province, Baptist and Methodist missionaries from the United States followed after them. The Rev. Asahel Moore preached at Oxford on the Thames in 1807. Here, the Methodists left their own meeting to attend "so that the whole settlement was together in the afternoon." Baptists and Methodists were sufficiently alike, in methods at least, to find no difficulty in thus fraternizing. The "Governor's Road," first projected by Governor Simcoe, was the means of access to these more remote settlements and Moore describes travelling through the woods on this primitive highway "which we were able to keep, sometimes by marked trees, and sometimes by small brush which was cut and strewed along by the intended path." In those early days Baptist churches were too few in number and too remote one from the other to permit any form of association, nor was this possible until the close of hostilities with the United States. Church records of the war years are meagre, but in general the effect, as with the Methodists, was to weaken the American connection. By 1837, however, the Western Baptist Association (London and Western Districts) and the Eastern Baptist Association (Niagara and Gore Districts) had 1,071 and 1,248 members respectively. The Eastern Association reported twenty-one ministers. Baptists were strongest in the townships of Townsend and Walsingham (Norfolk County) and in Bayham and Malahide townships (Middlesex County). All these settlements were along Lake Erie. In the whole province there were reported to be about fifty churches, the majority of the ministers being from the United States, from which came also some financial support.[5] The American Baptist Home Missionary Society, at work in Upper Canada since 1833, had seven itinerant missionaries in the province in 1837, of whom three were in the western section, at Toronto, Brantford, and St. Catharines.[6]

Baptist churches in Upper Canada were not immune from the anti-mission agitation which affected the churches in the neighbouring western states. This movement, most noticeable where educational facilities were meagre and cultural influences

[5] *Canada Baptist Magazine and Missionary Register*, I (1837), 17, 165.
[6] *Ibid.*, 93.

lacking, was a distinctly frontier phenomenon. Missionary societies were opposed on the ground that they were unscriptural, but behind this argument were such factors as fear of the expense and the resistance of illiterate ministers who anticipated loss of influence if missionary and educational efforts were supported.[7] The prejudice in the western states extended also to Sunday schools, Bible societies, theological schools, temperance movements, and indeed all organizations beyond the individual congregation. Canadian records of the late thirties and early forties reveal some instances of opposition to organized missions and even occasionally to education expressed in demands for "God-ordained and not man-made ministers."[8]

The Rev. F. A. Cox was sent to America with the Rev. J. Hoby in 1835 by the Baptist Union of England on a mission of inquiry, and spent some time in Upper Canada. He found four Baptist Associations in the province, comprising upwards of sixty churches and forty ministers. Many of the ministers were poorly supported and few had any learning, though education was not in general despised in Upper Canada as among the western American Baptists. Indeed, a recent meeting of the Upper Canada churches had sanctioned missionary and educational societies, Sunday schools, and tract societies, and had passed resolutions calling for prayer and effort against slavery.[9] In the Niagara District, at the time of their visit, the English visitors found three ordained ministers and one licentiate. In London District the churches were described as "generally young and feeble, wanting ministerial aid and support." Appeals had been made to both England and the United States for help but in each case the petitioners had been advised to look elsewhere. English Baptists suggested that the United States should look after these Canadian churches because of their proximity while American Baptists pointed out that as Canada was a British possession they should not be expected to provide for its spiritual welfare.[10] The visitors from overseas thought that Baptist churches in Upper Canada should have English rather

---

[7] See W. W. Sweet, *Religion on the American Frontier: The Baptists, 1783-1830* (New York, 1931), chap. IV.

[8] A. L. McCrimmon, *The Educational Policy of the Baptists of Ontario and Quebec* (Toronto, 1920), pp. 6-7.

[9] F. A. Cox and J. Hoby, *The Baptists in America; a Narrative of the Deputation from the Baptist Union in England to the United States and Canada*, 2nd ed., revised (London, 1836), p. 222.

[10] *Ibid.*, pp. 222-4.

than American preachers. "Americans are usually, in most respects, men of the right stamp," they wrote, "but as the Canadas are under the British government, and the people in general have strong political prejudices, an Englishman would have the readiest access to the ear and feeling of the multitude." It was suggested, however, that preachers sent out from England should be free from any strong national prejudices, and because of the large immigration from the United States and elsewhere should avoid all disparaging comparisons.[11]

The American background of the Baptist churches in the western part of the province has already been pointed out. One of the difficulties in bringing about unity of effort lay in the divergence of views between the churches in the west with their American background and the churches in the Ottawa Valley which had a Scottish background. Since 1816 there had been a vigorous Baptist growth in the Ottawa Valley so that by 1836 it was possible to organize an association. The churches in this association held open-communion views in contrast to the tendency towards close-communion views of the western groups, so that it was difficult to reconcile the sections. At the middle of the century the Baptists in what is now central Canada were without a missionary society, a paper, and a college. The first of these deficiencies was in 1851 remedied in part by the organization of the Regular Baptist Missionary Convention of Canada West; a new church paper, the *Christian Messenger*, came three years later, and in 1860 a Baptist college was opened at Woodstock. The pioneer era of Baptist history in Upper Canada had ended; a new chapter now began to be written.

The early Baptist preachers in Upper Canada were men who lived and worked for their own support among those to whom they preached on the Sabbath. In general they had little opportunity to obtain education and their preaching often consisted of loosely connected comments upon a chapter of the Bible. The case of Peter Fairchild in Charlotteville, already mentioned, illustrates the process by which a preacher was "raised up." Here was a member of a Baptist group who felt called upon to preach. He was known to his fellow-members as one with the necessary "gifts." With their consent and approval he was ordained to the ministry but ordination did not alter his social status. He continued to work on his farm but in addition he preached on Sunday and perhaps also during the week,

[11] *Ibid.*, pp. 233, 237.

attended at funerals and baptisms, and in general did the work of a pastor. Licensed Baptist preachers, like the itinerant preachers in the Methodist church, ministered more or less at large. They were sometimes called to take charge of congregations, in which case they were usually ordained so that they might administer the sacraments. Both the Methodist itinerancy and the Baptist farmer-preacher plan were well fitted to the needs of a pioneer society. In each case the minister was thoroughly familiar with the life of the people among whom he lived and whom he served.

Baptist churches exercised a close supervision over the conduct of their members and did not hesitate to expel from membership those whose lives did not meet the standards established by the Articles of Practice. Records of the Oxford Baptist church between 1810 and 1820 show exclusions for intoxication, for fighting, for adultery, for lying, for railing against the church and minister, and for "joining with the world in plays and sham marrying." Nancy Brink was excluded in 1819 for leaving the church and joining a Methodist class. Sometimes the persons expelled were received again if they showed a proper penitence. Differences arising between members were often settled by the vote of the members of the church.

Many of the customs and practices of the Baptist churches in Upper Canada were introduced from the United States. In some of the Baptist churches in the western part of the province one week day in each month was set aside as an occasion for confessing orally to the Articles of Faith which were read aloud by the church clerk. After a sermon the individual members were expected to "improve their gifts" by addressing the meeting. Elder W. H. Landon, of Oxford, has left the comment that the people had to be taught cautiously that the Holy Spirit had not conferred the same gifts upon all men and women. It took many years to have this comprehended. The Baptist covenant meeting had some likeness to the Methodist class meeting where the members related their religious experiences and were admonished or encouraged, as the case might require, by the leader of the class.

Presbyterianism was introduced in the western section of Upper Canada by missionaries from the United States, some of whom had a Scottish background, but after 1830 ministers began to come directly from Scotland so that by the middle of the century the majority of the churches had become distinctly Scottish in character. This condition was hastened by the large Highland immigration after 1830 which provided the old country ministers with congregations larger in number than they could easily serve. Another reason for the change lay in the disturbing effects of the Rebellion of 1837. In the Niagara Presbytery all but one of the ministers left the province during the uprising, their American nationality subjecting them to the suspicion of the authorities. Though several returned when order was restored, their influence was never as great as before, and within a few years this presbytery ceased to exist. After 1840, the American background of Upper Canada Presbyterianism disappeared and such American characteristics as revivalism and support of temperance measures were no longer prominent.

The Rev. Jabez Collver was the first Presbyterian clergyman to arrive in western Upper Canada. He was an ordained minister from New Jersey who settled in Norfolk County in 1793 where he formed a congregation unconnected with any presbytery but along Presbyterian lines. A year later the Rev. John Dunn, of Scottish birth and training but for some time resident in New York State, arrived at Niagara where the Rev. Robert Addison, Anglican, had been rector since 1792. Mr. Dunn preached at Niagara and at Stamford, but after two years relinquished both charges and went into business. His successor was the Rev. John Young, also a Scot but who had received ordination in New York State and had held charges at Schenectady and Montreal. His stay in Upper Canada was of short duration. Then in 1804 came the Rev. John Burns, another Scot who had been in the United States. By this time Presbyterians were increasing in number about Niagara, the Rev. Robert Addison observing in 1807 that "almost all the settlers about Niagara are Presbyterians."

More influential than any of those so far mentioned was the Rev. Daniel Eastman, a native of New York State, who after receiving his licence to preach came directly to Upper Canada in 1801 and settled on a small farm near Beaver Dams. He was ordained in 1802 and thenceforth, for many years, he traversed the Niagara District preaching and visiting the people in their homes. It was probably Mr. Eastman's church which was described by the traveller Howison when he visited St. Catharines around 1820. After noting the American appearance of the people he continued:

Presently an old man, dressed in showy blue coat, white pantaloons, boots, and plated spurs, made his appearance, and to my astonishment, proved to be a priest. The form of service was Presbyterian; and during the whole course of it people continued going out and in without any regard to silence or decorum; while the schoolmaster of the village, with a string of pupils, made his appearance only a few minutes before the blessing was pronounced. At the conclusion of the service, the clergyman gave out a hymn, which was sung by a party of young men who sat in the church gallery. The sound of a miserably played flute and a cracked flageolet, united with the harshness of the voices, produced a concert both disagreeable and ludicrous. When the hymn was finished, the preacher proclaimed several marriages, and dismissed the congregation.[12]

In common with the other religious bodies Presbyterianism was much disturbed by the War of 1812, the church at Niagara being destroyed by the American forces and the Rev. John Burns held a prisoner for several months. The Battle of Beaver Dams was fought close to the home of the Rev. Daniel Eastman, his family taking refuge in the cellar. After the war American immigration ceased for a time and since the large Scottish emigration to Upper Canada had not yet begun the Presbyterian cause languished. By 1822 the Rev. Daniel Eastman alone remained in the field. After 1830, however, when immigration was again active, ministers and missionaries re-entered from New York State and a new era opened. The Rev. A. K. Buell settled in St. Catharines in 1831 and soon established a second congregation at Drummondville. The Rev. Edward Marsh came to Hamilton in 1832 and quickly added Barton to his preaching circuit. These men, fresh from the great revivals in New York State, promptly inaugurated similar efforts in Upper Canada. They were also strong advocates of temperance and active in organizing temperance societies. In 1833 they joined with the Rev. Mr. Eastman in establishing the Niagara Presbytery, the first in what is now Western Ontario. By 1837 this Presbytery had ten ministers and five missionaries, all from New York State, revivalists, advocates of temperance, and supporters of Sunday schools. This Presbytery was distinctly a by-product of the American revivals. The same force was responsible for the entry after 1820 of a second group of American missionaries,

---

[12] John Howison, *Sketches of Upper Canada* (Edinburgh, 1821), pp. 133-4.

commissioned by the Associate Presbyterian Church of the United States. They organized congregations at Galt, Stamford, and other places which were joined in 1836 to form the Stamford Presbytery in connection with the Associate Synod of North America. The ministers of this group seldom remained in Canada more than a year, an exception being the Rev. John Russel who was minister at Stamford from 1825 to 1854. During the decade after 1820 this branch of Presbyterianism had almost a clear field in the western part of the province. Its ministers were strongly missionary in spirit and were welcomed by the people among whom they laboured.[13]

The Church of Scotland, "the Kirk," had no minister in the western part of the province prior to 1828 when the Rev. George Sheed settled at Ancaster and the Rev. Alexander Gale at Amherstburg. By 1831, however, there were three new men in the field, supported in part by the Glasgow Colonial Society: the Rev. Alexander Ross, who went to Aldborough on Lake Erie in 1829; the Rev. Robert McGill, who settled at Niagara in the same year, and the Rev. William Rintoul who became minister at York in 1831. In June, 1831, the Kirk ministers in the province formed a synod in which were four presbyteries. Two other ministers arrived in 1832 and were placed at Amherstburg and Guelph, while in 1834 five came, bringing the total in the western counties at that time to thirteen settled pastors, all natives of Scotland.[14]

A fourth Presbyterian group active in Upper Canada between 1825 and 1840 was the United Synod of Upper Canada, made up of some Canadians who had received ordination in Canada, some members of the Scotch secessionist churches, and some men from the Presbyterian Church in Ireland. At its organization in 1831 the United Synod of Upper Canada was divided into two presbyteries, Brockville for the east and York for the west, the latter having eight ministers, two of whom had been ordained in Canada. None was of American origin except the Rev. Daniel Eastman, who, as has already been mentioned, had been in the province since 1801. A more important group, so far as Western Ontario was concerned, consisted of the ministers of the United Secession Church of Scotland who appeared

---

[13] On the early period of Presbyterianism in western Upper Canada see H. E. Parker, "Early Presbyterianism in Western Ontario," *London and Middlesex Historical Society, Transactions*, part XIV (1930), 10-79.
[14] *Ibid.*, 40-5.

on the scene in 1832. The first men to arrive in the west were the Rev. William Proudfoot, who settled in London, and the Rev. Thomas Christie who took charge of congregations at West Flamborough, Dumfries, and Beverly. Other men came from year to year so that at the end of 1843 there were nine missionaries of the Secession Church in the western part of the province. All the new ministers did missionary work for a year before settling in a charge and in 1844 a small theological college was opened in London. This Missionary Presbytery on two occasions supplied ministers for churches in the State of New York, at Madrid in 1840 and Rochester in 1843.

Presbyterianism in western Upper Canada prior to 1830 was following a course not unlike that of the church in the western states. Thereafter, the arrival of Scottish ministers tended to modify the development until 1837 when the forced departure of the American missionaries left the field almost entirely to the old-country men. It was from that time that such American features as revivalism tended to disappear. The Scottish clergy were critical of this American practice and were inclined to view the activities of the more emotional religious groups as dangerous to public morals. "I deeply lament the ascendency which Methodists have acquired in this country," the Rev. William Proudfoot wrote in 1833. "Their doctrines are frightfully in opposition to the grand, the glorious doctrines of the gospel. . . . The country will never become Christian till these fellows be dislodged."

The Upper Canada settler who attended church service was probably more partial to shouting than reasoning and probably preferred a graphic picture of hell fire to the elucidation of abstruse passages from the sacred volume. Judged by results, Presbyterian practice was less effective than that of the Methodists in building up church membership. The description given by an American historian of the contrast between the methods of Presbyterians and Methodists on the American frontier can be applied to those two bodies in Upper Canada without the alteration of a single word:

The Presbyterian missionary went out looking for Presbyterians, and Presbyterianism prospered best where there was to be found the largest number of Presbyterian settlers. . . . On the other hand, to the Methodist circuit-rider all communities were alike. He did not expect to find Methodists in the early settle-

ments, but he was sent out to make Methodists of the raw material which the frontier presented. The difference in approach is doubtless partially responsible for the relatively slow progress of frontier Presbyterianism, in comparison with the more rapid growth of the Methodists and Baptists.[15]

In contrast to Presbyterian conservatism the Methodists had a genius for adapting themselves to changing conditions in the new communities. Wherever they found a group of believers they quickly organized them into a church and then sought new fields to conquer, leaving the oversight of the group to the local preachers from whom also they often recruited ministers. The feature of the local organization was the class meeting where, between the visits of the itinerants, the church members assembled for prayer and expression of their individual religious experience. The high emotion of conversion was sustained and refreshed by these gatherings while at the same time the ministers were enabled to cover a wider field without feeling that what they had gained today was lost tomorrow.

In contrast to the emphasis placed by the Methodists upon spiritual emotion was the large measure of attention given by the Presbyterian sessions and clergy to the matter of discipline. In this also there is an interesting parallel to the churches in the American West. Records of Upper Canada sessions abound with instances of members being dealt with by the little church courts. The session of West Gwillimbury Presbyterian church met on July 18, 1824, "to take into consideration what steps would be most proper to take with John Faires, a member of said church, and Robert Armstrong, also a member who was acting unchristianlike at the raising of Andrew McBeath's barn. The Session agreed that two of the members of Session, viz:– Alexander Bannerman and Adam Goodfellow should go and speak to Robert Armstrong and James Sutherland and John Mathieson to speak with John Faires, who acknowledged his offence to their satisfaction, and Robert Armstrong who was found not to be in the fault." Harsher measures were used against Vesta McKay, who came before the Session on May 8, 1830 and "declared before Mr. Jenkins, minister, and Elders that Christopher Armstrong was the father of her child. . . . Also the said Vesta McKay desired the ordinance of baptism to be

[15] W. W. Sweet, *Religion on the American Frontier*: II, *The Presbyterians, 1783-1840, a Collection of Source Materials* (New York, 1936), 60.

administered to her child. The Session unanimously agreed that ordinance should be delayed for some time until the Session observed some change in her future conduct and behaviour, likewise, the Session Clerk was to give her a statement of her confession who was the father of her child. Concluded with prayer."[16]

The Presbyterians guarded with utmost care the administration of the sacrament. The Methodist table was open to all who did "freely repent of their sins" but the Presbyterian table was carefully "fenced" which meant that it was not only restricted to those belonging to the church but even within the church to those who had not been guilty of breaking the commandments. "There were between sixty and seventy communicants," wrote the Rev. William Proudfoot after one service. "In spite of all our care there found her way to the Lord's Table . . . a member of the Church of England." More pleasant is the description he has left us of the first communion which he held in the village of London:

June 1st 1833. When I went into London, the meeting house was full and many outside. It was judged proper to have the service outside. The people in a twinkling made a pulpit outside – boards laid upon two casks – seats were placed all around and the audience all comfortably seated. Preached from Luke 23: 33, "And they crucified Him." The sermon went off well. I fenced the tables also out of doors. . . . After the fencings we went into the meeting house. There were four table services. I gave also an address after the service was over. The place was not very convenient for the service, but I never saw a Sacrament conducted with more external decorum. I was much afraid of disorderly behaviour at the outdoor service, but was happily disappointed. I did not give an evening sermon – lest I should weary the people, I had already spoken for six hours.

In Upper Canada, as in the western states, there was a distinct value in the measure of social control which was exercised by the churches. Almost all denominations had some form of punishment, usually deprivation of church privileges, and it was the ignominy of this which made it effective. Marriage regulations were enforced and irregularities were frowned upon. Sabbath observance was difficult to regulate but was continu-

[16] The original Session Book is in the possession of the United Church at Bond Head, Ontario.

ously stressed, especially by the Presbyterian clergymen who were shocked by the violation of the Sabbath in Upper Canada. In the pioneer society the church did what it could to establish patterns and no doubt the very existence of a church in a settlement attracted a better class of people, perhaps also at times causing some less desirable elements to go elsewhere.

8: The Religious Scene in the 1830's

When I reflect that not one in a hundred came here to get religion; but rather to get plenty of good land, I think it will be well if some or many do not eventually lose their souls.

—BISHOP FRANCIS ASBURY (1821)

There is nothing which surprises a tourist in America more than the variety of religious sects and persuasions that exist and flourish over the vast continent.

—DAVID WILKIE (1835)

The War of 1812 gave a sharp rebuff to the American influences which up to that time had been bringing Upper Canada into striking social likeness to New York State. By 1830, however, similar influences were again active in many aspects of social and religious life, though now rivalled and challenged by British immigration and the ideas which it imported. Although Methodism had broken off its American connections in 1828 and American Presbyterianism ceased to have influence after 1837, minor religious bodies continued to cross over from New York State, preaching their peculiar doctrines and making converts. Before dealing with these minor groups, it will be profitable to survey the general state of religion in Upper Canada during the decade after 1830, observing the extent to which the churches met the needs of the times.

The Church of England at home began to realize during the 1820's that its ministry in Upper Canada was seriously rivalled by other denominations. This caused some uneasiness. A writer in the *Quarterly Review*, in 1820, discussing Canadian conditions, gave this warning: "If we slumber we must expect that Anabaptists, Methodists and sectaries of all descriptions from the United States, who are already making great progress in Canada, will completely supplant the church. Their exertions cannot be blamed since they are, in many instances at least, not sowing divisions among Christians, but making Christians; nor is their success even to be deprecated, unless we exert ourselves, since any form of Christianity is better than none." The *Quarterly Review* article was called forth in part by a statement of one Captain Charles Stuart that the twelve or fifteen clergymen of the Established Church in Upper Canada[1] were as almost nothing to the mass of the people and that it was the Methodists and Baptists, particularly the Methodists, who were keeping alive the worship of God. The *Quarterly Review* writer, while in general agreement with Captain Stuart, did not accept the latter's good opinion of the American Methodists but regarded them as "for the most part gross and ignorant enthusiasts, and actuated by a spirit of bitter hostility towards the English Methodists who are a far more respectable body of men."[2]

Until 1830 the Church of England in Upper Canada had been entirely dependent upon aid from England for its support. In 1831, however, the British government announced the gradual withdrawal of its annual parliamentary grant of £15,500 to the Society for the Propagation of the Gospel, and the church in Upper Canada faced the prospect of having to assume at least a part of its own support. Recognition of this task was shown in the formation at York, in October, 1830, of the Society for Converting and Civilizing the Indians, a name which within a month was extended by adding the words "and propagating the Gospel among the Destitute Settlers of Upper Canada." The addition to the name was significant. It indicated that the Church of England was preparing to adopt the means used by the Methodists and Baptists, and instead of confining its work to settled parishes would now go out to the more remote communities and carry its message to the people. Little was achieved before 1834, but in that year the Rev. W. J. D. Waddilove, a resident of England who had never been in Canada, took upon himself to raise funds for the Canadian work and did so over a a period of years with conspicuous success. Most of the men who were thus supported became itinerants who had preaching circuits like the Methodists and held services in houses, barns, schoolhouses, not infrequently in a Methodist meeting-house. It was a striking change in Anglican policy in Upper Canada and a move towards that greater freedom from English tradition which the church in Canada was to assume in later years.

By 1836 the movement within the church in Canada for greater freedom of action had so far progressed that at a visita-

---

[1] Actually, in 1820, there were twenty-two Church of England clergymen in Upper Canada. Stuart had been in Upper Canada just before the expansion of 1819-20.

[2] *Quarterly Review*, XXIII (1820), 383.

tion of clergy, held in Toronto in that year, the way was paved for the creation of a new diocese of Upper Canada and the right was asked to hold annual conferences. In addition, steps were taken at this time to provide for theological training, for systematic support of missions, and for the launching of a church newspaper. Within six years all of these latter aims had been achieved and the new diocese had been constituted. The annual conference, or synod, was longer delayed, the first being held in 1853, at Toronto, although in 1851 an unofficial conference was held.

The Rev. William Proudfoot, on his arrival in Upper Canada from Scotland in 1832, noted at once that the Church of England contained the gentry. The Lieutenant-Governor and his staff were members, as were also the military officers and a majority of the officials. A British traveller at York in 1835 has left us this little picture: "The Sunday morning here always presents a gay scene of military parade; the colonial governor, accompanied by the military from the garrison in full dress, with the band playing, march to church, and a great part of the population, from a feeling of decorum, respect or convenience perhaps, slip from their houses and walk in company to the place of worship."[3] Elsewhere throughout the province, in a score or more of villages like London, St. Thomas, Amherstburg, Woodstock, and Delaware, similar respectable little congregations of Anglicans gathered from Sunday to Sunday to join in the familiar lessons and listen to a sermon, short in comparison to those of other denominations but probably longer than today. Any one of them might have been a village congregation in rural England. Good order and decency were their characteristics, in contrast to the curious disorder in some other churches, as recorded by their ministers and by travellers.

In other ways there were noticeable differences between the Church of England and the other denominations in Upper Canada. In contrast to the bare meeting-houses of most dissenting groups, with the men seated on one side of the room and the women on the other, the little Anglican churches, some of them of fine architecture, had their family pews which were sold and could be resold by their parishioner owners. J. C. Goodhue advertised in 1833, " a first class pew in St. Thomas Church, being No. 5 on the east side. It will be sold low for cash, or on

---

[3] D. Wilkie, *Sketches of a Summer Trip to New York and the Canadas* (Edinburgh, 1837), p. 194.

a short credit."[4] In the matter of clerical dress there was also a contrast between the Anglican clergy and those of other denominations. T. W. Magrath, a respectable Irish settler in Adelaide Township, noted that "the Archdeacons in the towns of Canada, I suppose from the absence of higher Dignitaries, affect the episcopal appearance as much as possible, observing the costume of the standing collars, short cassocks, and rosettes in the shovel hats."[5] The non-Anglican clergy displayed only minor distinctions in dress and this was true also of the humbler Anglican clergy who, as Magrath described them, "when riding through their parishes . . . carry a valise containing gown, surplice, books, communion elements, chalice and cup, with a great coat and umbrella strapped on it." Magrath compared their appearance to that of Methodist clergymen in Ireland. The British Wesleyan ministers who arrived in Upper Canada in the early thirties affected a distinct clerical dress and the first conference president sent out from England in 1833 rivalled the archdeacons in ecclesiastical splendour. But other Methodists continued as hitherto plain even to drabness in dress.

Magrath's comments upon the religious conditions of the province are of interest. He appreciated the energy of the Methodist itinerants, "whenever a settlement is formed there they are to be found." He recognized the worth of the dissenting preachers, "many of them are excellent men, and all of them are really or apparently zealous." He feared that the time had already passed when his own church could recover its lost ground: "The Methodist dissenters have obtained an ascendancy over our infant population. Their habits of domiciliary visitation, their acquaintance with the tastes and peculiarities of the Canadians, their readiness to take long and fatiguing rides, in the discharge of their self-imposed labours, render them formidable rivals to our more easy going clergy." From the political point of view as well he felt concern that the Anglican Church was not more active: "The Episcopals are, one and all, attached to the British constitution. In the democratic principle (wherever it appears), in the instigation to discontent, and in disaffection to the laws, may always be traced the absence of Church of England principles."[6] Magrath observed that the simple service

[4] St. Thomas *Liberal*, February 7, 1833.
[5] T. W. Magrath, *Authentic Letters from Upper Canada* . . . (Dublin, 1833), pp. 202-3.
[6] *Ibid.*, pp. 194-6.

of the dissenting groups, a hymn, a prayer, and a sermon, was preferred by the common folk of Upper Canada to the long prayers and frequent changes of posture in the Church of England. The length of the Episcopal marriage service rendered it also unpopular. He suggested that amid so much denominational rivalry it might be prudent "to make some concessions as to mere points of Form, when they do not involve any vital principles of our religion."

It was unfortunate for the Church of England in Upper Canada that through so large a part of its early history the chief effort seemed to be directed to the setting up of an establishment linked to the state as in England. Four years before the British Parliament passed the Constitutional Act, with its provision for a state church in Upper Canada, the Constitutional Convention at Philadephia, devising a form of union for the thirteen independent states, had adopted a clause forbidding the setting up of any establishment of religion. American immigrants consequently brought with them a conception of religious freedom which was opposed to the aims of the Church of England. In the new western states, where there was an abhorrence not only of establishment but even of ritual, the camp meeting and the revival were the most typical forms of religious expression. The same was largely true in Upper Canada.

The phrase "religious destitution" occurs repeatedly in descriptions of Upper Canada in the 1830's particularly in reports of the churches. Anglicans, Presbyterians, Methodists, and Baptists all lamented the impiety about them. Granted that there was much irreligion in the province, it is nevertheless true that the lamentations sometimes had reference to the activities of rival denominations rather than to an entire lack of religious exercises. Anglicans and Presbyterians lamented the inroads of Methodists and Baptists; Scottish Presbyterians looked with displeasure upon the revival methods of their American brethren; the two divisions of Scottish Presbyterians were as watchful and jealous of each other as they were of the Methodists or Baptists, while the Methodists, in their turn, had a poor opinion of the Christian Church and denounced the Universalists as if they were infidels.

When the Synod of the Church of Scotland in 1837 made a survey of religious conditions in Upper Canada, the western counties were described as "a moral wilderness." The London

District was said to be the home of teachers "fostering wild, visionary and fanatical views among their ignorant followers." A great part of the population, classified as of Canadian or American origin, was described as belonging to the Methodists or to no denomination, the inference appearing to be that there was not much difference between these two groups. Better conditions were said to exist in the Gore and Niagara districts where the population was more Scottish and Presbyterian.[7] The Rev. William Proudfoot, when told in 1833 that Methodists and Baptists had been increasing rapidly in number but that not many Scotch people had joined them, made the comment in his diary: "God only knows, I hope in His mercy so to bless my labour that they and all who hold errors will not increase." After he had had an argument with a man who threatened to leave his church, he wrote: "I lectured him and succeeded I think in preserving him from the fangs of the Baptists and Methodists."

Despite all that was written and said about the irreligious state of Upper Canada in the 1830's, there was without doubt a considerable interest in certain aspects of religion. Parents who were themselves living in what the ministers would term "a state of sin" were anxious that their children should be baptized. The consolation which the clergy might offer was sought in times of distress, while in most cases the visit of an itinerant or other minister was welcomed. The large immigration of the period made it difficult for the churches to reach all the people. The back townships might be visited by a minister only a few times in a year; on the other hand, in the more settled districts church organizations were sometimes more in number than the population could properly support. The Rev. D. McKenzie reported in 1834 that in the village of London, with a population of about a thousand people, the Church of England, the Methodists, the Presbyterians, and the Roman Catholics all had meeting places. A Baptist clergyman who visited York in 1835 found six places of worship but despite this did not think that actual religion was thriving. St. Catharines in 1832 had Presbyterian, Methodist, and Anglican churches. Brantford, on the other hand, if one may judge by the comments of ministers who visited the place, was a veritable Sodom and without a place of worship in 1833. The Church of England missionary to the Indians on the Grand River told the Rev. William Proudfoot that the report of its wickedness sometimes came to him "as a roar of distant thunder."

Desecration of the Sabbath, in part due to the lack of any regular religious services, was vigorously denounced by the ministers of all denominations. Proudfoot, on his first preaching Sunday in London, saw a mill in operation and was disturbed when told that this was common in Canada. Later he was to see many instances of labour on the Sabbath and of sports and games also occupying the leisure hours of the day. On the other hand, pleasant pictures have come down to us of Sabbath observance and the utmost decorum prevailing. Wilkie, describing a service held in a log school-house in the backwoods, says: "The farmers as they arrived, some from many miles distance, threw the bridles of their horses over a convenient stump or branch at the door, quaffed a bowl of water from a pailful placed at the roadside, on the root of a fallen tree, and then, Bible in hand, slipped into their places with all the unobtrusive simplicity of the covenanters of old."[8]

The most striking feature of the religious scene was the variety of religious sects, all busily engaged in advancing their particular beliefs. Travellers from other countries recorded this among their observations. Every new form of belief which came in from the United States seemed to find adherents, though often only by drawing away the more curious-minded from some other church body. The American origin of most of the sects, as well as their occasional eccentricities, made them objects of suspicion to more orthodox religious groups, even when they themselves, as in the case of the Methodists, had an American background. The civil authorities also became uneasy at times over the American sects whose members were usually reformers in politics. In the troubled days of 1837-8 their loyalty was much questioned. The rough treatment accorded to the Quakers of Norwich after the uprising of 1837 indicated the Tory dislike of their opinions and attitude. The Christian Church also fell under suspicion at that time and its members were subjected to much petty persecution. The variety of religious bodies in Upper Canada during the 1830's was so extensive that not all can be described in detail. It is not difficult to discover, however, with what ease religious ideas from New York State and elsewhere made their way into Upper Canada and there found people not

[8] Wilkie, *Sketches of a Summer Trip*, p. 163.

only receptive but ready to disseminate these ideas yet further.

Universalism of American origin, holding the doctrine of the final holiness and happiness of all mankind, was introduced into Upper Canada from New York State as early as 1831, a Universalist Society being organized at London on September 10 of that year. Thirty-one male members were enrolled.[9] The chief centres of Universalist thought in the western part of the province were the Niagara Peninsula, the London District, and an area north and south from Brantford. These were districts in which the Baptists and Methodists had laboured from the early days of the province and presumably the Universalist doctrines found receptive minds and hearts chiefly among these groups, just as in New York State. The Rev. William Proudfoot, who came to the village of London in 1832, makes several references in his diary to the presence of Universalists in the community. A preacher of this sect from the State of Ohio who journeyed through the western part of Upper Canada in the summer of 1844 found groups of his people in London, St. Thomas, Sparta (a Quaker settlement), Brantford, Jersey Settlement, Hamilton, Toronto, and Smithville, and preached to them in all these places.[10]

In 1849, the Rev. J. R. Lavell, Universalist minister in London, began the publication of the *Gospel Messenger or Universalist Advocate*, a monthly journal devoted to the propagation of the liberal doctrines. From the notices of preaching appointments appearing in the *Gospel Messenger* it is possible to determine where the doctrines were most appreciated. Among the places where regular preaching took place in 1849 were London, Westminster, Beamsville, Smithville (to which Lavell went from London), Berlin, Galt, Brantford, Waterford, Louth, and Jordan, while in several other places occasional services were announced. The *Messenger* quoted extensively from American Universalist journals such as the *Universalist Register*, the New York *Christian Messenger*, the *Universalist Miscellany* and the *Star in the West*. In June, 1849, the Council of the Christian Universalist Association for Canada West was held in the eastern part of the province and was reported in Lavell's

[9] *Evangelical Magazine and Gospel Advocate* (Utica), November 12, 1831, 361. Alvaro Ladd, who was the first secretary, was arrested during the Rebellion of 1837 and sentenced to death but was later pardoned.
[10] *Memoranda of the Experience, Labors and Travels of a Universalist Preacher*, written by himself (Cincinnati, 1845), pp. 383-6.

paper. It was described as the fifth annual session of the Association.[11]

Universalism in Upper Canada, as in the United States, made a greater appeal to men than to women. It was its misfortune, like other newly organized religious bodies, to draw to itself many eccentric characters. In the years immediately preceding the Rebellion of 1837 many Universalists were in the reform ranks, exactly where their liberal tendencies might be expected to place them. Elijah Woodman, sent to Van Dieman's Land in 1839 from London as a political prisoner, was a Universalist. Marcus Gunn, editor of the St. Thomas *Observer*, the *Middlesex Standard*, and the *Western Liberal*, all published at St. Thomas between 1848 and 1852, was a convert to Universalism from the Congregational body. In 1853 he published a pamphlet replying to attacks on the doctrines of Universalism which had been made by a Methodist clergyman, the Rev. William Pollard.[12] Universalism gradually declined in the province and in 1940 there were but two small congregations, both in the southwestern part of the province and served by one minister.

Pennsylvania contributed an extensive Mennonite emigration to Upper Canada, beginning as early as 1786 when several families, attracted by cheap land, settled on the Twenty Mile Creek, so named because it flowed into Lake Ontario at that distance from the Niagara River. These Mennonites were not Loyalists though they probably felt more at home under British rule than under the régime which had been inaugurated after the Revolution. Following the first settlement in 1786 other groups moved into the Niagara Peninsula, and also into what is now Waterloo County where a block of land, comprising about sixty thousand acres, practically the whole of Waterloo Township, came into Mennonite ownership. The brethren in Pennsylvania sent $20,000 in silver coinage overland to make the first payment. In the years 1803-4, when there was some difficulty over the Waterloo land title, Mennonites arriving from Pennsyl-

---

[11] The *Gospel Messenger* in its issue of January, 1849, stated that at that date there were in the British American provinces nineteen societies or churches, seven meeting-houses, and ten preachers. No estimate of members or adherents was given. A file of this journal for 1849 is in the library of the University of Western Ontario.

[12] M. Gunn, *An Address to the Public, Introducing a Letter to the Rev. Mr. Pollard with References to His Recent Attacks upon the Universalists and Unitarians of London, C. W.* (1853). A typescript copy of this pamphlet is in the library of the University of Western Ontario.

vania tended to go to the Markham settlement in York County but by 1805 the movement was again towards Waterloo and continued so down to the War of 1812.[13]

The Amish group of Mennonites in Upper Canada dates from 1822 when Christian Nafziger, a Bavarian, secured a tract of land in Wilmot Township, Waterloo County, upon which he planned to place a colony from his homeland. Before he was able to achieve this aim he was preceded by families from Pennsylvania who were attracted by the cheap land. These people organized a church in 1824 and later spread into the neighbouring counties of Perth, Oxford, and Huron. Members of the Reformed Mennonite Church, a conservative branch which originated in Lancaster County, Pennsylvania, in 1812, settled in Welland County, Upper Canada, in 1833, while congregations later arose in Waterloo County and elsewhere.

Members of the Brethren in Christ (Tunkers) migrated to the Niagara District of Upper Canada shortly after the founding of this sect between 1778 and 1780 in Lancaster County, Pennsylvania. John Winger is said to have settled in what is now Pelham Township in 1788, later removing to Bertie Township where he took up land on Black Creek. Winger, who became a bishop, is generally considered to be the founder of the Tunker Church in Canada. As early as 1794 application was made to the provincial administration for the right of solemnization of marriage by Tunker ministers and this was granted by legislation which came into force at the end of 1798, Tunkers being included under the term Calvinists. Also, by the legislation of 1793, they, in common with Quakers and Mennonites, were exempted from military service but were required to pay a fine annually to the government. The Tunkers held as a fundamental belief that war was wrong and that Christ's teaching emphasized non-resistance.[14]

The Christian Church, springing into existence almost simultaneously after 1800 in three different sections of the United States, entered Canada in the year 1821 when the Rev.

[13] L. J. Burkholder, *A Brief History of the Mennonites in Ontario* (Toronto, 1935) is the chief source of information on the history and development of the separate congregations.

[14] See *Evangelical Visitor*, anniversary number, Nappanee, Indiana, August 28, 1937, 42. This sect has continued active in the province and in 1938 held its General Conference near Welland when close to a thousand delegates were present from the United States and Canada.

Allen Huntley, of New York, answered a Macedonian call from Mrs. Mary Stodgill, an American woman residing near New-market. From Newmarket he went on to Lake Simcoe where he also preached. He made a second visit to Upper Canada in October of the same year, accompanied by other ministers, and on October 21, on the shore of Lake Simcoe, Huntley was ordained, a church of forty-three members, later known as Keswick, was instituted, and the rite of baptism was administered. Keswick was the first church of this sect in Canada. A second was formed a year later in East Gwillimbury under the ministry of Nathan Harding and A. C. Morrison, both members of the New York Conference. Eight other churches were organized before 1830.[15]

The entry of the Christian Church into Upper Canada seems to have aroused pronounced Methodist antagonism. As already mentioned, this church was under much unjust suspicion in 1837 and many of its members left the province at that time. Some of the smaller preaching places completely disappeared. Because of its American connection the Christian Church also found difficulty in securing the legal recognition accorded to other religious groups. As early as 1835 the annual conference appointed Thomas Henry to draft and circulate a petition to the Assembly asking that the right to solemnize marriage and hold property be granted, but not until 1845 was this fully conceded. In the rebellion period it was even threatened that American preachers might be excluded from Upper Canada, this being given as a reason why the petition should not be granted. When coalition took place in the United States in the 1830's between groups of the Christian Church and the Disciples of Christ, there was some resulting unsettlement in Upper Canada, congregations in a few instances becoming divided and two churches arising in place of one. The Christian Church continued its separate existence, however, and by revival methods, in which it was assisted at times by preachers from the United States, added to its membership.[16]

The Christian Church in Upper Canada had its most marked growth in the years of struggle between 1825 and 1845.

---

[15] Mrs. P. A. Henry, *Memoir of Rev. Thomas Henry* (Toronto, 1880), pp. 187-8.

[16] The census of 1851 showed 3,093 members of the Christian Church and 2,064 Disciples, followers of Alexander Campbell, in the province. During the next decade the Christians increased only 925 while the Disciples added 2,083 to their number.

When its major difficulties were removed, it seemed to languish and fewer churches were opened between 1850 and 1890 than in the earlier period. During this time also the church suffered severely from the drain of its promising young men to the United States. When sent there for education and training, they tended to accept invitations to American pulpits. This was remedied in more recent years when training in Canadian universities was available. An important step was taken in 1877 in the incorporation of the Conference of the Christian Church in Ontario.

The Millerite movement, with its definite prediction of the date on which Christ would return to the earth, found response in various parts of Upper Canada in the early forties. Meredith Conn, leader of a Methodist class in the Talbot Settlement, has recorded that the membership was almost entirely carried away by the Millerite movement. His own family and one or two others were all who stood fast and it was only after some years that Methodism was properly re-established at Tyrconnel.[17] The influence of the Millerite doctrine appears to have been more marked in the eastern section of the province than in the west, though at a later date Adventist doctrines were again preached and Adventist churches were organized. In 1869 and later James Caleb McIntosh, of Centralia, Ontario, a sort of second William Miller, published pamphlets in which he predicted the second coming of Christ in the spring of 1873. When this did not happen he changed the date to the spring of 1884, forty years after the earlier excitement. His argument was that as the Israelites wandered forty years in the desert so there was also forty years wandering for "the true Israel after they came out of Egypt, or Babylonial church in 1843-44." Unlike his American predecessor, McIntosh attracted little attention.

Mormonism quickly spread from its birthplace in New York State into Upper Canada. Missionaries were reported at work in the Kingston district as early as 1833[18] while between 1833 and 1835, when Canadian Methodism was somewhat upset by the competition of Wesleyan missionaries, the Yonge Street circuit lost heavily to the Mormons, the membership declining from 951 in 1833 to 578 in 1836.[19] Through the

[17] St. Thomas (Ontario) *Times*, January 9, 1892.

[18] *Canadian Emigrant* (Sandwich), July 27, 1833.

[19] C. B. Sissons, *Egerton Ryerson: His Life and Letters* (Toronto, 1937), I, 260.

decade after 1830 there are frequent references in the press to Mormon activities in the province. The village of Churchville in the Home District was a stronghold of the belief with frequent meetings and baptisms. At Mersea in the Detroit River area the Mormons were apparently unpopular, for an attack made upon them in 1838 was recorded in the *Western Herald*, published at Sandwich.[20] In Lambton County, near the St. Clair River, the preaching of Thomas Borrowman led to an emigration of Canadian Mormons, and the road by which they made their exodus to the United States in 1846 is still known as the Nauvoo Road. The emigrants were chiefly Scottish people who had come to Lambton from Lanark County in the eastern part of the province.[21] Joining their fellow-religionists at Nauvoo, Illinois, the Mormon "New Jerusalem," they became a part of the larger migration to the new city of refuge in the valley of the Great Salt Lake. The gaunt framework of an old mill on the Sydenham River near Alviston, Ontario, is all that now remains to recall this Mormon community of 1846.

Ebenezers, the name commonly given to members of the Community of True Inspiration (Amana), founded settlements in southwestern Ontario in the 1840's, Kenneberg in Haldimand County and Canada Ebenezer nearer the Niagara River, both of considerable value through their fine stands of timber. A correspondent of the New York *Tribune* wrote in 1851 that at Kenneberg there were about fifty members holding seven hundred acres of land. "They are socialists," he wrote, "and a young man and his sister teach school. . . . Each family lives by itself, and may take out its stock and leave at will. They have a sawmill, and it is now in active employment."[22] Four years later the *Tribune* reported that the Canadian communities were preparing to remove to Iowa. During the summer of 1855 the first Amana village in the new western state was laid out and the migration of the several communities from New York State and from Canada was carried out gradually during the next few years.[23]

Unlike most other Protestant denominations, the Congre-

[20] Issue of October 9, 1838.
[21] Recollections of William Nisbet, of Sarnia, read before the Lambton County Historical Society.
[22] New York *Weekly Tribune*, March 22, 1851, p. 7.
[23] See Bertha M. H. Shambaugh, *Amana the Community of True Inspiration* (Iowa City, 1908), pp. 61, 77. Also New York *Daily Tribune*, October 9, 1855, p. 6.

gational Church in Upper Canada owed almost nothing to that body in the United States. One reason for this was that the American church, feeling that its form of organization was unsuited to frontier conditions, took only a minor part in missionary work in the western states, contenting itself with the Plan of Union whereby Congregational and Presbyterian settlers in a new community might unite and call a minister of either denomination. The results greatly favoured the Presbyterians, especially in the region north of the Ohio River where the union scheme was most widely adopted.[24] The Plan may, however, have suggested the formation in 1827 of the Canada Education and Home Missionary Society which had as its objective "to provide for destitute places, faithful evangelical ministers, either Presbyterian, Congregational or Baptist." The Rev. Henry Wilkes, a Congregational minister, was the first secretary of this Society.[25]

The Congregational Church appeared in Upper Canada later than in the other provinces, the earliest organized church being established at Frome, in what is now Elgin County, in 1819, under the name "The Congregational Presbyterian Prince of Peace Society."[26] Joseph Silcox, the local school-teacher and recently come from England, was chosen as pastor and continued in that office with but one interruption until his death in 1850. As late as 1840 there were but sixteen Congregational churches in the province. Complaint was made that whenever a Congregational church was established in a new settlement, other rival denominations would also set up their churches and thus weaken the pioneers in the field. No doubt most of the religious groups suffered to some extent from this practice.

Despite its English background and affiliations, the Congregational Church in Upper Canada showed surprising indepen-

---

[24] W. W. Sweet, *The Story of Religions in America* (New York, 1930), pp. 307-9.

[25] John Wood, *Memoir of Henry Wilkes, D.D., LL.D., His Life and Times* (Montreal, 1887), p. 43. The American Missionary Society, from its organization in 1826, gave some financial support to the Canada Education and Home Missionary Society but by 1835 the Congregational leaders in both Upper and Lower Canada were looking to England for aid and continued to do so.

[26] Michael Smith, in his *Geographical View of Upper Canada* (Hartford, 1813), mentions the presence of Congregationalists in two townships of the Long Point country, Windham and Townsend. Nothing further is known of these groups which probably had no minister and did not continue as a separate church body.

dence at times. During the troubles of 1837 two ministers were forced to resign because the congregations disagreed with their strong sympathies for the provincial administration at Toronto. In the year after the Rebellion, when a day of fasting and prayer was proclaimed on account of the disturbed state of the country, it was made in the old form of command and threatening – "as ye fear the wrath of God and the Queen's displeasure, ye shall all assemble in your respective places of worship." The Rev. Henry Wilkes called his church together and while asking it to concur in the observance urged it also "respectfully to protest against any interference of the civil power in such matters, beyond naming the day, and exhorting the faithful subjects to observe it in the manner proposed." The protest was approved by the congregation and published by the pastor in its name.[27]

Quaker migrations from the United States to Upper Canada were, as A. G. Dorland has pointed out, simply the fringe of the great westward movement "which by 1820 had brought more than twenty thousand Friends into the Great Plains beyond the Alleghanies and established in the middle west one of the most populous centres of Quakerism in the world."[28] The Friends who came to Canada were not Loyalists, as has often been stated, though their migration was mixed and intermingled with a migration of Loyalist relatives, friends, and neighbours. Chiefly they were impelled to leave their old homes in New Jersey and Pennsylvania by that same restlessness and unsettlement which was moving so many others to go west. Most of them were probably attracted by the cheap land in Upper Canada or by the prospect of bettering their material position. Religious persecution played no part in their migration, though some may have felt that religious freedom would be more assured under the British government which they had known than under the new republican rule whose future course was less certain.

Settlements of Quakers began on the Bay of Quinte and in the Niagara District at about the same time, probably in 1783. Ten years later there were twenty-five or thirty families in the neighbourhood of Niagara at Black Creek and Pelham, and by 1799 the settlement had sufficiently increased in number to organize a Monthly Meeting. This was the first Monthly Meet-

[27] Wood, *Memoir of Henry Wilkes*, p. 106.
[28] A. G. Dorland, *A History of the Society of Friends (Quakers) in Canada* (Toronto, 1927), p. 55.

ing in Upper Canada. One hundred miles west of Niagara, another Quaker settlement had its beginnings in 1808 when several families, chiefly from Dutchess County, New York, took up land in Norwich Township in the London District. Still further west, other groups of Friends settled in the townships of Yarmouth, Malahide, and Bayham, now portions of Elgin County. During this period similar growth had been taking place in the eastern section of the province. By 1808 it was felt that a wider measure of organization was needed for the province and with the consent and approval of the Yearly Meetings of Philadelphia and New York the Canada Half Year's Meeting was instituted and held its first session in January, 1810. At this time it was estimated that there were about 1,000 members of the Society of Friends in the province, a number which was increased by continued immigration from the United States to about 2,500 by 1830. Thereafter, the growth of the Quakers in Upper Canada slowed down and eventually ceased.

The Quakers were but little affected in their intercourse with the United States by the War of 1812. This was in striking contrast to the Methodists and other sects having connections with the Republic. Representatives in 1813 from Canada to the New York Yearly Meeting found it impossible to get through but this was the only difficulty of the kind which was recorded. Within the province, however, they frequently found themselves in difficulty over the payment of fines demanded in lieu of military service. To pay these fines, which would go to the expenses of the war, was, in the minds of the Quakers, quite the same as joining the militia. When they refused to pay, as they often did, the authorities seized goods to the amount of the fine or sent the protesting Friends to jail. During the troubles of 1837 the Quakers were subject to much suspicion as the western districts in which many of them lived were centres of unrest.

Revivals and camp meetings, which proved so effective in the United States in the conversion of great numbers of people, were introduced in Upper Canada by the Methodists soon after 1800 and were later utilized in religious effort by almost every Protestant denomination except the Church of England and the Scottish Presbyterians. In form and methods the revivals and camp meetings in Upper Canada differed not a whit from their counterparts in New York State, from whence they were derived, and the results corresponded also, chiefly because the same sort of people came under their influence. Fear played a large part in the experience of the pioneer, fear of accident or starvation, storm or drought, sickness or death. Revivalists, therefore, played upon a sensitive area of their hearers' minds as they portrayed death and hell, eternal punishment or eternal bliss.

While there are records of Methodist camp meetings in Upper Canada as early as 1805, it was not until the 1820's that they were at all common and the heyday of the institution came during the next two or three decades. In later years arrangements for camp meetings were carefully planned but in earlier days they seemed to spring up almost spontaneously. The Rev. Alvin Torry tells in his autobiography of religious services held in a farm home in the Long Point country which were so marked by fervour that "the mighty flame spread rapidly and we soon commenced a camp meeting within the bounds of our charge." Camp meetings in Upper Canada, as in the United States, were most commonly held in June or in the early autumn, thereby avoiding the busy harvest season. The opening service was usually on a Friday and the duration was commonly from five to eight days. The place of meeting was selected in a wooded portion of a church member's farm and in some cases the same place was used year after year. A considerable space was cleared of trees and brush and inequalities in the ground levelled. Surrounding the camp area in the earlier days was a fence or stockade, built of brush or boards to a height of eight or ten feet but in later years, when there was less disturbance by rowdies, the fence disappeared and the bounds of the camp ground were formed by the tents of the attending worshippers.

The central feature of any camp meeting area was the preacher's stand and the altar or mourner's bench immediately in front of it. The preacher's stand was a platform built of small timbers, elevated at least six feet and sometimes provided with a canopy. Half a dozen preachers might be seated upon it at one time as it was customary to call in the ministers from nearby churches or circuits for the big effort. The mourner's bench was often merely a long pole on short supports, a place at which the penitents might kneel, but at large camp meetings it became an enclosure twenty feet or more square within which were seats, the entrances being from the pulpit side. The area was covered with sawdust or tanbark and at the commencement of a meeting a further layer of straw was sometimes added since people in time of conviction often fell or threw themselves prostrate on the ground and might remain there for hours. Sometimes a wave of excitement would sweep over a gathering of this kind and as if moved by one impulse scores would rush to the altar, throwing themselves down, sobbing or groaning. This was the objective of the preaching and far into the night the ministers would move from group to group praying and exhorting the penitents. From time to time also a revival hymn would begin, echoing through the forest:

> *Come all who would to glory go,*
> *And leave this world of sin and woe,*
> *Forsake your sins without delay,*
> *Believe and you shall win the day.*

The reactions of those under conviction differed greatly, some earnest and composed, others in a frenzy, some apparently unconscious of all about them. Yet in Upper Canada, if we may believe the contemporary descriptions of camp meetings, there was much less of the wild hysteria which so often accompanied the camp meetings on the western American frontier. Young children were particularly susceptible to revival excitement and revivalists rather gloried in their hysteria, accepting it as an indication of divine power.

Revivalism in the United States produced an extensive hymnology, much of which was used in the camp meetings and revivals in Canada. Many of these hymns, crude but expressing vividly the emotions of conversion and the changed life, remained in use in Methodist and Baptist churches long after the pioneer period had passed, and some of the better ones, "A Home beyond the Tide," for example, are sung to this day in Ontario. Many revival hymns were never printed but were merely passed on from group to group by the itinerant Methodist and Baptist ministers who found them efficient instruments for the conviction of sinners. Collections of these revival hymns sometimes went into several editions. One such collection, widely used in Canada, was *The Golden Harp*, of which G. W. Henry was editor. An examination of the hymns in this book shows how distinctly they reflected the life of the frontier. Travel and pilgrimage, military life, ships and the sea, danger and death are all pictured vividly and given a spiritual significance. In Henry's collection there are more than a score of hymns presenting life as a voyage, with such titles as "The

Gospel Ship," and "The Gospel Life-boat," "The Old Ship of Zion," "The Ship Bound for Canaan," and "The Christian Sailor." One example may be quoted, to be sung to the tune of "The Mistletoe Bough":

> *What vessel are you sailing in?*
> *Declare to us the same.*
> *Our vessel is the ark of God,*
> *And Christ's our Captain's name.*

> *Chorus, –*
> *Hoist every sail to catch the gale,*
> *Each sailor ply the oar;*
> *Though storms and tempests may arise,*
> *We soon shall reach the shore.*

Death and the joys of Heaven offered copious themes for revival hymns, many of them of morbid type dwelling heavily upon deathbed scenes or youth untimely cut off in the midst of pleasure. There were also a few revival hymns in ballad form, recalling some incident or figure of the past. One such hymn, of American origin, "The White Pilgrim's Grave," was widely sung at revivals in parts of Western Ontario after 1850, although the story upon which it was based was probably unknown to most of those who sang it. The temperance theme was also common and Henry's collection even includes a hymn which may have been reminiscent of the panic of 1837:

> *I have a never failing bank,*
> *A more than golden store;*
> *No earthly bank is half so rich –*
> *How then can I be poor?*

> *I know my bank will never break –*
> *No, it can never fail;*
> *The firm – Three persons in one God;*
> *Jehovah – Lord of all!*

> *Should all the banks of Britain break,*
> *The Bank of England smash –*
> *Bring in your notes to Zion's bank,*
> *You'll surely have your cash.*

The early revivalists, like the Salvation Army in more recent times, were quick to utilize popular secular melodies for their hymns. In the supplement to *The Golden Harp* there are hymns to be sung to such melodies as "Highland Mountains," "The Mistletoe Bough," "Freemasons' Hymn," "Poor Mary Ann" (utilized for the hymn "Look to the Cross"), "What's the News," and the well-known "O Susanna." Very rarely do the names of the authors appear with their hymns. Like the Negro spirituals they came out of travail of soul and were the expression of deep emotion. Few were of sufficient merit to last beyond the memory of the generation that had sung them, and their crudity of thought and expression were out of harmony with later times. Nevertheless, they were in their day the spiritual heart-beats of men and women who found in them a lively expression of the most sacred things in life.

9: Social and Humanitarian Influences

Our House of Assembly for the most part have violent levelling tendencies which are totally different from the ideas I have been educated with. The neighboring states are too often brought in as patterns and models which I neither approve or countenance.

—DAVID W. SMITH to JOHN ASKIN (1792)

The Americans wish to do everything in their own way in order that it may be entirely American. Rifles, steamboats, glass lamps, stoves, elections, marriages and religions must all have the shape, the color, the taste, the flavor of Americanism.

—THE REV. WILLIAM PROUDFOOT (1833)

Less than a quarter-century intervened between the close of the War of 1812 and the Rebellion of 1837. The period was characterized by a deep prejudice on the part of the Upper Canada administration against all things American and particularly against American political ideas, every effort being made to exclude them. The task was not an easy one in a province whose southwestern region was virtually a highway between the older East and the new West. Between the Niagara and the Detroit rivers there was a steady flow of people so that as early as 1830 a stage line ran regularly three times a week across this portion of the province. At intervals there were hotels or inns where passengers might spend the night. A majority of the proprietors of these inns were Americans.[1] Around the firesides, where discussion ranged free, many an Upper Canadian must have gained wider acquaintance with the political and social changes which were under way in the Republic, both at Washington where Andrew Jackson held sway and in the newer western states where political experimentation in wide variety was in progress. The Upper Canadian inn must, indeed, have been one of the most effective of the various agencies spreading ideas.[2]

[1] We have an account of such a journey made in 1832 from the Niagara River to Detroit in the narrative of Benjamin Lundy, printed in his abolitionist journal, the *Genius of Universal Emancipation*, March, April, and May, 1832. This narrative was reprinted in the Ontario Historical Society, *Papers and Records*, XIX (1922).

[2] An anonymous correspondent of the Montreal *Herald* described "barrooms of taverns" in 1838 as "hot beds of sedition and treason." Mrs. Anna Jameson recorded at about the same time that the taverns were practically the only places of assembly or amusement in Upper Canada. See her *Winter Studies and Summer Rambles in Canada* (New York, 1839), I, 293. Reprinted in the New Canadian Library (1965) p. 84.

Nor were these new ideas necessarily all of American origin for immigrants from the British Isles, moving to the western counties of the province or to the western states beyond its borders, might bring tidings of movements and events in the older lands which were not without meaning and significance for Upper Canadians.

Newspapers form so important a source of information and of ideas for people of today that it is easy to exaggerate the influence of the press in the spread of ideas during the thirties. Though there were more than a score of newspapers published in the province at that time, they were all weeklies and most of them had comparatively small circulation. Furthermore, not all of them attempted any serious comment upon public affairs and there were some which were as diligent as the most Tory officials in suppressing or combating anything that savoured of American democracy. Some American and some English newspapers made their way into the province but few of these reached the great mass of the inhabitants, the majority of whom may only occasionally have seen a newspaper of any kind.

British travellers who entered Upper Canada after journeying in the United States were struck by the similarity between the ways of living, the manners, and the speech of the neighbouring peoples. Edward Allen Talbot in the 1820's noted that although the inhabitants of Upper Canada were of the most diverse races the tendency was towards assimilation to one type – the American. John MacTaggart, in the same period, thought that the feeling in the province was "totally Yankee."[3] An Oxford man who was in the province during the thirties saw nothing more degrading than "the affectation of Yankee airs and idioms by the newly-imported English settler, the Anglo-Canadians seeming to copy the worst and most prominent features of American character, and the British settler in Canada caricaturing the copy."[4] Patrick Shirreff, a visitor from Scotland, was equally emphatic. "I shall renounce all pretensions to discernment," he declared, "if the inhabitants of Upper Canada are not the most accomplished Yankees on the other side of the Atlantic."[5] Similar observations were recorded during the next

[3] John MacTaggart, *Three Years in Canada: An Account of the Actual State of the Country in 1826-7-8* (London, 1829), I, 207-8.
[4] *Six Years in the Bush, or Extracts from the Journal of a Settler in Upper Canada, 1832-38* (Huntingdon, England, 1838), pp. 21-2.
[5] Patrick Shirreff, *A Tour through North America . . .* (Edinburgh, 1835), pp. 408-9.

decade. John R. Godley, who visited the province in the early forties, remarked on the exceedingly heterogeneous and exotic character of the population, so that there seemed to be no groundwork for native population at all. "The Canadians," he wrote, "are neither British nor American: the local circumstances and situation of the country . . . tend towards the latter and the tendency is increased by the vicinity of, and intercourse with the States. . . . I think they are more American than they believe themselves to be, or would like to be considered; and in the ordinary course of things, as the emigrants cease to bear so large a proportion as they do now to those born in the province, they must become more so."[6]

The extent to which the inhabitants of the province had become Americanized in speech and in manners shocked visitors from overseas, many of whom came expecting to find a little England. Yet while manners and customs seemed alike, there was sometimes a lack in Upper Canada of little refinements which softened the picture in the United States.[7] Moreover, among the immigrants from Great Britain and Ireland there were many who seemed, in the words of one traveller, "to have left home for the purpose of indulging their vicious propensities without encountering the scorn and censure of their friends and relations." This element affected Yankee airs and idioms and copied the worst features of American character, sometimes being mistaken for actual immigrants from the United States.

Hundreds of words and phrases of American origin were carried into Upper Canada and became a part of the vernacular. A surprising number of these may still be heard in rural Ontario.[8] The Rev. William Proudfoot, on his arrival in the province late in 1832, noticed that in certain localities there were "many who guess and calculate and expect." The American words and phrases were well understood by the majority of those who heard them, but must have been puzzling to some of the newcomers from older lands. But how expressive they were:

[6] John R. Godley, *Letters from America* (London, 1844), I, 200-2.

[7] Patrick Shirreff, at Niagara in 1833, recorded: "The bar-rooms of the hotels we entered were filled with swearing tipsy people, and the establishments badly conducted, from the stage-coach to the presenting of butter; which, instead of being, as in the States, hardened by means of ice, was an unclean fluid" (*A Tour through North America*, p. 94).

[8] Le Roy G. Davis contributed to *Minnesota History* (September, 1938) an article "Some Frontier Words and Phrases." Of the scores of examples which he assembled at least three-fourths were in fairly common use in Ontario until recent times and many are still in use.

"hold yer horses," "like a thousand of brick," "crazy as a bed-bug," "blind as a bat," "it ain't what it's cracked up to be," "if ye don't like it ye can lump it," "like all possessed," "a regular bigbug," "let er rip," "like all git out," "it ain't tuh be sneezed at," "don't git on yer ear," "half-baked," and "hasn't the gumption of a louse." Substitutes for swearing were found in such expressions as "by gosh," "gosh all fishhooks," "by cracky," "what the Sam Hill," "by General Jackson," and "so help me Jumping Joshua" or "so help me Jumping Judas." There were endless shades of meaning conveyed by the tone of voice used by the speaker. James Taylor, an English visitor in the early forties, described the speech of Upper Canadians as rapid, vehement, and nasal, "delivered in a majestic manner as though with each and every statement a matter of the greatest importance was being communicated."[9] John R. Godley in 1844 met a Canadian farmer who had been in the Michigan and Illinois country and who gave a graphic description of the lack of money there. "Well he would not live in such a country," he *expected*. "They managed to *hook* eighteen dollars out of him; and he was glad enough to *clear* with what he had left." Godley was struck by the anti-American prejudices joined up with exceedingly American manners.[10]

The persistent curiosity about other people's business which occasionally annoyed British visitors in Upper Canada, but more frequently in the United States, was often merely an evidence of friendliness, as was also the habit of addressing others without an introduction of any kind. Patrick Shirreff when in Canada found himself quickly falling into the habit of nodding to strangers whom he passed on the street. The same easy friendliness appeared in the common practice of stage-drivers and others addressing their passengers by such military titles as Captain or Major. This was as common in Upper Canada as in the United States. As an instance of the ease with which newcomers fell into the ways of the country the traveller Howison relates that two Scotsmen whom he had seen at Montreal and who lifted their hats to him there did not do so when he saw them again at Kingston.

The Rev. William Proudfoot noted in his diary after a church service at Clinton Township in 1833 that he did not like

[9] James Taylor, *Narrative of a Voyage to and Travels in Upper Canada* (Hull, 1846), pp. 49-50.
[10] Godley, *Letters from America*, I, 212-13.

the appearance of the congregation: "There was an air of Yankeeism about them." This dislike of Yankee characteristics was ever present in the minds of the officials, of old country clergy and half-pay-officer settlers. The officials resented the contrasts drawn by travellers and others between conditions in Upper Canada and in the neighbouring states. Patrick Shirreff, after a few days at Niagara in 1833, wrote: "I could no longer conceal the disappointment experienced with Canada and its inhabitants. . . . The manners and customs of the people were essentially Yankee, with less intelligence, civility and sobriety. The houses and fences were inferior to those of any district yet seen, and instead of the youthfulness and non-ceasing activity of the States, there seemed the listless repose of doating age." Howison had noted similar conditions at an earlier date: "There, bustle, improvement and animation fill every street; here, dullness, decay and apathy discourage enterprise and repress exertion." Lord Durham in 1838 wrote of "the striking contrast between the American and British sides of the frontier line in respect to every sign of productive industry, increasing wealth and progressive civilization." In the same period Mrs. Jameson, at the Detroit River, noted on one side "all the bustle of prosperity and commerce," and on the other side "all the symptoms of apathy, indolence, mistrust, hopelessness."

The general urge to be up and doing which was so characteristic of the United States after 1830, and which reflected the optimism of the times, gradually communicated itself to Upper Canada and during the forties began to be remarked upon by visitors. John R. Godley, when he was at Toronto in 1842, wrote:

In this country all the world is in a whirl and fizz, and one must be in the fashion; every thing and every body seem to go by steam; if you meet an acquaintance in the street he is sure to have just arrived from some place three or four hundred miles off, and to be just starting upon a similar expedition in some other direction. After a short experience of this mode of life one quite forgets that there is such a thing as repose or absence of noise, and begins to think that the blowing of steam is a necessary accompaniment and consequence of the ordinary operation of the elements – a Yankee music of the spheres.[11]

[11] *Ibid.*, I, 199-200.

Upper Canada had its "whirl and fizz" but it was always mild as compared with the bustle of the United States. When Adam Fergusson called on President Jackson in 1831, he was asked by Jackson if he preferred Canada or the United States as a field for emigration. Fergusson replied that he was much pleased with what he had seen in Upper Canada and that he did not believe the President would think worse of him for having some bias for his own country's settlements. "Certainly not, sir," said Jackson, "and I have no hesitation in saying that, so far as regards climate and soil, it is a matter of indifference whether settlers go to Upper Canada or to us; but I will say (with some emphasis) that, in the States, they will find more stirring."[12]

In manifold ways the influence of the United States upon the social life of the province was visible. Even the high-pressure eating habits of Americans, which furnished British travellers with excuse for copious satire, were evidently not unknown in Upper Canada. When Shirreff was at Cobourg in 1833 he wrote: "We found the young men swallowing their food at the table of the hotel as fast as those of Albany did. It is almost a universal practice in the United States and Canada to board men, such as clerks and shopmen, in hotels. A large bell or horn is sounded half an hour before meals, and again when served. Hence the rush to table and expeditious eating."[13]

The architecture of the province during the first half of the nineteenth century showed unmistakably the influence of the United States. The first houses were of log, hastily put together as a rule, but sometimes of such excellent workmanship as to survive to the end of the century. The log house in Upper Canada was of the traditional North American type, first introduced in the colony of New Sweden but later adopted generally because of cheapness and the ease with which it could be erected. Loyalists and other American immigrants set the pattern which was followed by thousands of newcomers from the British Isles who had never seen such a type of building before their arrival in North America. Mennonite immigrants from Pennsylvania who settled in Waterloo County are credited with having introduced the bank barn which has continued practically unchanged in type during almost a century and a half. The

---

[12] Adam Fergusson, *Practical Notes Made during a Tour in Canada and a Portion of the United States in 1831 . . . The Second Edition, to Which Are Now Added Notes Made during a Second Visit to Canada in 1833* (Edinburgh, 1834), pp. 213-14.

[13] Shirreff, *A Tour through North America*, p. 122.

Mennonites who entered the Grand River district around the year 1800 found the country suited for livestock and immediately fashioned farm buildings on Pennsylvania lines. The barn with a bank (or sometimes the bank with a barn) was an idea that in later years spread through surrounding townships and counties and became a distinctive feature of the Ontario landscape. The Rev. William Proudfoot remarked that in St. Thomas and Brantford, where there was a considerable American element, better taste was shown in store fronts and business premises than elsewhere.[14]

The era of humanitarian effort or "benevolence" which was ushered in during the second and third decades of the nineteenth century in the United States communicated itself quickly to the Province of Upper Canada. The great religious revivals which had swept over portions of the eastern states gave impulse to the formation of societies and the inauguration of movements designed to care for all who were the victims of misfortune or injustice. "The present age," said the *Christian Examiner* in 1825, "is distinguished for publick spirit and benevolent enterprise, manifested in every possible form. There is one way of doing good, in particular, which never before was carried to anything like the same extent – namely, by associating for this purpose. We have societies for everything. The consequence is that scarcely a month passes in which we are not called upon to join, or aid, some benevolent association."[15] Counterparts of these American societies soon appeared in Upper Canada wherever similar objectives existed.

The temperance movement was one of the earliest of the American reform activities to affect the province, the medium of communication being the Methodist, Baptist, and Presbyterian bodies having connections with the United States. These churches gave encouragement to the formation of temperance societies and even advocated total abstinence on the part of their members. They had ample scope for their activities since Upper Canada, during its first fifty years as a province, must have been one of the least temperate countries in the world. Distilleries and breweries were proportionately as common as the gasoline

---

[14] One of these early store fronts in St. Thomas still survived in 1938 and was pictured in Eric Arthur, *Early Buildings of Ontario* (Toronto, 1938), p. 17.

[15] *Christian Examiner* (Boston), II (1825), 241.

stations of a more modern era and a cheap, bad whisky was everywhere available. Even as early as Simcoe's time the evils of intemperance had become so noticeable that official regulation of the sale became necessary.[16] Simcoe had hoped that by encouraging brewing he might provide a substitute for the hard liquor so generally in use but he was unable to break down the established custom, and consumption of whisky grew year by year after his day. Some measure of the intemperance was probably due to the presence of discharged soldiers, men who had lived in an environment where heavy drinking was common. Among soldiers in garrison towns there was also widespread drunkenness. The traveller Godley noticed this condition, attributing it to the soldier's comparative idleness, his command of money, and the want of any inducement to save it.[17] John J. Bigsby, who was in Upper Canada during the 1820's, found the evil also prevalent among men of higher social standing: "Strong drink is the bane of Canada West," he wrote, "especially on outlying farms, and still more especially, I fear, among half-pay officers."[18]

Patrick Shirreff, coming to the province in the early 1830's from Scotland, a land where liquor was by no means shunned, was amazed at the consumption of whisky in Upper Canada and shocked by the effects which it produced. On a July day near Rice Lake he remarked that two-thirds of the people whom he met on the road were tipsy – "a painful sight." On a Sunday journey by steamboat between York and Hamilton he found many of the passengers drunk and quarrelling. The bar-room of the hotel at Newmarket he described as filled with drunkards of the lowest class, "part of them in rags and swearing in a disgusting manner." He makes several references also to the prevalence of drunkenness in the Niagara District.[19]

In the United States, from the period immediately after the close of the War of 1812, there arose a demand for united action

---

[16] "Many inconveniences having arisen from the Number of Tippling houses and some irregularities in the manner of licensing them, the Justices in their several divisions are by this bill enabled to meet once a year for the purposes of granting such licenses as they may think proper" (*Simcoe Papers*, III, 3-4).

[17] Godley, *Letters from America*, I, 241. After 1840 temperance societies were organized in a number of the British regiments in Canada. See *Temperance Advocate*, VII (1841), 7.

[18] John J. Bigsby, *The Shoe and Canoe, or Pictures of Travel in the Canadas* (London, 1850), I, 262.

[19] Shirreff, *A Tour through North America*, pp. 117, 118, 123, 125.

to check the growing use of liquor. Eventually a general temperance movement swept over the land. Newspapers printed lengthy communications on the subject while local temperance societies sprang up in great numbers, to be united later in state-wide organizations. In 1833 the movement became national with the founding of the United States Temperance Union. At first interest was in temperance rather than in total abstinence but within a decade the second phase dominated the effort. By 1830 there were probably more than a thousand temperance societies in the United States and the movement had spread into Canada, receiving warm support from the Methodists, Baptists, and American Presbyterians. The first societies were established in 1829 in the Niagara Peninsula, at Stoney Creek, Ancaster, Beverly, and Pelham, the latter a Quaker stronghold. At about the same time a society was formed at St. Thomas, one of the first in the London District. In May, 1830, the *Christian Guardian* reported that upwards of twenty societies had been formed in the province, with probably about two thousand members. During the next two years this number increased to about one hundred societies with an aggregate membership of ten thousand. By 1836 district temperance societies were appearing and in that year Canadians became associated with the American Temperance Union. Thenceforth the work was conducted in a more organized way. Canadian societies were brought closely into touch with the movement in the United States during 1835 by the visit of an agent of the New York State Temperance Society who spoke at more than twenty places in the province.[20] The St. Catharines *Journal* reported that more than five hundred persons were pledged to total abstinence at his meetings. Young Men's Temperance Societies and societies for Negroes and for children were also a feature of this period.

In Upper Canada, as in the United States, the temperance movement was furthered by the publication of journals. In Canada the earliest of these was the *Temperance Advocate*, established in 1835. It greatly extended its influence after 1839 by sending copies free to every minister and school-teacher in the province. The *Advocate* printed in each issue what it termed a "Catalogue of the victims of alcohol in Canada," resembling the record of slavery horrors in Garrison's *Liberator* and in

---

[20] See St. Catharines *Journal*, November 12, 19, 23, December 17, 1835. The first Total Abstinence Society in Canada was formed at St. Catharines in June, 1835.

Theodore Dwight Weld's *"Slavery as It Is: Testimony of a Thousand Witnesses."* The *Temperance Record*, established in 1836 by Jesse Ketchum, a Toronto businessman, was a further aid to the cause, as was also the *Challenge*, issued from time to time between 1854 and 1863 by J. J. E. Linton of Stratford who, in addition to his activities in the temperance ranks, was a profound anti-slavery man. Temperance literature from the United States was also widely circulated.

The temperance movement in Upper Canada influenced the carrying on of certain lines of business. In the St. Catharines *Journal* of June 2, 1836, Charles Marsh of Chippawa advertised the opening of the Temperance Mansion House: "Every exertion will be made to render this establishment in reality the 'Travellers' Home,' undisturbed by the noise and turmoil incident to those places more or less where spirituous liquors are sold." The *Western Herald* of January 8, 1839, contained an announcement by the firm of J. and J. Dougall of Windsor that their vessels plying between Sandwich and Kingston were "sailed upon temperance principles." This firm was one of the first mercantile houses in the province to abandon completely the traffic in liquors. A news item in the St. Thomas *Liberal* in 1834 strikes a note familiar to this generation with its drunken motorists when it says: "The mail stage route from London to Sandwich has very lately been filled with double teams to run every day. The carriages and horses are in excellent condition, and the drivers, certainly without a single exception, are temperate. This is admirable – of all the requisitions and appendages to a stage concern – give me a sober driver."[21]

Baptists and Methodists were the most consistent supporters of the temperance movement, but even these groups were not more opposed to the liquor traffic than those early Presbyterian churches which had connection with the United States. In the Presbyterian church at Hamilton in 1831 none was received or retained as a member who made, sold, or used ardent spirits. As early as 1833 the Western Association of Baptists passed a resolution recommending to the churches that they form themselves as a body into temperance societies and receive none as members but such as would agree to temperance principles.[22] This Association in 1840 strongly commended the support of

[21] Quoted from St. Thomas *Liberal* in *British American Journal* (St. Catharines), December 11, 1834.
[22] St. Thomas *Liberal*, July 18, 1833.

the temperance cause to the churches.[23] Similar sentiments were expressed on various occasions by the Methodist conferences.

Fraternal temperance societies appeared in the province about the middle of the century. The Sons of Temperance, established in Quebec and the Maritime Provinces in 1847, entered Upper Canada a year later and spread rapidly. The Independent Order of Good Templars, organized in the United States in 1850, was active in Canada by 1854, while the Royal Templars, founded at Buffalo in 1877, entered Canada a year later. These fraternal societies were social centres for the communities where they were organized and through debates, spelling matches, and other forms of entertainment offered young people opportunity for intellectual development. Sir George Ross, former Premier of Ontario, has recorded with gratitude in his memoirs the training which he received in public speaking when as a young man in Middlesex County he was a member of the Sons of Temperance.

Upper Canada produced no Dorothea Dix to carry on a crusade for better treatment of the insane but at an early date the need of such reform was realized and inquiry was made concerning the methods of treatment in use in the United States. In 1835 Dr. Charles Duncombe, member of the Assembly for Oxford, moved a resolution providing a grant for the expenses of three Commissioners who should obtain information with regard to lunatic asylums. He was himself appointed as one of the Commissioners and drew up the report which was presented a year later. Heretofore there had been no public provision for the care of insane persons other than placing them in the jails where they received no special medical attention and but little attention of any kind. Responsibility for their care lay with the Courts of Quarter Sessions and these bodies sometimes arranged with private parties to look after the unfortunates. In 1830 the Grand Jury of the Home District had suggested that some place other than the jail should be obtained for the accommodation of the destitute insane, and this probably helped to bring about action by the Assembly. Dr. Duncombe in his report recommended the building of an asylum similar to that in Worcester, Massachusetts, the details of which he set down minutely. But quite as important as the building, in his opinion, was the method of treatment, and here again he found much to be admired in the Worcester institution. He particularly commended the separation of patients into classes according to the nature and seriousness of their condition and emphasized the "mild and gentle means, without violence in any instance" which he had found at Worcester and also at some other asylums. The similarity of several of the recommendations of 1836 to methods still accepted is noticeable.[24] There were but few American institutions of high standard at this time but Duncombe drew upon the experiences of the best in suggesting policies that might be followed in Upper Canada. His own deep interest in the subject and the growing feeling of public responsibility for the insane would probably have brought early action had not the outbreak of 1837 intervened. When that disturbance was over Dr. Duncombe was an exile in the United States and men's thoughts were on other matters than those of humanitarian character. Not until 1850 was provision made for the proper care and treatment of the mentally afflicted, the new Toronto Asylum opened in that year being modelled both as to building and methods of treatment on similar institutions in the United States. From the time of Duncombe's report the province has deliberately looked to the United States for ideas on the care of the insane, both in the matter of buildings and in methods of treatment.

The Commissioners who visited the United States seeking information on the care of the insane gave attention also to prisons and penitentiaries and presented their observations in a separate report, also written by Dr. Duncombe.[25] This document urged a more enlightened attitude towards the problem of the criminal and particularly towards the problem of the juvenile offender, so often a product of his environment. Duncombe presented a grim picture of children to be seen on the streets of the capital city of the province, ragged, uncleanly, using vile language, and degraded by their idleness and bad habits. "Is it possible," he asked, "that a Christian community can lend its sanction to such a process without any effort to rescue and to save?" In Duncombe's report may be seen an indication of the growing humanitarian spirit within the province which had

---

[24] Duncombe's report on the treatment of the insane is printed in the Appendix to the *Journal* of the Assembly, Upper Canada, session of 1836, I, no. 30.

[25] "Report of Commissioners on the Subject of Prisons, Penitentiaries, etc.," Appendix to the *Journal* of the Assembly, session of 1836, I, no. 71.

already found practical application in work for children carried on by Jesse Ketchum in Toronto.

When Duncombe and his fellow Commissioners visited the United States there were two schools of thought on prison methods. The Pennsylvania Prison Society, founded in 1787 and the oldest prison society in the world, had conceived and developed the penal philosophy of separate confinement of prisoners and had introduced it in 1829 in the Eastern State Penitentiary. The other system was the Auburn plan of work in company but with enforced silence and an absence of all communication among the prisoners. The Auburn plan gave a higher degree of profit from the labour of the convict though the Pennsylvania plan was regarded as bringing about a greater degree of reform. The Upper Canada Commissioners recommended the Auburn plan, which was adopted and three years later the first prisoners were received at buildings erected near Kingston. William Powers, a deputy-keeper at Auburn, was brought to the province to supervise the work of construction and remained with the institution for four years. He then resigned, being unable to agree with the warden, a political appointee who knew little of prison work. John R. Godley, when in Kingston in 1842, visited the penitentiary and noted its likeness to the New York State prison at Auburn, the prisoners being employed at different trades or at labour on the buildings.

The organized movement for peace, stimulated in New England by the federalist attitude towards the War of 1812, soon influenced Canada. At an early date there was communication between Massachusetts and the Maritime Provinces and in 1826 it was reported that there were already twelve peace societies in Upper Canada.[26] This was two years before the organization of the American Peace Society gave the subject national significance. In Upper Canada the Quakers were stout supporters of the ideal of universal peace, though not generally leaders in the organization of the societies. In 1827 John Casey, apparently a resident of Upper Canada, published a volume on universal peace, having been brought to a conviction of the importance of the subject, he said, by reading three peace tracts

[26] The *Friend of Peace* (Boston), I, 37; III, 159. The New England theologian, Noah Worcester, who took an active part in the Massachusetts Peace Society, wrote September 11, 1821, from Brighton, Mass., to Sir Peregrine Maitland inviting his attention to the objects of the Society "to prevent another war between Great Britain and the United States." See Royal Society of Canada, *Transactions*, XVI (1922), sec. II, p. 14.

printed in the State of New York, the first writings on the subject which he had ever seen. In his work he quotes such journals as the *Friend of Peace* and the *Herald of Peace*, the former an American and the latter an English publication, and also mentions the presence of peace societies in the other British American provinces.[27] An agent of the Peace Society of New York who visited Upper Canada in 1839, shortly after the Rebellion, declared that the aims of the Peace Societies should be: "To act as committees of vigilance, to inculcate peace among the people, and to arrest and hand over to the constituted authorities such persons as they may find committing breaches of the Laws."[28] The Societies were to do more, it would appear, than to preach the ideal of peace; they were to be active in maintaining it when discord was threatened.

The American Missionary Association, organized at Albany in 1846 and openly opposed to slavery, found a field for work among the Negroes who entered Upper Canada from the United States. Between 1848 and 1864 the Society maintained its own missionaries or supported those of other organizations in the southwestern part of the province where the coloured people were most numerous. The work was difficult and the results far from encouraging if one may judge by the tone of the annual reports. Agitators constantly raised doubts concerning the motives of the white missionaries while self-constituted Negro collectors gave the Negro churches a bad name in the minds of many people who might otherwise have been sympathetic.[29]

Though not connected in any way with the missionary movement which followed the great revivals, mention might be made of the Moravian Indian mission which was established on the Thames River as early as 1792 and was known as Fairfield. This mission was unique in that the Delaware Indians, of whom it was comprised, had migrated along with their Moravian teachers from the State of Ohio. Lands for these Indians were granted by the Upper Canada administration in 1793 in which year also Simcoe visited the place, being much pleased with the

---

[27] John Casey, *Universal Peace; Being a Rational and Scriptural Vindication of the Establishment of Permanent and Universal Peace; upon the Immovable Basis of Christian Principles . . .* (Black Rock, 1827). The preface to this book is dated from Upper Canada, October 10, 1826.

[28] St. Catharines *Journal*, October 31, 1839.

[29] See Fred Landon, "The Work of the American Missionary Association among the Negro Refugees in Canada West, 1848-1864," Ontario Historical Society, *Papers and Records*, XXI (1924).

conditions which he found. At the end of the century Fairfield consisted of fifty houses with on hundred and fifty inhabitants. The Indians for some years were able to furnish the North West Company with a large quantity of provisions, according to the traveller Latrobe.[30] The principal settlement at Fairfield was destroyed by the Americans during the War of 1812 but when peace came the work was resumed at another site known as New Fairfield. The Rev. Christian Dencke, one of the Moravian missionaries, in 1818 produced a translation of the Epistles of John in the Delaware tongue. This was printed by the American Bible Society in an edition of one thousand copies, of which three hundred were sent to New Fairfield. It was announced at this time that Dencke had also completed a translation of John's Gospel and was at work on the Gospel by St. Matthew. In the same year the American Bible Society printed one thousand copies of the translation of Mark made by the Indian chief, Joseph Brant, and of a translation of the Gospel of John made by Captain John Norton.[31]

A further development of the humanitarian spirit may be seen in the changes which were made in the Criminal Code in 1841, at which time the pillory was abolished and the punishment for various offences considerably reduced. Banishment for crime ceased in 1842 when legislation was passed providing that instead of transportation there should be imprisonment in the provincial penitentiary or elsewhere. This put an end to a form of punishment not under Canadian control since the penal colonies were under the supervision of the British government. The last conspicuous instance of transportation was the sending to Van Diemen's Land in 1839 of 139 prisoners who had been implicated in the troubles of 1838 in Lower Canada and along the border of Upper Canada. There had been some moderation of the criminal laws in the early thirties but not all the barbarous features had been removed. Wilkie, when at York in 1834, saw "a poor and wretched female with her feet confined in the stocks, set for public gaze on a piece of vacant ground at the side of the public thoroughfare, and raised upon a platform,

---

[30] C. J. Latrobe, *The Rambler in North America, 1832-1833*, 2nd ed. (London, 1836), II, 180.

[31] See extracts from the second annual report of the American Bible Society in the *Panoplist and Missionary Herald*, XIV (Boston, 1818), 555. John Norton, translator of the Gospel of John, was a Scotsman who, coming to Canada early in life, settled among the Mohawks by whom he was made a chief. He took part in the War of 1812.

that all might see her in passing."[32] Imprisonment for debt was abolished in Upper Canada in 1835, at about the same time as in most of the northern states.

[32] D. Wilkie, *Sketches of a Summer Trip to New York and the Canadas* (Edinburgh, 1837), pp. 196-7. The pillory had been in common use during the 1820's.

10: The Background of the Rebellion

The chiefest authors of revolution have been, not the chimerical and intemperate friends of progress, but the blind obstructors of progress; those who, in defiance of nature, struggle to avert the inevitable future, to recall the irrevocable past; who chafe to fury by damming of its course the river which would otherwise flow calmly between its banks, which has ever flowed, and which, do what they will, must flow forever.

—GOLDWIN SMITH

The unrest in Upper Canada which culminated in the uprising of December, 1837, can be traced back to the years immediately following the War of 1812. The immediate fall in prices when hostilities ceased brought hardship to farmers while the prohibition of American immigration handicapped the land speculators and other business interests. Much uneasiness resulted from delays in fulfilling the promise of land grants to men who had served in the militia. The war was not five years in the background before there were charges of pension frauds, the Select Committee on Public Accounts informing the Legislature in 1819 that in their opinion "most shameful" impositions had been practised in recommending individuals to be placed on the lists. Leading officials were also charged with feathering their nests through salaries and emoluments which, when compared with those paid to officials in the nearby American states, seemed disproportionately high. Reform newspapers from time to time made such comparisons.[1]

Out of such grievances as above mentioned, and out of the ever-present question of obtaining land, came the setting for the

[1] The St. Thomas *Liberal* made the statement in 1837 that while the average salary of a state governor in the United States was only a little over $2,000 a year, four governors in British North America received nearly $92,000, made up as follows: Lord Gosford in Lower Canada, $44,000; Sir Francis Bond Head in Upper Canada, $22,000; Sir John Harvey in New Brunswick, $13,000; Sir Archibald Campbell in Nova Scotia, $13,000. The *Liberal* added that New York State with a population of two million people paid only $4,000 to its governor while Upper Canada with only 300,000 people paid five times as much. The *Liberal's* arguments were reprinted in the St. Catharines *Journal*, August 24, 1837.

agitation led by Robert Gourlay after 1817.[2] When he issued his famous circular, seeking information concerning conditions within the province, the replies which he received convinced him that the affairs of Upper Canada were administered chiefly for the benefit of a select group and that it was his job to set things right. Gourlay's subsequent agitation and the persecution which it brought down upon him had far-reaching consequences. The land question was particularly brought to public attention and from his day until 1837 it grew in importance. The pioneer farmer might have little comprehension of constitutional issues but he did know when his living and comfort were interfered with and, if the interference were sufficiently harmful or too long protracted, he was likely to strike back.

The possible political effects resulting from the impact of American ideas was a matter of much concern to the authorities in Upper Canada, but travellers who visited both countries were, more often than not, surprised at certain differences between the two. While Upper Canada was becoming Americanized in many other ways, it seemed unable to catch the enterprise and energy which were so characteristic of the Republic. Contrasts of this kind were sometimes unfair in that they did not take into consideration certain fundamental differences between the communities. Toronto, the most important town in the province, was after all but a local community, whereas Buffalo, with which it was frequently compared, was the terminus of the Erie Canal and the jumping-off place for tens of thousands of people migrating to the West. Nevertheless, contrasts with the United States were always in the minds of observant people, and since it was natural to attribute economic conditions to the relative forms of government there was bound to develop the belief that application of the American formula might cure Upper Canada's ills. More than one traveller suspected that envy of conditions in the United States had something to do with the

[2] The persecution of Robert Gourlay by the Family Compact is a *cause célèbre* in the early history of Upper Canada. Gourlay, a Scot of good education, came to the province in 1817. He was interested in the possibility of increased British immigration and decided to prepare a statistical account of Upper Canada. His questions addressed to local officials excited alarm among the members of the governing group who feared loss of their special privileges. Having failed by legal proceedings to quiet Gourlay, resort was had to an old Alien Law passed in 1804 and after a trial which was scandalous in character he was banished from the province. The Gourlay affair was an example of an administration making criticism of its actions a crime.

prevailing discontent in the province and suspected also that discontent was by no means confined to the Reformers. Mrs. Jameson, for example, found "among all parties a general tone of complaint and discontent," even those who were enthusiastically British seemed to be as discontented as the rest.[3] The Montreal *Herald*, in 1838, after lauding the loyalty of the British population in Lower Canada, "as staunch as it is undeserved," remarked that conditions were different in Upper Canada, where "besides that numerous portion of the population which are many of them Americans in fact, and all of them republicans at heart, there is a large portion of the British population in a state of dissatisfaction, which they no longer attempt to conceal."[4]

As unrest developed in the province and dissatisfaction with the form of government became more widespread, it was only natural that there should be increased interest shown in the political machinery in the United States, particularly in the forms of administration set up in the newer and neighbouring states of the West. In the eight years which preceded the uprising in Upper Canada, the Republic was going through one of the most exciting political periods in its history. Jackson's victory in the presidential campaign of 1828 was the prelude to democratic innovations wide in variety and extent, news of which was carried to Upper Canada by the press and by visitors from the Republic. Canadians who journeyed in the United States likewise brought back reports of the changes which were going on. William Lyon Mackenzie made an extended trip in the United States in the summer of 1829, in the course of which he met many public men and had the privilege also of an interview with President Jackson. Mackenzie was much impressed with the simplicity and apparent cheapness of American government.[5] But it was not the policies of Jackson's administration which chiefly affected the British province; rather it was the political theories of the newer western states with their yet unshaken belief in the wisdom of elected legislatures and their tendency to glorify that branch of government at the expense of the execu-

---

[3] Anna Jameson, *Winter Studies and Summer Rambles in Canada* (New York, 1839), I, 76-7. Reprinted in the New Canadian Library (1965), p. 50.

[4] Quoted in *Western Herald* (Sandwich), October 9, 1838.

[5] See R. A. MacKay, "The Political Ideas of William Lyon Mackenzie," *Canadian Journal of Economics and Political Science*, III (February, 1937), 12-13.

tive. What the Upper Canada Reformers could not foresee was that within a decade the western states would find their confidence in the legislative branch badly disturbed and that instead of adding to the powers of their elected representatives they would actually be taking steps to check them. This latter tendency was to be particularly marked in the forties when the states were seeking means of recovery from the financial disaster of 1837.[6]

In the years just after 1830, however, the western states must have seemed to many Upper Canadians to furnish the model upon which they should proceed in their political development, and the Upper Canada Reform programme of 1836, with its demands for an elective Legislative Council, control of all revenue by the Assembly, and freedom from interference with its legislative activities, could very easily be described by its opponents as "American." It was an alien principle which the Reformers were seeking to introduce into the existing imperial system and to admit it was to change the character of that system.

The County of Middlesex, in the London District, may serve to illustrate the growth of unrest in a community over a period of years.[7] In this area the dominant figure was Colonel Thomas Talbot, member of a notable Irish family, who had received his first grant of land in 1803 and had so added to it that by 1830 he had become the largest individual owner in the western part of the province. Talbot, who was a member of the Legislative Council of Upper Canada, acted also as a government land agent in a number of townships and for some years his arrangements with the government were such that for every farm he allotted to a settler he himself received an even larger acreage.

By 1832 discontent had become so openly displayed that Talbot was alarmed and decided to take action. Plans were made for a rally of his supporters at St. Thomas on St. George's Day at which it was hoped to make such a display of force as would still the Reformers. In a letter addressed to the Hon. Peter Robinson, at York, a week before the event, Talbot predicted

[6] See Bayrd Still, "An Interpretation of the Statehood Process, 1800 to 1850," *Mississippi Valley Historical Review*, XXIII (September, 1936), 189-204.

[7] The County of Middlesex until 1852 included also the townships now forming the County of Elgin.

"hot work." Contemporary newspapers have preserved for us a detailed account of the St. Thomas meeting, the central feature of which was Colonel Talbot's own speech. It consisted chiefly of a coarse tirade against Reformers in general, with special denunciation of the temperance societies – "Damned Cold Water Drinking Societies" he termed them – in which he found "poisonous and seditious schemes" being hatched to deceive the unwary.[8] One section of the Talbot Settlement in which there were numerous people from New York State was also singled out for special attack. Talbot's biographer has properly described the address as "one of the most extraordinary prepared speeches, both as to form and matter, ever delivered." It began with the military command "Silence and attention," it included an incitement to personal violence against Reformers individually, and it closed with a benediction imploring the Deity to bless and preserve "all you that are true British subjects." Others were apparently to be excluded from the Divine care.[9]

Talbot's vehemence may have been excited in part by a cleverly written circular which had been printed and spread throughout the townships as soon as public notice of his St. George's Day rally appeared. It was signed "A Freeholder" and was addressed to the inhabitants of the County of Middlesex. After setting forth the recent party changes in England and the success which was there attending reform movements, the writer charged the administration of the province with being entirely out of line with English progress: "The Legislative Council of this Province is composed of men whose views are diametrically opposed to the views of the Imperial Government. . . . The leaders of the Tory party are well aware that recent dispatches from England demonstrate that the views of the British Ministry respecting the Legislative Council are directly opposed to their wishes." The writer then proceeded to deal specially with Colonel Talbot whose party zeal was attributed to the fact that he had received more than 60,000 acres of land which if sold at the price he had often asked would amount to the sum of $360,000.

[8] Talbot's dislike of the temperance societies may be attributed in part to his own drinking habits, but was probably due also to the fact that the temperance movement had come in from the United States and was supported by the Methodists. This, in itself, would be enough to damn the movement in his eyes.

[9] C. O. Ermatinger, *The Talbot Regime or the First Half Century of the Talbot Settlement* (St. Thomas, 1904), pp. 162-9.

If the Tories say this was for services in the army I can correct this misrepresentation for I have heard from his own lips that he never did much actual service and sold his commission for the trifling sum of 10,000 guineas, add to this a pension of £400 Sterling a year he now receives and then say Tory whoever you are if he has not received liberally from Tory administrations and is he not bound to humbug the people if by so doing he can in any degree oppose the measure of the King and Ministers so long as those Ministers are not of the Tory party.

Col. Talbot may be the father of the Talbot settlement, but he will find on the 23rd April that he has many sons who are of age and think and act for themselves and who are not afraid to tell grey beards the truth.[10]

Talbot's supporters cheered him at St. Thomas but discontent was not lessened and by the end of the year Reform political organization was proceeding apace in the area over which he held sway. Activities of the "political unions," as they were termed, were recorded from week to week in the St. Thomas *Liberal*. The activities of the Tory group also received attention. In its issue of January 10, 1833, the *Liberal* reprinted a Tory broadside calling for volunteers to disperse a Reform meeting which had been announced for January 17 at St. Thomas. The broadside, calling for an attack on the Reformers, who were described as "Yankees," read as follows:

NOTICE

The Ripstavers, Gallbursters, etc. with their friends are requested to meet at St. Thomas on the 17th of January, at 12 o'clock, as there will be work for them on that day. The Doctors are requested to be in readiness to heal the sick and care for the broken-headed. Let no rotten eggs be wanting. As the Unionists are all Yankees, a few pieces of pumpkin will not be amiss.

Whatever Unions may be in England, it must be remembered that in this country, with Republicans at their head, they are the next step to Rebellion. The object of the nasty Republican Trio, that is to say of the Hypocrite, the Atheist and the Deist, in their intended meeting is to wheedle weak and simple souls so far into the paths of Rebellion, that they cannot afterwards retreat even if they wish to do so. Therefore, most noble Ripstavers, check the evil in the beginning, that is, hoe them out

[10] A copy of this circular is in the library of the University of Western Ontario.

– sugar them off – in short sew them up. The Dastards may think to screen themselves from the public fury by holding their meetings at a private house; but public or private put yourselves in the midst of them. You have a right to be there. It is a public meeting.[11]

The insinuation in this document that Upper Canada reform and American republicanism were one and the same thing is typical of much of the criticism directed against the Reform group. It was most natural that the American settlers, being generally excluded from office, should gravitate to the Reform ranks, but their presence there actually complicated the movement by providing so convenient a target for opponents. They might be Reformers with the best of intentions and the purest of motives but their known leanings provided the Tory group with one of the best weapons in its arsenal. Reform was often checked by simply raising the cry "American."

By 1833 a very considerable number of inhabitants of the County of Middlesex had come to associate their grievances with the policies of Colonel Talbot. His extensive acquisitions of land, his truculent manners, and the large measure of control which he could exercise over the individual farmer's welfare combined to make him a rather sinister figure. This feeling was expressed by the *Liberal* in an article published during the summer of 1833 in which it said:

The county of Middlesex, from its first settlement up to this moment, has been controlled by two distinguished individuals, as absolutely and despotically as is the petty sovereignty of a German despot. This they have been enabled to do through the immense influence their high official stations give them. Magistrates, officers of the excise, surveyors, and militia officers, commissioners to carry the appropriations of public money into effect, all are appointed through the recommendations and influences of these sages of the District – thus forming a host of worthies who are ever at the back of their Patrons. We assert without fear of contradiction, that the Hon. Colonel Talbot

---

[11] The *Liberal* advised Reformers so to conduct themselves that if their opponents disturbed the peace, on their heads would fall the disgrace. In its issue of February 14, 1833, the *Liberal* reported a political gathering at Yarmouth where Tory partisans broke windows and committed other excesses which "would have disgraced a band of Sioux Indians."

rules with a more absolute sway, and his power is infinitely more to be dreaded than that of the King of Great Britain.[12]

No general statement could possibly comprehend the manifold reasons for individual unrest in Upper Canada, so widely did they vary. The specific grievances of one individual in Middlesex County have been preserved for us in the writings of Robert Davis, a resident of Nissouri Township, and however much his extravagance of language and bitterness of feeling may be discounted there is clearly discernible the feeling of frustration by which he was moved. Davis was a potential rebel when he wrote in 1837 and a year later he died from wounds received in the fighting at Amherstburg. In his book he says of himself:

. . . the author has been in Canada since he was a little boy, he has not had the privilege of a classical education at the King's College, or the less advantages derived from a District school. The greater part of his time has been spent in close confinement in the wilderness of Nissouri Township. Indeed, it has been confinement enough, to watch over and provide for a tender and increasing family. He had in most instances to make his own roads and bridges, clear his own farm, educate himself and children, be his own mechanic, and except now and then, has had no society but his own family. Has had his bones broken by the fall of trees, his feet lacerated by the axe, and suffered almost everything except death. He waited year after year in hope of better days, expecting that the government would care less for themselves and more for the people. But every year he has been disappointed, and instead of things getting better, in many instances they have been getting worse. The Church ascendancy has been getting worse and worse, till they have at last got fifty-seven rectories established, and what next, who can tell. The Orange mob is worse every election, so that it is impossible for any honest, peaceable reformer to give his vote for a member of parliament without the fear or realization of having his head broken. Also, honest reform magistrates are almost daily getting their discharge from the commission of the peace, and Court of Requests: while the most ignorant and worthless of the tories are becoming magistrates.[13]

[12] *Ibid.*, July 25, 1833.
[13] Robert Davis, *The Canadian Farmer's Travels in the United States of America . . .* (Buffalo, 1837), preface, pp. 3-4.

The political temper of the province at large was revealed in the election contests, which from 1828 on were characterized by extreme bitterness. The Reformers, who had secured a clear majority in 1828, lost control of the Assembly in 1830, regained it in 1834, and then in 1836 were once more defeated; on this occasion, they believed, by the unjust and illegal tactics of their Tory opponents. When Sir Francis Bond Head dissolved the provincial Assembly in 1836, it was recognized that the coming trial of strength would be of unusual importance. Newspapers in the United States made comment on the rift between Governor and Assembly, a situation remindful of their own colonial disputes in days gone by. *Niles' Register* in April saw a storm brewing in Upper Canada: "The executive council have all resigned because the 'Algerine government,' as it is called, that is the governor, did not consult them in carrying on the government."[14] In June the *Register*, commenting upon the dissolution of the Upper Canada Assembly, said: "The affairs of the province are in a very disturbed condition, and the disposition manifested by the 'mother country' to force the popular will, is daily severing the ties of feeling, and must soon eventuate in an outbreak that will bring the people and authorities into serious collision. Experience is not always admonitory to nations and individuals."[15]

The village of London appears to have been one of the special storm centres of 1836 and there remain several accounts of the disorder which prevailed. Robert Davis, already mentioned, said of the contest: ". . . If you had been in London at the last election, you would have seen a set of government tools called Orange men, running up and down the streets crying five pounds for a liberal; and if a man said a word contrary to their opinion he was knocked down. Many were knocked down in this way and others threatened; and all this in the presence of magistrates, Church of England ministers and judges, who made use of no means to prevent such outrages."[16]

Dr. Charles Duncombe, one of the members for Oxford,

---

[14] *Niles' Weekly Register*, XIV (April 2, 1836), 73.

[15] *Ibid.*, XIV (June 11, 1836), 249.

[16] Davis, *The Canadian Farmer's Travels*, p. 14. W. H. Merritt, of Welland Canal fame, wrote in after years: "The election occurred on the first of July, 1836, and the author, who was present, has for remembrance a gathering which for riot and drunkenness, though his own village could get up no mean display, exceeded everything he had ever seen before" (*Biography of the Hon. W. H. Merritt . . .*, St. Catharines, 1875, p. 161).

subsequently brought the details of the London election to the attention of the British government. In his memorial he stated that when he came near London on the last polling day he encountered one of the Reform candidates, Elias Moore, fleeing for his life from Tory Orangemen and found the Reformers generally being driven from the polls. This, he declared, was being done in the presence of officers of the law and of the rector of the endowed Church of England parish. Tory partisans, he charged, were "constantly hurrahing and cheering on the Orangemen who were seen running through the streets, intoxicated, with clubs, threatening the Reformers with instant death if they shouted reform." Duncombe charged also that when the rioting commenced two of the local magistrates had sworn in twenty special constables to keep the peace but that the returning officer forbade the use of this force and even threatened to commit the magistrate to prison if he interfered with proceedings.[17]

These charges were of so serious a character as to be later investigated by a Select Committee of the Assembly. The Rev. Benjamin Cronyn appeared before the Committee on December 21, 1836, and agreed that there had been violence, though he said he had often seen more fighting on a militia training day than during the whole election. However, after full allowance had been made for the rough manners and love of fighting which might characterize a pioneer community, it still remains evident that there was a violence in this contest which was countenanced by the authorities and for which they must bear a portion of the blame. The Rev. William Proudfoot, the Presbyterian clergyman in the village, after witnessing the election tumult, wrote in his diary that it was "a scene."

Sir Francis Hincks in after years expressed the opinion that if the Reformers had won in 1836 there would have been no rebellion. Whatever may be the measure of truth in that statement, it is undeniable that from July of 1836 to December, 1837, there was a steady growth of political bitterness on the part of the Reformers and increasing anticipation of troubles on the part of the governing group. Reform political organization now tended to take on a militant character, particularly in the Home and London Districts. In the election of 1836 Reformers carried

[17] Appendix ot the *Journals* of the Assembly, Upper Canada, session of 1836-37, no. 5, pp. 3-4.

twelve seats in York and in the counties to the west but secured only five seats in the eastern section of the province. The most distinctively Reform section of the whole province was to be found in three western counties, Middlesex, Oxford, and Norfolk, which among them sent six Reform members to the Assembly. Except for the London seat, these three counties formed a solid Reform block.

The governing group constantly charged the Reformers with seeking to introduce American political ideas in place of British. Before the election of 1836 the *Canadian Emigrant*, published at Sandwich in a Tory district and itself strongly Tory in sentiment, printed an article deriding the Reformers then in the Assembly and concluding: "Such and such will be our members until the emigrant population is fairly represented. At present, although the emigrants of the last ten years exceed in number, property and knowledge, the whole population besides, the elective franchise is almost entirely in the hands of the Yankee faction. This can be proved by a single glance at the present members. Is there one who has arrived in the country within the last fifteen years? There is not, and yet at least half the members ought to be men who have emigrated within that period and made the country what it is."[18] After the election of 1836 Dr. Thomas Rolph classified the membership of the Assembly: for British supremacy and monarchical government, 44; for republicanism and elective institutions, 18. Viewed in this way, the election had been a referendum as between British and American institutions.[19]

Prejudice against things American was skilfully utilized by Lieutenant-Governor Sir Francis Bond Head in 1836 and 1837. His method of appealing directly to the people was in itself an unconscious acknowledgment of the power of democracy. In the election of 1836 he was able to spread the idea that British connection was threatened and that Reformers were in some way in league with the United States. When he opened the Legislature a few months after his victory in the election, he commended the "loyal feeling" and the "stillness and serenity" of the public mind, even though at the moment when he uttered

[18] *Canadian Emigrant* (Sandwich), April 12, 1836.
[19] Thomas Rolph, *A Brief Account, together with Observations, Made during a Visit in the West Indies and a Tour through the United States of America, in Parts of the Years 1832-3; together with a Statistical Account of Upper Canada* (Dundas, U.C., 1836), p. 266.

the words there existed a bitterness of feeling which within a year would lead to open rebellion. Against the Reformers, whom he boasted he had completely defeated, he made outrageous charges. Marshall Spring Bidwell, one of the most high-minded men in the province, was pictured as aspiring to become "President of the republican state of Upper Canada" while others were charged with plots to rob the banks and abscond to the United States. Coming from high sources these tirades against Reformers tended to perplex the public mind.[20] Early in his career in Upper Canada Sir Francis Bond Head had confused the real issue of his quarrel with the Assembly. When the members of that body expressed a lack of confidence in his advisers and refused to vote the necessary supplies for carrying on government, he had retaliated by reserving the money bills passed during the session, thereby preventing the carrying out of public works and incidentally creating some measure of unemployment. The unfortunate effects of his policy he at once attributed to the actions of the Reform Assembly and this charge was accepted in many quarters as true. In the election of 1836 Head also raised the bogey of an American force threatening Canada. Replying to an address from the electors of the Home District he announced in bombastic words: "In the name of every regiment of militia in Upper Canada, I publicly promulgate – let them come if they dare." With these words fresh in public memory it is easy to see how rumours of American intrigue and American invasion were accepted as true during the troubled days at the end of 1837. Writing of the situation at Toronto, Samuel Thompson said: "Every idle report was eagerly caught up, and magnified a hundred-fold. But the burthen of all invariably was, an expected invasion by the Yankees to drive all loyalists from Canada."[21] With memories of 1812 still keen, it can be imagined how effective this appeal would be in circles already antagonistic to the United States. For years after the Rebellion the conception of an American plot against Canada was reiterated in English journals. The *United Service Journal* in 1840 paid a glowing tribute to Head's services in reviewing his *Narrative* while the *Colonial Magazine* of the same year, in citing causes for the late uprising, referred to a "Texian spirit"

[20] Samuel Thompson, *Reminiscences of a Canadian Pioneer for the Last Fifty Years: An Autobiography* (Toronto, 1884), pp. 117-18.
[21] *Ibid.*, p. 120.

in the United States, of which the Reformers had been fully cognizant. Press and pulpit in the United States, said the writer of the article, had been engaged in "urging and inciting a general movement to seize the Canadas from the Queen of Great Britain" and this more forcibly than they were at the same time inciting their people to wrest Texas from Mexico. The article, which had apparently been written by some person connected with the administration in Upper Canada, spoke of Mackenzie's "address" as having been adopted at various meetings of "Americans" held in Upper Canada and in general insinuated that American influences had intruded upon a people who hitherto had been satisfied and happy.[22]

The Rev. William Proudfoot, at London, has recorded that after the political contest of 1836 there was a breaking down in social relations within the village. "The Tory party have become insolent," he wrote, "and seem determined to take vengeance on all who are not of their way of thinking. . . . The influence of the election has eradicated everything amiable in it." Mrs. Anna Jameson noted an unattractive atmosphere also in the official society at Toronto when she visited the town early in 1837. After attending a dinner party which was graced by the presence of the Lieutenant-Governor and other notables, she wrote to her father: "The cold narrow minds, the confused ideas, the by-gone prejudices of the society, are hardly conceivable."[23]

Political unions, which had made their appearance in the Talbot Settlement in 1832-3, and had later tended to diminish in number, came into public notice again during 1837. Following a meeting held at St. Thomas on November 17 for the purpose of organizing a local union, John Talbot, the editor of the *Liberal*, wrote to William Lyon Mackenzie at Toronto:

Some of the good folks in these parts are about to form Political Unions and some have already formed them. Would you favor me with a copy of your "Printed documents and Blank lists" in order that we may advance "decently and in order." A little advice on the subject would do us no harm. The Tories in this part of the parish are beginning to think that something must be done to satisfy the Reformers or – they must

[22] *Colonial Magazine* (London), II, 462-4.
[23] Anna Jameson, *Letters and Friendships, 1812-1860*, ed. Mrs. Stuart Erskine (London, 1915), p. 150.

be put down at the point of the bayonet – or revolution will take place. What think you?[24]

Meetings for similar organization purposes were held at this time in Westminster, Dorchester, Delaware, Yarmouth, Norwich, and other townships in the west. At a meeting held in Dorchester, Nathaniel Deo of Westminster urged correspondence with the Reform leaders at Toronto. Dr. Charles Duncombe addressed a meeting in Norwich at the beginning of December. Abraham Sackrider of that township told the magistrates, when under examination later, that a Methodist preacher named Bird had addressed Dr. Duncombe's followers at a place called Sodom early in December and had encouraged them to take up arms and "fight for their freedom." A Reform rally which was held at St. Thomas on October 6, 1837, declared its strong sympathies with the Patriots of Lower Canada and set forth its own grievances in a resolution, the concluding phrases of which recall the wording of the Declaration of Independence:

That, time after time, both in this province and in Great Britain, most loyally, nay most servilely, have we petitioned for a redress of the long and frightful catalogue of the wrongs of Canada. Our prayers have been spurned, and our feelings have been deeply wounded by the insults that have accompanied the contemptuous disregard of our most humble supplications for justice; that we have too long hawked our wrongs, as the beggar doth his sores, at the fastidious threshold of haughty oppression, when, derided and mocked, we have been sent empty away. That, since our iron-hearted rulers have turned a deaf ear to the voice of our complaints, we, confiding in the goodness of our cause, resting as it wholly does on reason, truth and equity, for its support, will call upon the God of Justice to aid us in our holy struggle as Britons and as men.[25]

It is easier to understand the restless spirit of reform among common folk of the province than to explain the belligerent

---

[24] Public Archives of Canada, Papers re examination before magistrates at London of persons taken up for treasonable and seditious practices (1837).

[25] *An Impartial and Authentic Account of the Civil War in the Canadas . . .* (London, 1838), pp. 109-10. The resolution was reprinted from a report of the meeting which appeared in the St. Thomas *Liberal*. "When the business of the meeting was over," said the *Liberal*, "several rounds of heart-stirring applause were given for the friends of Canada in the British Parliament, and for Papineau and the Lower Canadians."

Toryism of others in the same social scale. Talbot in 1832 was able to rally several hundred supporters, most of whom must have been undergoing quite the same experiences which agitated the minds of others. The British traveller Wilkie was in Toronto when Mackenzie printed Joseph Hume's "baneful domination" letter and was struck by the character of the resulting demonstration in favour of the provincial authorities:

> *A body of the Constitutionalists – as they denominate themselves – came down from the Gore district in one of the Hamilton steamers, and preceded by a band, banners and all the noisy attributes of a procession, marched to the Governor's house and presented a true and loyal address, professing their staunch purpose to support the crown, and expressing, we are informed, their detestation of the rebellious tendency of the said letter. The day, it was the 17 July, turned out to be a very busy one for all idle people about town, and a dollar-making event for the taverns and bar-rooms. Down near the wharfs, an ox was roasted bodily – horns, tail and all – and formed a chief point of attraction to those who were curious in the wholesale manufacture of beef-steaks.*[26]

Patrick Shirreff, visiting the province in 1833, remarked upon the extreme Toryism of many humble folk newly arrived from Britain. "Whig and radical in the mother country," he wrote, "after becoming possessed of a few acres of forest in Canada they seem to consider themselves part of the aristocracy, and speak with horror of the people and liberality."[27] But communities varied oddly in their political preferences and even within a family there was sometimes division so that when the outbreak came in 1837 it was literally true that relatives were to be found fighting each other, thereby giving to the struggle some of the characteristics of a civil war. In this respect the uprising in Upper Canada differed from that in Lower Canada where the struggle was racial.

It would be difficult to determine with any degree of accuracy what proportion of the population of Upper Canada was seriously disaffected in 1836-7. In the earlier stages of the American Revolution it was estimated that one-third was loyal

---

[26] D. Wilkie, *Sketches of a Summer Trip to New York and the Canadas* (Edinburgh, 1837), p. 206.

[27] Patrick Shirreff, *A Tour through North America* . . . (Edinburgh, 1835), p. 104.

to the Crown, one-third inclined to independence, and a remaining third uncertain or waiting to see which way the political winds might blow. Possibly a somewhat similar division existed in Upper Canada prior to the events of December, 1837, though the Rev. John Radcliff, Anglican rector of Warwick, wrote to the authorities in June, 1838, that from his own knowledge of the western parts of the province and from information supplied by reputable persons elsewhere he judged that the disaffected were to the loyal in the proportion of three to two.[28] No estimate of the disaffected could properly be made upon the basis of the number of those who were in arms. Considering the risks of life, reputation, and property involved in rebellion, it is surprising how many actually did take up arms. On the other hand, how many more must have weighed the matter and decided that the risks were too great. Since the number of those in arms was greatest in the Home and London districts, it is safe to conclude that the number of those who were potential rebels must also have been greatest in those sections. It was in these two districts that the authorities made the greatest number of arrests during subsequent months.

For those who basked in the sunshine of official favour, the unrest preceding the Rebellion seemed to be basest ingratitude, if not disloyalty, and only explainable as contamination from the United States.[29] Colonel Charles Eliot, a retired officer and magistrate in the Western District, wrote to the *Canadian Emigrant* in 1832: "Talk of grievances, yes we have our grievances, there is no perfect felicity in this subluminary sphere – nothing without alloy. And Upper Canada has its grievances. It harbors the fierce and deadly rattlesnake in our wilds, in its habited places it gives sustenance to that creeping Cobra Cappello, Mackenzie, and the Macoushi Indian of the South, Ryerson, with his 10 foot blow-pipe and Wourali poison – even Upper Canada has its grievances."[30] Unrest was present, however, in Colonel Eliot's own community at this time, for on April 2, 1832, a public meeting was held at Sandwich for the purpose of presenting an address of loyalty. William Elliott, one of the

[28] Public Archives of Canada, Series C, 609, II, 52.
[29] The London *Gazette* of September 7, 1839, quoted the St. Catharines *Journal* as blaming the unrest in that section of the province upon the machinations of "Yankee loafers and Yankee school teachers" who had "soft-soldered and hoodwinked" the parents and taught the children republicanism.
[30] *Canadian Emigrant* (Sandwich), February 23, 1832.

speakers, said such action was necessary because certain people were "disseminating discord and disaffection throughout the province and misrepresenting the feelings of the people." From the notices of the meeting which appeared in the press it was evidently non-payment of war claims dating from 1812-14 which was at the bottom of the agitation in that locality.

Apart entirely from questions of a political character there were certain social conditions which made for unrest. The heavy loss of life occasioned by the cholera epidemics in 1832 and 1834 created a depression of spirit in many of the survivors. Grim records of the ravages of the disease have come down to us, such a picture, for example, as the deaths at Dumfries, thirty within thirty hours, with men digging graves and burying their dead at night "by torches and fires built in the graveyard." Whole families were wiped out, in other cases parents were taken and children left to the mercy and care of neighbours. The *Courier of Upper Canada* described London in 1832 as a deserted town, families having removed and closed up their houses.[31] At Sandwich the publication of the *Canadian Emigrant* was suspended for four months during the summer of 1832 and intercourse with Detroit was prohibited. In 1834 London was again the scene of an epidemic but in no such degree as was Galt where the disease was brought to the town by an employee of a travelling menagerie. The hundreds of people who had attended the circus carried the cholera to many nearby communities.[32]

Poverty and the drabness of pioneer farm life were other factors producing unrest in the thirties. Romantic pictures of early days in Upper Canada do not always agree with the facts. There were numerous misfits in the province, men who had come with dreams of making a fortune in Canada, but who found themselves quite unsuited to the labour and hardships of bush life. There were others who lacked physical strength to meet the test of the backwoods or were among the shiftless class who drifted about the country getting their living off others. These, and even many of the more enterprising, tended to go off to the United States in times of stress.

---

[31] *Courier of Upper Canada* (York), August 4, 1832.
[32] James Young, *Reminiscences of the Early History of Galt and Settlement of Dumfries* (Toronto, 1880), pp. 97-107.

11: The Western Phase of the Rebellion

> It certainly appeared too much as if the rebellion had been purposely invited by the government, and the unfortunate men who took part in it deliberately drawn into a trap by those who subsequently inflicted so severe a punishment on them for their error. It seemed, too, as if the dominant party made use of the occasion afforded it by the real guilt of a few desperate and imprudent men, in order to persecute or disable the whole body of their political opponents.
>
> —LORD DURHAM

> The rebels of Gallows Hill and the militia of Toronto were literally brothers and cousins.
>
> —SAMUEL THOMPSON

From an early date the London District, in the western section of the province, showed more of the characteristics of the American frontier than any other portion of Upper Canada. It lacked the steadying influence of a Loyalist element and its population included a considerable number of American settlers, some of whom were of questionable character, as was shown during the War of 1812 when there was disorder, disloyalty, and even some difficulty with the militia. In the years after the war a new restlessness developed and from 1832 onward the London District moved steadily towards rebellion. Thus, when Mackenzie raised the banner of revolt in the Home District in 1837, there was an auxiliary force in the London District ready also for the attempt to change by force the character of government within the province.

The Duncombe uprising, so named after the man who was its leader, was a hopeless affair from the beginning but it demonstrated the extent of the unrest in the west. Several hundred men, poorly equipped and poorly led, took the chances of death or imprisonment, loss of reputation and property, with all the accompanying risks for their families or relatives, and marched out in semi-military order at the call of Dr. Charles Duncombe. If such a number of men were prepared to face the risks involved, we may well ask how many more hesitated only at the final step of rebellion. For Duncombe himself it brought loss of citizenship, reputation, and property, and had he been captured there is little doubt that he would have been sent to the gallows. For scores of the men who joined him it meant similar loss of reputation and property together with the stigma of disloyalty and even of treason.

Duncombe was an American by birth. A gravestone in the old City Cemetery of Sacramento, California, records his death there on October 1, 1867, at the age of seventy-five. The family[1] removed from Connecticut to Upper Canada some time after the War of 1812 and Charles Duncombe appears in the public records in October, 1819, when he came before the Medical Board and having passed the necessary examinations was admitted to practise in the province. He was described at that time as of Delaware Town in the London District.[2] In 1825 he became surgeon to the 2nd Middlesex Militia and in 1832 was appointed a member of the Medical Board. Two years earlier he had been elected to the Assembly from the County of Oxford. His ability was soon recognized and in 1836 he was appointed a Commissioner to visit the United States and collect information which might be used in improving the provincial school system. This he did with great thoroughness and while in the United States also collected valuable information upon the conduct of prisons and insane asylums. His reports upon these subjects had considerable influence upon policies which were later adopted in Upper Canada (see chapter 9). After the election of 1836, with its disastrous results for the Reform party, Dr. Duncombe visited England in company with Robert Baldwin, seeking to lay the case of the Upper Canada Reformers before Lord Glenelg, the Colonial Secretary. They failed to secure a hearing but their grievances were brought to the attention of the House of Commons by Joseph Hume. Glenelg at once sent out to Lieutenant-Governor Sir Francis Bond Head a copy of the charges which had been made against him and the latter was promptly exonerated by a compliant Tory Assembly. Duncombe's experiences during 1836-7 were therefore not of a character to allay his feelings of injustice.

This was the man who in December, 1837, headed the farmers and artisans of the London District marching out to join Mackenzie at the provincial capital. There is no need to go into details of the adventure which within a few hours became

---

[1] David and Elijah Duncombe, like their more famous brother, were both doctors of medicine, the former receiving his certificate of fitness to practise in the province in January, 1828, and the latter in April, 1830.

[2] Delaware was an early settlement on the Thames River about ten miles southwest of the present city of London. Settlement had not yet begun at London in 1819.

a complete fiasco. Actually, a force under Colonel Allan Mac-Nab was on its way to meet Duncombe and his men before the latter received their first word of the defeat at Toronto. The rallying place was the little village of Scotland, in Brant County, but when MacNab reached Scotland on December 15 Duncombe's force had vanished. A proclamation promised a reward of £500 for the capture of Dr. Duncombe, £250 for the capture of Eliakim Malcolm, Finlay Malcolm, or Robert Alway, and £100 for the capture of one Anderson or of Joshua Doan. Dr. Duncombe, after romantic adventures, crossed into the United States, aided in his flight by relatives and friends who did not shun risk on his behalf.[3] Jacob Yeigh, who had been his chief lieutenant, also escaped to the United States as did Malcolm, Doan, and others who were prominent in the movement.[4] Robert Alway, Duncombe's fellow-member from Oxford, was not a participant in the uprising, for although a warm friend of Mackenzie he was opposed to any resort to arms. He was arrested, however, on Christmas Day of 1837 and confined in Hamilton jail for about three months, his wife being also detained for two weeks. When released he sold his property in Upper Canada and removed with his family to Rochester, New York. In March, 1839, an attempt was made in the Assembly to declare his seat vacant but this appears to have failed since on April 8, 1839, he was reported to be in his place in the Assembly and the motion to declare him unseated was withdrawn.[5] Later he removed with his family to Texas but before he had time to establish himself in any business he and his youngest daughter died of yellow fever.[6]

The collapse of the uprising in the west was so complete that there was really no reason for further military action, but MacNab saw the opportunity of teaching a lesson to the Quakers in Norwich, people who had emigrated from the

---

[3] Dr. Duncombe, after some years in the East, went to California, probably at the time of the gold rush. He was in Sacramento County at least as early as 1852 since in that year he was one of the founders of Washington Lodge of the Masonic Order.

[4] Joshua Doan was a participant in the Patriot attack upon Windsor a year later and in January, 1839, was hanged at London after trial before a court-martial.

[5] *Journals* of the Assembly, Upper Canada, session of 1839, 29, 88, 140.

[6] Information supplied by his grandson, Professor F. J. Alway of the Department of Agriculture, University of Minnesota. After the death of Robert Alway, the widow with her seven children returned in 1844 to Upper Canada and settled on an uncleared plot in Norfolk County.

United States and who by their religious belief were opposed to all military activities. This settlement, moreover, was largely Reform in politics, a third reason why such an extreme patriot as MacNab might feel that it needed a lesson in loyalty. Echoes of the "march through Norwich" were heard for many years. Writing in the *Oxford Star* of December 15, 1848, one who signed himself "An old settler" said: "When that part of the late rebellion which was more intimately connected with our county comes to be written and well understood, the name of Duncombe himself will lie under lighter and less general execration than some who early made themselves hoarse with cursing the rebels and crying 'God save the Queen'." The writer described the leaders of the invading loyalists as "swearing and swaggering in front of raw recruits" and leading raids into Norwich "in which some scores of Quakers' farmyards were reduced, as many pigpens carried by storm, and bleaching yards sacked and rased."[7]

An equally unpleasant feature of the MacNab campaign was his use of Indians to capture disbanded members of Duncombe's force. The correspondent of the Rochester *Daily Democrat* told of meeting a company of about a hundred Indians, "bearing the royal standard, with faces painted in a most frightful manner, well armed, headed by two British officers, who were leading them in a circuitous route to attack the rebels in the rear." MacNab, he said, used about two hundred Indians in the search for fugitives "with directions to take all prisoners who had not in their caps a badge of red flannel, which was worn by all the loyalists, and to shoot every man who attempted to escape."[8]

The use of armed bands of Indians, little removed from savagery, in the capture of fellow-citizens reveals the extreme bitterness which characterized the civil struggle of 1837. This phase of the Rebellion, when brought to the attemtion of the Colonial Secretary, caused him to express the hope that the only motive in enlisting the Indians had been to keep them from unofficial warfare. "If it were really designed," he wrote, "to bring these people into active service as auxiliaries of H.M.

[7] The events in Norwich were recorded in a series of five articles written by Stella Mott and contributed to the Woodstock *Sentinel-Review* during May and June, 1937.

[8] Reprinted in an extra issue of the *Palladium of British America*, January 8, 1838. The *Palladium*, a Toronto weekly newspaper, was founded by Charles Fothergill in December, 1837.

forces I must express entire repugnance to such a measure. It is scarcely possible to conceive any necessity which would justify it and nothing would in my opinion tend more to alienate the inhabitants of Upper Canada and to irritate the people of the United States than the attempt to let loose on the assailants of the government the horrors of savage warfare."[9] Sir George Arthur hastened to assure the Colonial Office that no improper motive had suggested the use of the Indians, but the records indicate that there was little if any hesitation in utilizing their services. When rebellion losses claims were being settled in 1845, several men from the London District asked compensation for their aid in handling Indian allies. Peter Schram, for example, testified that he had been in charge of twenty-eight Indians, adding that "the service was a dangerous one and proved beneficial to the government in intercepting some of the rebel leaders on their endeavoring to enter the country in disguise, one of which was killed by the Indians on endeavoring to make his escape." His claim of twelve pounds was approved.[10]

The actual military operations of the Rebellion covered only a brief period but disturbing effects of the uprising continued throughout the whole of 1838 and even into 1839. The majority of the actual leaders were able to make their escape to the United States[11] but hundreds of followers were confined for varying periods in the jails of the province. During these months of hysteria persons were arrested whose worst offence had been the utterance of some criticism of the administration; in other cases people were denounced merely to pay off private grudges. There were outbursts of patriotic fervour from Tory partisans as well as from some who hoped in this way to obliterate the memory of former radical leanings. Tory newspapers outdid themselves in describing the patriotic spirit of the province, an example being the London *Gazette*'s description of a rally of troops in that village in the early part of January: "This town on Wednesday and Thursday last presented the appearance of one vast camp. . . . On Thursday evening the splendid scene rose to its highest grandeur. The public square of four acres was thickly

[9] Public Archives of Canada, Series Q, 425 A, 52, 109.
[10] Minute book of the Commission on Rebellion Losses Claims in the London District, in the library of the University of Western Ontario.
[11] The St. Catharines *Journal* of January 4, 1838, had a note from a London District correspondent dealing with the escape of several of the more prominent figures in the Duncombe uprising. Most of them made their way to Michigan.

studded with immense columns of daring spirits. . . . The sublimity of the spectacle was still heightened by the departure of Col. Radcliff's company, to join their comrades in arms who are now guarding the western frontier. The cheering of the multitude was past description."[12] A contrasting picture of conditions in London appears in a letter written from that village in May, 1838, by Mrs. Dennis O'Brien, wife of the principal merchant in the place: "London since December last has been one continual scene of confusion, crowded with soldiers and large numbers were billeted on each house for want of barracks, and it has been but recently since we got rid of them; and arrests of persons suspected of being implicated in the rebellion were going on through the winter. . . . Great dissatisfaction and excitement prevails in the country and many are daily leaving."[13]

A report made by W. H. Draper, Solicitor-General, upon the arrests in the London District showed that in April there were still seventy prisoners in the small London jail, while 130 others had been admitted to bail. The crowded condition of the London jail was attributed by Draper to the zeal of local loyalists whose charges in most case were supported by little more than suspicions.[14] A veritable reign of terror existed for a time in the province, the old statute of misprision being evoked, under which it was judged an offence to have withheld from the authorities information as to treason. At the end of the summer, however, the *British Colonist* at Toronto was able to announce that only three state prisoners remained in jail there, two of these, Enoch Moore and Ebenezer Wilcox, being from the London District. Moore had received the death sentence when tried at London but was afterwards reprieved. Wilcox had likewise been tried and convicted at London and afterwards sentenced to death at Toronto, but he was also later released.[15] In treason trials at Hamilton during March, 1838, nine men received the death sentence but were later pardoned. Charles Lindsey, biographer of William Lyon Mackenzie, listed the names of 885 persons who were arrested or absconded in 1837-8. Almost half of these, 422 to be exact, were residents of the Home District, at the centre of government. The second largest number, 163, were from the London District, while 90

[12] Reprinted in St. Catharines *Journal*, January 16, 1838.
[13] Original letter in the library of the University of Western Ontario.
[14] Report of W. H. Draper, Solicitor-General, Durham Papers, Sect. 3, I, 684.
[15] *Western Herald* (Sandwich), October 16, 1838.

were residents of the Gore District. There were less than a hundred arrests in the whole eastern section of the province.[16]

Lord Durham, in his famous report, remarked on the lack of unity of interest or opinion among the inhabitants of the province. There was no real centre to which all the separate parts were connected and which they might follow in sentiment and action, nor was there any general intercourse which would diffuse knowledge of the opinions and interests of others. This helps to explain why in 1837 there was a major uprising at the capital of the province, a smaller uprising in the London District, and numerous tiny eruptions elsewhere developing out of purely local issues. Even within a single small area the opinions of separate groups varied. In Middlesex County, for example, the attitudes of the Quakers in Yarmouth Township, the English settlers in London Township, and the Scotch in Lobo Township differed radically. In Wellington County four neighbouring communities varied almost as widely. Fergus, aristocratic and militantly Tory, was quite satisfied with conditions and when rebellion came its militia was ready to support the government. Elora, with a mixed population, was restless and discontented. Bon Accord, described as solidly Scottish, decided the matter by debate and when the crisis came its inhabitants joined neither the militia nor the rebels – they stayed at home. The men of Eramosa did likewise. They met, discussed the situation, and resolved – "that we return home, remain neutral, and mind our own business." James Peters, the township clerk, worded the resolution. But the men of Eramosa were not left alone. Armed loyalists descended upon the settlement, arrested seven of the best-known Reformers, and placed them in jail at Guelph. They were tried three months later and acquitted. Their homes, however, were meanwhile subject to raids by militia from Guelph which, says the historian of the community, were little better than looting expeditions in some cases.[17]

[16] Charles Lindsey, *The Life and Times of William Lyon Mackenzie* . . . (Toronto, 1862), II, 400.

[17] See Hugh Templin, *Fergus and the Rebellion of 1837*, condensed from a series of articles printed by the Fergus *News-Record*, December, 1937. The Hamilton *Bee* of February 28, 1845, commenting upon a petition of Lieutenant-Colonel John Burwell for grants of land to those who served in the militia in 1837-8, said: "What in the name of all that is honest do these fellows want? In the 'Reign of Terror' they had their own way. They pillaged everything – even clothes necessary for young patriots in expectancy."

In the Huron Tract, where the Canada Company held sway, there was deep and bitter feeling over the policies of that great land corporation. Though the issue was local there was sufficient agitation within the townships to bring about the organization in 1835 of the "Huron Union Society," its object being the protection of its members against wrong and injustice and the obtaining of redress if wrongs or injustices should be committed. Colonel Anthony Von Egmond, a veteran of the Napoleonic Wars, was elected President of the Union and the list of officers and members, containing as it did the most important people in several townships, is evidence of the widespread discontent which existed in the district. Though no body of armed Reformers from the Huron Tract joined Mackenzie's force, it was old Colonel Von Egmond who commanded the rebel band on Yonge Street on that fateful December afternoon of 1837. When the brief conflict was over Von Egmond was a prisoner. He died a few days later in the Toronto prison.[18]

Among the Scottish settlers in Waterloo County there was much sympathy for Mackenzie and his cause. The provincial authorities evidently had doubts concerning the loyalty of Dumfries Township and inquired as to the feelings of the people before calling out the local militia. They were informed, in effect, that the inhabitants were mostly Scotch, most quiet and inoffensive, but "it would be better not to put arms in their hands." The only portion of the township in which any military organization took place was in the neighbourhood of the present village of Ayr. Yet even at Ayr there were persons suspected of disloyalty and a company of militia was sent from Fergus to arrest five leading Reformers. Two made their escape but the other three were sent to Hamilton jail. At their trial in March, 1838, one was acquitted, one found guilty though allowed his liberty upon finding security to keep the peace for three years, while the third, Horatio Hill by name, was sentenced to death. This was later commuted to transportation for life but confinement and worry had so affected his health that he died in prison.[19]

There were comparatively few arrests at first in the Western District, adjacent to the Detroit River and far removed from the

[18] See W. B. Kerr, "Colonel Anthony Von Egmond and the Rebellion of 1837 in Huron County," a series of articles contributed to the Goderich *Signal* between October 1 and December 24, 1931.

[19] See James Young, *Reminiscences of the Early History of Galt and the Settlement of Dumfries* . . . (Toronto, 1880), chap. XIV.

provincial capital. Lindsey lists but eleven who were taken up by the authorities. The *Western Herald* (Sandwich) charged that no special effort was made by the magistrates to intercept the followers of Mackenzie and Duncombe who made their way out of the country at that point, but this seeming apathy may have been due to the excitement created by the presence of hostile armed forces on the American side of the Detroit River. During the whole of 1838 there were disturbances and threats of aggression, culminating in actual invasion at Windsor by a Patriot force in the first week of December. The excitement during January, 1838, was so great that the *Western Herald* temporarily suspended publication.

In the settlements which were removed from the frontier wild rumours of invasion from the United States kept the inhabitants in a state of suspense. Elijah Woodman, at London, wrote on June 28, 1838: "News arrived that the rebel army was coming and would be in London on the 4th July to take dinner. Of course, all was confusion and bustle. Families began to move, goods and all." Three days later, on a Sunday, there was another alarm:

The court house square was covered with regulars and militia all under arms. All the bridges leading into the town were put into preparation for defence and if obliged to retire were arranged to be cut away. At ten o'clock in the evening sixteen waggon loads of prisoners, seventy-two in number, drove up to the door of the jail. This filled the jail to overflowing. An examination took place in a day or two, many were released, some got bail for their appearance at court, while others got bail for three years for their future good behaviour, and some were held in jail as rebels for high treason.[20]

The London [U.C.] *Gazette* of May 26, 1838, commenting upon the threats to which the province had been subjected, declared that it had hitherto been inclined to discount the rumours but professed now to have definite proof that an invasion was being planned and that since the United States government was indifferent to what was going on the proper policy would be to pursue the invaders into their own land: "Let the ruins of their own frontier stand as a memorial that a peaceable though brave people are not to be injured and the offendors escape. . . . We

[20] Original manuscript of Elijah Woodman in the library of the University of Western Ontario.

are not advocates of war on slight or unjustifiable grounds; but are we thus ever to be tormented by the unrestrained violence of a lawless democracy – that land of slavery, mobs and lynch-law – that government of numbers and consequently of ignorance and poverty, rags, dirt and alcohol."

Anger created by these constant alarms was no doubt responsible for the continuance of arrests within the western part of the province even as late as the summer of 1838. The Toronto *Mirror* of October 26, 1838, printed a letter written by Alexander Ledbeater of Howard Township stating that on June 29 he and twenty-five of his neighbours had been arrested and taken to London jail where, after being detained for three weeks, they were examined and allowed to go without even being informed as to the charges preferred against them. Their captors, he declared, terrorized the women and children by informing them that the men would be executed. It was probably this incident to which the Rev. William Proudfoot of London referred when he wrote in his diary on November 28, 1838: "Mr. Jennings brought accounts of the insolent tyrannical doings of the Magistrates about Chatham. How richly these deserve a recompense for their conduct." In the same issue of the *Mirror* there appeared a proclamation calling upon twenty-one men, residents or former residents of the London District, to surrender. Among the names were Dr. Charles Duncombe, Eliakim and James Malcolm of Oxford County, John Talbot, former editor of the St. Thomas *Liberal*, Samuel Edison, the grandfather of Thomas A. Edison, and Joshua P. Doan, who a few months later went to the scaffold at London following the Patriot invasion at Windsor.

Fear rather than loyalty governed the conduct of many people in the western section of the province during the months of 1838. A despatch to the Colonial Office late in the year expressed the opinion that "most of the settlers in the London District, being natives of the United States, would join the Rebels if they were successful" and added: ". . . there are many disaffected persons scattered throughout the province ready to assist the American brigands should they invade in any form." The Rev. William Proudfoot wrote in his diary on November 23, 1838: "The loyalty of the people is very different this year from what it was last. Every person considers military service a burden; most young persons are going off to the States." Sir George Arthur noted a reluctance on the part of the militia to come forward for the defence of the province but attributed it to grievances of which they had complained.[21] At the same time he was puzzled to explain why the militia in the London District were unable to assemble for lack of arms when no such want existed among the disaffected element. "It is a matter of the deepest moment to enquire into whose custody those arms have fallen," the Colonial Secretary warned him when informed of the situation.[22]

Amid the confusion of this period one minor group within the province was ardent in its loyalty to the administration, a loyalty which was combined with vehement antipathy to the United States. This group consisted of the Negroes, chiefly runaway slaves, who were domiciled in Upper Canada. Sir Francis Bond Head, in his *Narrative*, tells of the Negroes hastening to the Niagara frontier in waggon-loads and asking that they might be allowed to be foremost "to defend the glorious institutions of Great Britain." Allowance must always be made for the exuberance of Head's writing but there is other evidence that the fugitives in the province were prompt in offering their services. Several companies of blacks were mustered, the famous Josiah Henson being captain of an Essex company which assisted in the defence of Fort Malden (Amherstburg) from December, 1837, until the following spring. The extreme loyalty of the Negroes was recorded by James G. Birney, the abolitionist leader. When in Toronto in 1837, he found that the coloured people generally belonged to what he termed the government party. We have also the testimony of no less a personage than William Lyon Mackenzie. Answering an inquiry from the American Anti-Slavery Society in 1837 as to the condition and prospects of the coloured people in Upper Canada he wrote: ". . . Nearly all of them are opposed to every species of reform in the civil institutions of the colony – they are so extravagantly loyal to the Executive that to the utmost of their power they uphold all the abuses of government and support those who profit by them. . . . I regret that an unfounded fear of a union with the United States on the part of the colored population should have induced them to oppose reform and free institutions in this colony whenever they have had the power to do so. The

[21] Glenelg to Arthur, December 13, 1838, Public Archives of Canada, Series Q, 425 A, 162.
[22] Glenelg to Arthur, August 22, 1838, *ibid.*, pp.53-4.

apology I make for them in this matter is that they have not been educated as freemen."[23]

There is ample evidence to show the ill effects of the rebellion period upon morals and organized religion. During 1838 there was an unusual amount of crime in the western section of the province, arson, burglary, assault, and other forms increasing over preceding years. The militia who had been called out to suppress the Rebellion were under a minimum of discipline and the seizure of property for so-called defensive reasons was easily turned into looting. When the rebellion losses claims were dealt with at a later date, it was shown that at times there had been an almost childish destruction of property by companies of militia who were billeted in inns or private houses. Speaking of the military excitement of the times, a letter appearing in the *Canada Baptist Magazine* in 1838 said: "It is painful to witness the feelings of revenge that are abroad, to see how the morals of the community are injured by attention to the exciting and stirring events of war."[24]

"In a civil war," says John Buchan, "the loser is in a worse case, for the cause he opposed has become the cherished loyalty of a nation, and opposition to it is felt to carry a moral as well as an intellectual stigma." When the Rebellion in Upper Canada was over such a stigma was applied by certain church groups to other church groups, creating thereby a most unseemly religious controversy that persisted for some time. Religious bodies whose background connected them with the United States were particularly singled out for criticism and at times it seemed as if a deliberate effort were being made to blame them for the Rebellion itself. The American Presbyterian ministers of the Niagara Presbytery with but one exception left the country. It was impossible for them to stay in Upper Canada as their meetings were under surveillance and they were themselves viewed by excited Tories as suspicious characters. The congregations of the Universalists and of the Christian Church were similarly disturbed during 1837-8, the Christians being charged with having aided refugees of the Rebellion. Anglicans, Methodists, and Presbyterians joined in denunciation of the Universalists. A letter which appeared in the London *Times* pointed out that

---

[23] American Anti-Slavery Society, fourth annual report, published in the *Quarterly Anti-Slavery Magazine*, II (July, 1837), 350-1.
[24] *Canada Baptist Magazine*, II (December, 1838), pp. 159-60.

the Home and London districts were the only sections of the province in which disaffection could be said to have been widespread and charged that in these districts a large proportion of the disaffected population were Universalists. "Not a few also of the Quakers of Norwich have been suspected," the letter continued, "and very many professed Baptists have been found arrayed in the ranks against our Sovereign liege lady the Queen." After giving the Wesleyan Methodists, "as connected with the British Wesleyans," a clean bill of health, and expressing the belief that not one member of the Church of England was known to have participated in the Rebellion, the letter concluded:

We see who are the disaffected, and who are the contented. How desirable then by every means to increase the number of the latter and draw off from the ranks of the former. In a word, how all-important is it for the promotion of good order and peace in Upper Canada to look well to the provision existing for the sound religious instruction of the people there in the principles of the Church of England. Can it be doubted that the efficiency of the Church in Canada is important towards quelling existing disorders and promoting a healthier tone of society, harmony among the inhabitants and obedience to the laws? In the disaffected parts of Upper Canada it is evident it must be available to this end.[25]

When this letter was reprinted in the *Church*, the official organ of the Church of England in Upper Canada, it provoked an immediate reply from the editor of the *Canada Baptist Magazine*:

It is pretty broadly insinuated that no other instructions than those given in the Church of England are likely or adapted to promote true religion and secure good order in the state and that no other teachers are worthy to be entrusted with the guidance of the public mind. Such assumptions will not do here, and, we trust, not anywhere else in Protestant Christendom.

If there be any persons in the London District calling themselves Baptists who have ranged themselves under the standard of rebellion . . . they are as widely recreant from our principles as from those of our Episcopal brethren. How many churchmen

[25] This letter was written by the Rev. Thomas Green, a travelling missionary of the Church of England in the London District, and was copied in the *Church*, published at Cobourg. It thereby came to the attention of members of the other denominations in Upper Canada.

were concerned in the Rebellion, on the wrong side, is not known we presume to the correspondent of The Times *or the editor of The* Church, *nor would they willingly tell if they knew. Probably many were thus engaged – and we know of some among the leaders who were professed and acknowledged members of that community.*[26]

Not all the church bodies were as independent and stout-hearted as the Baptists when taunted on the issue of loyalty. The Rev. William Harvard, the British-born President of the Wesleyan Methodist Church, ordered his preachers to scrutinize their membership lists and to deal summarily with any who had been associated with the Rebellion. His policy reflected the subservient attitude which Wesleyans were wont to assume towards the Church of England, but it was out of step with the tradition of Canadian Methodism and was deeply resented. Presbyterians seemed particularly anxious to clear themselves of harbouring rebels and the Presbytery of Toronto in May, 1838, declared it was the duty of sessions to bring home to applicants for membership a sense of the "heinous wickedness" of having been connected in any way with the Rebellion. The Rev. William Proudfoot recorded in his diary in November, 1838, that two Presbyterian ministers in his vicinity had refused to baptize the child of a Reformer because they regarded the father as a rebel. "This shews their ignorance in the first place," Proudfoot wrote, "and in the next place their impiety in making political opinions a term of communion."

Many aspects of community life were disturbed by the troubles of 1837-8. The effect upon the schools may be illustrated by the report for 1839 from the London District. Attendance during the preceding four years was presented as follows:

1835	103 schools	1,771 boys	1,296 girls
1836	85 "	1,547 "	1,124 "
1837	96 "	1,698 "	1,111 "
1838	88 "	1,356 "	750 "

The decrease in 1838 was attributed to the Rebellion and to the continued disturbed state of the district. Included in the report was this statement: "The undersigned have much gratification in reporting that a number of persons who had been teachers in the years preceding, mostly of American birth, have left the

District, and gone it is believed to the United States from whence they came."[27]

James Thomson, an agent of the British and Foreign Bible Society, who visited Upper Canada in 1838-9, has left us some interesting sidelights on the condition of the province at that time.[28] He found social life much disturbed and remarked on the religious animosities which prevailed. His own work, however, received general support and at public meetings all the local clergy were usually present and on the platform. He noted that "perfervid loyalty often took the familiar form of abuse of Americans." At a meeting in Sandwich he was attacked as a "Yankee stroller" and the Wesleyan minister who sat beside him on the platform was denounced as a fellow "stroller." The local Anglican clergyman, who was also on the platform, was scolded for having permitted such "adventurers" to enter the town and get a hearing. Loyalists, said Thomson, preferred Bibles printed in Great Britain to those of American origin while in Lower Canada he found a reluctance to take any Bibles printed in the United States lest possession of the books might arouse suspicion on the part of the authorities. Customs officials carefully examined all consignments of books from the United States and Thomson found it highly advantageous in carrying on his operations to have officials and military officers named as patrons of the Bible societies.

[27] Appendix to the *Journals* of the Assembly, session of 1839, vol. II, part I, pp. 280-2.
[28] See Waldo Smith, "An Agent of the Bible Society in Canada, 1838-1842," *Canadian Journal of Religious Thought*, IX (December, 1932), no. 4.

12: The Aftermath of Rebellion

> The course of events have always been the same. First, unreasoning opposition to popular demands; next, bloody and protracted struggles; finally, but invariably, unlimited and ignominious concessions.
>
> LORD DURHAM (1832)

Had the uprising in December, 1837, been the last enterprise in which Mackenzie and his associates sought to achieve their ends, a vast amount of suffering would have been avoided and the name of Mackenzie himself would stand higher than it does today. He was not content, however, to accept defeat but proceeded to organize an expedition directed against the province from which he had fled. Through the whole year 1838 there were frequent threats and half a dozen actual invasions organized by the Hunters' Lodges which found members in plenty among the unemployed following the panic of 1837. With prospects of adventure and loot, and with promises of reward at the expense of the Upper Canada government, it was easy to draw into the ranks considerable numbers of the flotsam and jetsam of such states as New York, Ohio, and Michigan, who were supported by expatriated Canadians in attacks along the St. Lawrence, in the Niagara Peninsula, and on the Detroit River frontier of the province. At the end of January, 1838, Mackenzie was at Watertown, New York, and writing from that place to C. H. Graham, of Rochester, a sympathizer, he said: "From Belleville downwards, to the Cedars, a distance of 200 miles, an exposed and undefended frontier . . . is open to us as an enemy – to defend it adequately would be ruinous to the Govt. of Great Britain, still more to that of Canada, which has already expended one million of dollars within 2 months in the upper province alone!! And this with a lessening income, and a bankrupt exchequer! The end, with a little perseverance on our part will be a break up, and I mean to stick to them like wax – as do others of our party." Discussing the situation in the London District Mackenzie added: "The intelligence from the west, as I expected it would, disappoints expectation – but the grand object of distressing the enemy has been fully attained – and troops which would have harassed Papineau are on a goose chase west of the head of Lake Ontario. Perhaps your correspondent before many days go by will lunch at Toronto. The event would not surprise me."

In the same period men who had also sympathized with the Rebellion but who, with sounder judgment, saw that nothing could be gained by border warfare were expressing fervent hopes that the escaped leaders would accept the situation and do nothing that might increase the sufferings of those in prison or of their families. Francis Hincks, writing at this time to the Rochester sympathizer just mentioned, said: "I trust there is no danger of any invasion from your side. Surely the influential refugees will for the sake of the unfortunate prisoners keep matters quiet. We think on the arrival of Lord Durham more liberal measures will be pursued to the prisoners but the constant alarm of new invasions has a bad effect." William Lesslie, writing from Toronto in June, also to the same person, said: "All the efforts of Lord Durham to heal the wounds, the deep wounds of our distressed country, may become unavailing by the predatory warfare likely to go on on the frontier – last evening (Sunday) the military were called to arms by the sound of the trumpet in consequence it is said of some alarming symptoms on the lake or on the frontier. How long is such a state of things to continue?"[1]

Granted that there were some men in the Patriot ranks to whom the events in Canada seemed the latest chapter in man's struggle for freedom – the noble Pole Von Shoultz for example – the fact remains that the majority of those who engaged in the enterprises against Upper Canada quite deserved the opprobrious title of brigands given to them by the Canadian authorities. This was particularly true in connection with the raids along the St. Clair River which were marked by murder, thievery, and general banditry, with no apparent political objective in mind. With two or three exceptions the leaders of the invading bands everywhere were stupid, vain, and in the face of danger cowards. They quarrelled among themselves, confused their own plans, and in the end achieved nothing. Their misguided followers paid the penalty of their leaders' stupidity in imprisonment, exile, and death. Mackenzie himself was soon disillusioned as to the calibre of some of the men who were rushing to his aid. Writing from Watertown in February with reference to the man who had

---

[1] Photostats of the three letters to C. H. Graham, of Rochester, are in the library of the University of Western Ontario. The original letters are in private hands.

been his associate in the Navy Island episode he said: "Van Rensselaer would not go away. Our people believed him a great general – all I could say to the contrary went for nothing. So I gave in, they had their own way – their god turned out a kind of wooden one, got drunk, went to bed, got sober and stupid – called his votaries together and recommended them to go abt. their business. And they did so. Thus ended expedition the 1st, in this section. I need not say more."[2] There were others besides Mackenzie who were likewise disillusioned. Dr. A. K. Mackenzie, formerly of Hamilton, who had been elected chairman of the Canadian Refugee Relief Association, when it was organized at Lockport in March, 1838, was writing in April to Dr. James Graham, of Rochester:

I am informed that you are from Canada, if so you have your prejudices in favor or against the patriots, but from all I can learn you are a real friend, and have just views of our case. I am glad of this, for I find but few who have. What Dr. Duncomb, McKenzie, Papponow and Nelson are doing at the present moment I have not been advised, but while prudent steps are progressing in one way I wish to urge it in another. I am preparing a petition to Congress in the name of the Association, praying for a section of the western lands sufficient for 50,000 persons – about 13,000 we now have ready to go on – with liberty to buy all the necessaries to settle a new country. If successful with the government in this particular we shall yet do well, but I fear our boys will be too hot-headed to exercise patience, yet I know all depends upon deep plans, well digested and faithfully carried into effect. . . . You will please observe I am no friend to this pilfering work that some of our boys, in the warmth of their feelings, have carried on. I expect you will see Dr. Duncomb soon, and hope you will hasten him to this place for truly his advice is much needed.[3]

In the western section of the province the Patriot attacks were disjointed in character, reflecting the lack of any unity of plan among the several leaders. Fort Malden (Amherstburg) was the objective of an attack in January when Patriot forces

[2] W. L. Mackenzie to C. H. Graham, Watertown, New York, February 25, 1838. Photostat in the library of the University of Western Ontario. Original letter in private hands.

[3] Dr. A. K. Mackenzie to Dr. James Graham, Lockport, April 13, 1838. Photostat in the library of the University of Western Ontario. Original letter in private hands.

occupied Bois Blois Island opposite the town and initiated a miniature naval warfare by the use of the schooner *Ann*. The enterprise ended ingloriously when the schooner ran aground and was captured, together with the leader of the expedition, Dr. Edward Alexander Theller, of Detroit. In February another Patriot nest was broken up when British troops attacked a force assembled on Fighting Island. "General" Donald McLeod, a Canadian refugee who was the leader of this band, escaped capture only to fall later into the hands of the American authorities. In March there took place one of the strangest events of the year when a Patriot force landed on Pelee Island, eighteen miles out in Lake Erie, and was dislodged by a British force which crossed the ice on horses or in sleighs, taking along two six-pounder guns. Military history does not record many such unusual episodes as a cavalry charge across a frozen lake with the lines wheeling when the leader's horse breaks through. In June attacks shifted to the Niagara frontier where the nature of the country made it extremely difficult to learn the extent or nature of the invasion. Indeed, the Patriots who entered on this occasion were on Canadian soil for more than a week before the authorities learned of their presence. The party was almost entirely made up of Canadian refugees, among whom Jacob Beemer and Samuel Chandler were prominent. Over forty arrests were made. James Moreau, recognized as one of the leaders in the affair, paid the death penalty while sixteen others were later transported to Van Diemen's Land.

Ramifications of the plots against Canada extended beyond the immediate border, though few of those who were mixed up with the Hunters' Lodges had any clear idea of the Canadian situation. Even expatriated Canadians had confused notions of what was going on or what was being attempted, being fed with ideas of conquest and victory by their leaders. The opinions of Charles Latimer, a former resident of the London District, will illustrate this. Latimer was in Chicago in November of 1838 and wrote to Hugh O'Beirne, of Detroit:

The news from Canada is so encouraging that I feel it necessary now to write to ascertain what the plans are, what is going on, and what is to be done in your part of the world.

I am glad that the thing has broken out in Lower Canada and hope the lodges were in readiness to sustain them and that they have not been premature. . . . I have initiated several here;

but last night we had our first meeting including the most re-
spectable people in the town, we have lawyers, doctors, squires,
&c, &c. Whigs and Democrats.

On Saturday we meet again, last night we initiated at the
lodge; one of the gentlemen, Kentuckian, full-blooded is having
made for us a handsome rifle to fire eight shots with one charge.
On Saturday three young lawyers will join us; one of whom is
fitting up for the expedition whenever the word "march" is
given, I think you may safely calculate on two at least from this
place; it takes here uncommonly well.

England is now precisely on the eve of a revolution, the
people there must succeed or blood will be spilt in less than three
months and the first drop of blood that is shed British monarchy
will be prostrated and the Canadas will be free; at all events it is
clear England cannot go to war even with her own colonies, the
people will not allow in their present temper a man to leave the
country to war against Canada a moment after this news shall
reach them and I very much doubt whether all the troops in
Canada will not be required on the other side of the ocean.
Russia is eager to try her strength with her, the people of Eng-
land are ready to try theirs. I do think that under all circum-
stances she will at length be convinced of the necessity of giving
us peaceful possession.[4]

Less than two weeks after the above letter was written
there came the last and by far the most serious border attack in
the west. Patriots to the number of more than one hundred
crossed the Detroit River on the night of December 3-4 in a
small steamboat and landed on the Canadian shore above the
village of Windsor. Their commander, L. V. Bierce, a lawyer
from Akron, Ohio, was as ready with bombastic proclamations
as other Patriot leaders but like them incapable of planning or
carrying out any successful military operation. A small force of
militia under capable leadership had little difficulty in defeating
and scattering the invaders, a number of whom were killed in
the fighting while four others who had been taken prisoner were
shot in cold blood by Colonel John Prince, in command of the
militia. This atrocity became a subject of debate even in the
imperial Parliament at London, though in ferocity it was
matched by the killing by the Patriots of Surgeon John J. Hume.

[4] Public Archives of Canada, U.C. Duplicate dispatches, October- December 1838, folio 539 ff. This letter is stated to have been found on the
body of one of those killed at Windsor in December, 1838.

The majority of those who crossed the river managed to make their way back but forty-four were taken prisoner and sent to London for trial by court-martial. There, in the "Gothic" court-house, so much admired by visitors, they were all, save one, sentenced to death, though for five who had turned Queen's evidence and testified against their fellows there came a recommendation of mercy. Six were hanged in the court-house square during the early part of January, 1839, but the capital sentences were not carried out beyond this number. In April sixteen were sent to Quebec to be transported to Van Diemen's Land. The others were subsequently deported to the United States.

During the fortnight in which the six invaders were executed at London Sir George Arthur, the Lieutenant-Governor, was in the London and Western districts. At St. Thomas, replying to an address from the inhabitants, he said: "The brigands have been taught such a lesson of the character and loyalty of the people of this country as, it may be hoped, will henceforth leave these provinces in undisturbed tranquility."[5] At Sandwich proceedings were disturbed when two addresses were prepared, one by the belligerent Colonel John Prince, who was ready for war with the United States, and one of milder character prepared by a Colonel Elliott. Arthur declined to hear either of them and gave the inhabitants a bit of his mind with respect to their lack of unity. He particularly warned against anything in the nature of retaliations.[6]

Arthur's reputation has suffered much at the hands of writers dealing with this period of Upper Canada's history. He came to the province from Van Diemen's Land where, as administrator of a penal colony for twelve years, he was the head of a government quite unlike that of Upper Canada. While at Albany, on his way to Toronto, he had interviews with the exiled Marshall Spring Bidwell and with Governor Marcy which convinced him that there was a definite understanding and definite co-operation between the state authorities of New York and the disaffected element in Canada. Arriving in the province he found the jails full and military trials still in progress. Almost at once there were laid before him the death warrants of men convicted of treason against the state and he knew that most of his advisers were in revengeful mood, not only willing but

[5] Quebec *Gazette*, February 4, 1839.
[6] *Ibid.*, February 1, 1839.

anxious that the sentences should be carried out. Moreover, he was much concerned with fears of war with the United States, behind which he thought he could detect signs of Russian intrigue.[7]

In view of the excited condition of the times it is easy to understand the pressure which was brought upon Arthur to pursue a vindictive policy towards prisoners of the Rebellion and captured invaders from the United States. On one occasion he appears to have favoured the suggestion that every tenth captured invader should be shot. Such a proposal appears in a letter written to Durham in June, 1838, but may have been merely the passing on of a suggestion that had been made by some of the judges. Glenelg was prompt to rebuke the judges and their policy. "The rule of decimating is an arbitrary one," he wrote, "resting in truth on no sound principle. It excludes the exercise of that patient and mature deliberation which should in every case precede the execution of capital sentence and savors more of vindictiveness and passion than a calm and enlightened regard for justice." In a later communication he expressed the hope that Arthur would be spared "the distressing duty of making any considerable addition to the number of capital punishments."[8] In the autumn of 1839, when more than eighty prisoners were about to leave Upper Canada for Van Diemen's Land, Arthur wrote to Normanby at London: "Could I have ventured to follow the impulse of my personal feelings I should certainly have extended Her Majesty's free pardon to several others of the brigands but in the present excited state of the community, justly exasperated at the atrocious attacks upon their property and lives, which have for some time past been made and are still in practice, by a portion of the border population of the neighbouring states, a further extension of mercy to the brigands would have been viewed with extreme

[7] C. R. Sanderson's unpublished thesis, "Sir George Arthur, a Vindication" (University of Toronto, 1940), based upon the collection of Arthur papers acquired by the Toronto Public Library, presents a much more favourable view of Arthur than has hitherto prevailed. His conclusion is that there is no justification for the view that Arthur having been Governor of a convict settlement was necessarily tinged with callous inhumanity. He finds the record quite otherwise.

[8] Arthur to Durham, June 27, 1838, Durham Papers, section III, vol. I, 930. Glenelg to Arthur, August 22, 1838, Public Archives of Canada, Series Q, 425 A, 56, 216.

disapprobation by a great majority of the people of Upper Canada."[9]

A Canadian comment upon the invasions, made by the editor of a religious journal, may be quoted appropriately:

> It cannot be doubted that our own loud complaints, set forth in the darkest coloring by a revolutionary press, that obtained too much countenance among us, have actually awakened a pretty general belief in the United States that the Canadians are a people panting after republican institutions and on the eve of founding them on the debris of the monarchical of which they have grown tired. Such being the case, it is scarcely more than what might be expected that the Anglo-Americans south of the St. Lawrence should look with favor on an insurrection that promised to revolutionize this country after their own favorite model; that some of them would be inclined to assist it from their love of political theory, and some from the speculating pursuit of gain which forms so prominent a feature in their character. The grievances under which we were reported to be suffering awakened the sympathy of some, and the party divisions existing among us indicating weakness stimulated by the rapacity of others. To these causes we may fairly ascribe that banding of multitudes on their frontiers for the invasion of our territory, or in their own language "to assist the oppressed Canadians to obtain their freedom."[10]

The border troubles of 1838 had important and lasting effect upon the Upper Canadian attitude towards the United States. The inheritance of anti-American feeling from the Revolution, which had been increased and perpetuated by the War of 1812, was given new life by the border outrages and by the aid and sympathy tendered to Mackenzie and his fellow-exiles in the United States. John R. Godley, who visited Upper Canada in the early forties, expressed the opinion that the border troubles had been useful in preventing "far more effectually than any political reasoning or even abstract feelings of patriotism could do, all undue 'sympathy' between the Canadians and Americans,

---

[9] Arthur to Normanby, Toronto, October 14, 1839, U.C. Duplicate dispatches, October-December, 1839, folio 1. The Marquis of Normanby was Secretary of War and the Colonies.

[10] *Canadian Christian Examiner*, III (1839), pp. 2-3. The *Examiner* was a Presbyterian publication printed in 1839 at Toronto.

a sympathy which might otherwise have become dangerous to British connexion.'[11]

American influences were weakened after 1837 in the western section of the province by the presence of British regular troops. Amherstburg since the 1790's had been accustomed to seeing the redcoats but, beginning in 1838, London also became an important garrison town while St. Thomas and other places at times saw something also of imperial military activities. With the pageantry of British arms ever before them in parades, drills, and military observances, to which were added the quite material benefits which arose from supplying the needs of the garrison, London citizens lost the radical tinge which had been so noticeable before 1837 and at times became almost blatantly Tory. In 1841, though old party lines were somewhat shattered as a result of the changing political conditions, Hamilton Killaly, a Tory, who was later to become Commissioner of Works in the provincial administration, was elected over John Douglas, a merchant and Reformer. It was charged at the time that with the connivance of the officers votes were cast by soldiers in garrison who had no right to vote and that this support all went to the Tory candidate.[12] Another Tory was elected in 1844 in the person of Lawrence Lawrason, a narrowly partisan magistrate who had been foremost in tracking down radicals in 1837-8. In 1845 when the Hon. W. H. Draper as head of the administration under Lord Metcalfe found it necessary to secure a seat in the Assembly, Lawrason obligingly vacated his place and for a time London was represented by the government leader. The Toryism of the town had its worst manifestation in 1849 when, following the flare-up in the province over the Rebellion Losses Bill, London was one of the two places in Upper Canada where the Governor-General, Lord Elgin, met with a hostile reception when he made a goodwill tour of the province. That was the year in which the Tory party completely discredited itself by its annexationist manifesto.

A centre like London, with its garrison and its select social groups, might continue in election after election to choose Tory candidates but among the farmers of the western counties it was Reform policies which were adhered to and Reform candidates

[11] John R. Godley, *Letters from America* (London, 1844), I, 146-7. Godley was in Canada and the United States in 1842.
[12] This was not the only occasion when the military in London interfered in an election, an even more glaring case being recorded in 1850.

for whom the votes were recorded. If these policies gave evidence of the influence of the United States it was in part because these people in the west were better acquainted with the United States than those in any other portion of the province. It was not possible to lie in the path of westward American migration without absorbing some of the American political philosophy, and in no part of the province was there as large a proportion of people having kin in the neighbouring country as was the case in the western counties.

The departure from the province of a considerable number of people was one of the more serious aftermaths of the Rebellion in Upper Canada. Some left hurriedly in order to avoid arrest, others in fear that their Reform opinions might connect them with the troubles, while not a few made mental comparisons of the province and the nearby states and decided that they preferred the states. Estimates vary widely as to the number who left Upper Canada because of the Rebellion but it was sufficient to give serious concern to the authorities and to affect business adversely.

Emigration to the United States had been going on during the whole of the thirties, probably not more than one-third of the British immigrants who entered the province remaining, the others going on to the new western states. Adam Fergusson in 1831 found Michigan "quite the rage," even supplanting Ohio and Illinois in popular favour.[13] Patrick Shirreff in 1833 also voted the tendency to leave Upper Canada: "It is a knowledge of the Western States, joined to their pecuniary difficulties, which makes many farmers anxious to sell their properties."[14] The *Western Herald* (Sandwich) called attention to the serious loss sustained by the province in the departure of so many of the newcomers from Great Britain. It found a specific text for its discussion in the reported departure of some immigrants who had been brought to Upper Canada under the Earl of Egremont's scheme. These people, having been subjected to certain impositions upon their arrival in the country, had thereupon

---

[13] "The influx of emigrants at present to Michigan is quite remarkable. Seven steam-vessels ply from Buffalo to Detroit, and the decks have been swarming every day since the navigation opened for the season" (Adam Fergusson, *Practical Notes Made during a Tour in Canada and a Portion of the United States in 1831*, Edinburgh, 1834, p. 303).

[14] Patrick Shirreff, *A Tour through North America* . . . (Edinburgh, 1835), p. 366.

proceeded to the United States. Commenting upon this the *Herald* said:

> *Every emigrant who, smarting under injuries, crosses to the neighboring territory, is a loss beyond all computation. Our neighbors, with a calculating policy (from which we might learn some profitable lessons) receive him with open arms. He hears nothing but marvellous tales of the fertility of such and such a county, the advantage of oak openings – the astonishingly rapid settlement of St. Joseph's or White Pigeon Prairie – projected railroads, etc. If he has sufficient means he locates himself without any trouble. If he has not he obtains employment and liberal wages, and in a few months by economy acquires sufficient for the purchase of a lot and his support until he can raise a crop. . . . In the meantime he contrasts treatment which he received from his own countrymen with that he experienced from the people of the territory. He broods over his injuries and becomes absolutely hostile to the provinces. He recollects that such and such of his friends and acquaintances intended following him to Canada, if he reported favorably of the country. He writes them a detail of his injuries, of the difficulties and delays and disappointments they must encounter in procuring land under our present regulations – of the facility with which it can be obtained in the territory. . . . These representations induce his friends to emigrate to Michigan. . . . Thus the oppressed or disappointed emigrants become, as it were, the nucleus of an important settlement and numbers of industrious subjects are decoyed from our province.*[15]

Had Upper Canada during the thirties offered the same attractions as the West it might have added materially to its population from among the numerous Americans who journeyed through the province from Niagara to Detroit on their way to the new states. The Brantford *Sentinel* in the fall of 1835 estimated that not less than two hundred teams had passed through that town during the season, laden with the furniture and families of emigrants bound for Michigan territory. "It is obvious," said this newspaper, "that land in the western part of our Province is held at too high a value to encourage much American emigration to our shores – for instance a tract of 100 acres of good land in Upper Canada can hardly be bought for £100

[15] *Western Herald* (Sandwich), October 26, 1833.

whereas in Michigan the same quantity and quality of land can be obtained with as many dollars."[16] But cheap land was not the only factor in the situation for prior to 1837 the industrial activity of the United States lured large numbers of mechanics and labourers from the province. This movement was accelerated when Sir Francis Bond Head dismissed the Assembly in 1836 and held up expenditures on public works, thereby depriving many men of employment.[17] Some of those who left at this time were later found in the Patriot bands which gave trouble along the border. Robert Davis, of Nissouri Township, who received fatal wounds at Amherstburg in December, 1837, was one of this type.

The descriptions which have come down to us of waggon trains crossing the peninsula in 1836-7 do not as a rule distinguish between Canadians who were emigrating and Americans who were merely taking a short cut from New York State to the West. The Lewiston *Telegraph*, for instance, in March, 1837, computed that during the previous month not less than two hundred teams had crossed into Upper Canada at that place destined for the far West.[18] These were obviously Americans moving from one state to another. Major R. Lachlan, Sheriff of the Western District, addressing the local Agricultural Society on Februay 20, 1837, stated that an average of 200 waggons, 150 pairs of horses and 200 pairs of oxen and 800 persons with their movables crossed every month at the Detroit ferry, "having come up through Canada." These were probably also Americans but the extent of the migration led the *Western Herald* at Sandwich to remark: "While our neighbors on the other side of the river are rapidly going ahead we . . . seem to be nearly at a standstill – whether taken in a commercial or agricultural point of view."[19] The Rev. William Proudfoot, on his way to Chatham in October of the same year, also noticed people in waggons proceeding to Michigan. "These waggons are so constructed," he wrote, "that the whole family sleeps in them." Two weeks later, when he was in Woodstock, he wrote with regret of the

[16] Quoted in Montreal *Gazette*, October 13, 1835.
[17] The Cobourg *Star* in the spring of 1836 that nearly 1,000 men had left Toronto to seek employment in the United States, most of them being immigrants from the British Isles. See *Canadian Emigrant* (Sandwich), May 24, 1836.
[18] Lewiston *Telegraph*, March 1, 1837, quoted in Toronto *Colonist*, March 15, 1837.
[19] *Western Herald* (Sandwich), May 22, 1837.

departure from the province of a Canadian family: "Called at Mr. Aikman's to bait as usual, and was much disappointed to find that he and all his family have gone to the States – to Wisconsin. Mr. Aikman was one of those who felt dissatisfied with the government of the Province and in order to get out of reach of that system of misrule and oppression he sacrificed a valuable property for a mere trifle."[20]

Even Lower Canada contributed its quota to the westward movement. The Hamilton *Gazette* in August, 1838, reported that five or six waggons and a number of horses, together with about one hundred emigrants had passed through the town on their way to Illinois. These people were said to be from the Lower Province.[21]

The emigration to the United States, which had been continuous during the earlier 1830's, was much increased in volume by the troubled conditions during and after the Rebellion. Canadian and American newspapers alike made reference to the increased exodus. The Toronto *Mirror* in August, 1838, reported that the steamer *William IV* was taking two hundred emigrants and forty horses up the lake, with Illinois as their destination. "If matters go on at the present rate," said the *Mirror*, "one half of Canada will be in Illinois and the Far West before long. The whole people appear like the swallows in autumn – preparing for emigration."[22] The *Canadian Chrisian Examiner*, a Presbyterian publication, said in its issue of October, 1838: "It seems generally agreed that emigration from this country to the United States is going on to a considerable extent. If this involved only the removal of the politically disaffected – those absolutely hostile to British institutions and connexion there would be little reason to regret it. But it is to be feared that many good subjects and useful members of the community are also withdrawing themselves – some through timidity and a desire to be out of the way of apprehended trouble – others from the scarcity of profitable employment and the backward state of public improvement and of private enterprise."[23]

The Detroit *Free Press* of June 7, 1838, said of the incoming Canadians: "The emigration to the new states from our neighboring province of Upper Canada in the present season is

[20] *Proudfoot Diary*, October 19, 1837.
[21] Quoted in St. Catharines *Journal*, August 16, 1838.
[22] *Ibid.*, August 16, 1838.
[23] *Canadian Christian Examiner*, III (1839), 313. This journal, like most religious journals of the time, gave some attention to political affairs.

immense. A large number of families, well provided with money, teams and farming utensils, have crossed over to this place within the last few weeks. Twelve covered waggons, well filled and drawn by fine horses, crossed over yesterday." The *Buffalonian* of the same date said: "A cavalcade of 16 waggons, containing the effects of 150 emigrants from the Johnstown District, U.C. passed our office yesterday on their way to Indiana." During the same month the Lewiston *Telegraph* reported a procession of seven covered waggons, laden with as many families, which had passed through that town *en route* to the American West.[24]

Dr. Elijah Duncombe, a brother of the exiled Charles Duncombe, wrote in May, 1838, to a former resident of St. Thomas, then living in Connecticut:

> *Nearly one third of the Inhabitants have left and are leaving for the United States, all the leading Reformers are gone and a great many moderate Tories. . . . The Country is in a confused state, the Tories say there will be another skirmish in a few weeks. . . . There was about 120 Rebels as they called them in London jail – 50 from Yarmouth, 6 of whom were found guilty of High Treason and 3 – Harvey Bryant, old John Moor and Enoch Moor, brothers to Elias Moor – were condemned to be hung on the 25 of this month but they were respited till the Queen's pleasure is known, and 46 have petitioned to Leave the Province and their Property, under an Act that was passed this winter. The Liberal papers in the Province are all put down – not one goes, and we have no news but Tory news – and every letter is opened that there is any Prospect of conveying any Intelligence – hard times indeed.*[25]

Additional evidence as to the migration may be drawn from sources other than the newspapers. The Methodist Episcopal Church in Upper Canada reported a smaller growth in membership during 1838 than in previous years, "a large number of the members having emigrated to the United States during the year." The population of the town of Hamilton showed a decrease of 225 in 1838 as compared with the returns of 1837. The Rev. John Ryerson, Methodist minister at Toronto, wrote in 1838 to his brother, Egerton, at Kingston: "Many persons are leaveing & prepareing to leave the Province from these parts,

---

[24] Quoted in Toronto *Mirror*, June 23, 1838.
[25] The original letter is in the library of the University of Western Ontario.

many more than I had any idea of when I wrote you last. I was last week round through the townships of Markem, Vaugn, Chaugecushee & Toronto, attending Missionary Meetings & Qt. Meeting, & I find some of the best farmers in those parts have sold, & others are trying to sell, & leaveing & have left for the States. The most of the farmers who have sold have made great sacrifices of property."[26]

Much of the Canadian emigration to Illinois, Indiana, and other western states was a part of the general westward movement of the time. In the United States this movement had been stimulated by the panic of 1837 and tens of thousands of people moved to the territories that later became the states of Minnesota, Wisconsin, and Iowa. These territories, not having been caught in the throes of the extravagant public spending of the thirties, had low taxation and were thus destined to have a rapid growth. Missouri was likewise little affected by the depression in the East.[27] The pull of the West continued, therefore, irrespective of political conditions in Upper Canada, so that in the summer of 1839 a London District correspondent of the Detroit *Advertiser* asserted that nearly half of the population in that section of the province were prepared to emigrate, most of them being farmers. The Toronto *Examiner* in the same period expressed the opinion that the province would lose a fifth of its population by emigration to the western states.[28]

The reported prosperity in the West, as well as the widespread advertising which that section of the Republic was receiving at the time,[29] was probably a factor in bringing about the organization in 1838 of the Mississippi Emigration Society. The prospectus of the Society, issued at Toronto in May, 1838, stated that since many people were dissatisfied with political conditions in Upper Canada it was planned to purchase a large tract in Iowa and colonize it with Canadians. The leaders in this enterprise were Peter Perry, a former member of the Assembly from Lennox and Addington, Thomas Parke, member for Middlesex, James Lesslie, a Toronto merchant, and Francis

[26] C. B. Sissons, *Egerton Ryerson, His Life and Letters* (Toronto, 1937), I, 472. John Ryerson's spelling was always quaint.

[27] *Missouri Historical Review*, XXX (1936), 137.

[28] See St. Catharines *Journal*, July 11, 1839.

[29] Illinois in particular was becoming widely known through the writings of such men as Henry B. Fearon, John Bradbury, Patrick Shirreff, etc. A considerable literature on the American West came from the presses of England between 1820 and 1840.

Hincks, who was later prominent in the public life of the country. The new territory of Iowa, which was then much in the public eye, seemed to offer exceptional opportunities for emigrants and Perry, Parke, and Lesslie were sent west to choose a site for the new settlement. Hincks was meanwhile active in promoting the enterprise, some shares being placed with American sympathizers in New York State. Writing to C. H. Graham, of Rochester, in May, 1838, after explaining delays in getting the Society under way, Hincks said: "I am aware we shall lose many valuable settlers owing to the impatience to get away that prevails, but we shall have thousands and a constant drain for years to come."[30]

The deputation which had been sent to Iowa reported favourably and some people did remove to the western territory, though no such colony as had been planned was ever established. Naturally, there was criticism in official circles of this proposal to encourage emigration from the province and the Toronto *Patriot* branded the idea as a swindle, adding that those who left Upper Canada should write after their names the letters "I.O.A." which could be interpreted as meaning "I owe a great many debts which I cannot pay." In the end, however, the influence which chiefly nullified the colonization plans was the coming of Lord Durham and the hope that his policies would remedy the conditions which were driving people out of the country. When Durham's report substantiated the hopes of Reformers the western colonization project was soon but a memory.[31]

Concern was expressed in 1838, and rightly so, over the serious loss of population. It was not only a matter of numbers but also of quality, for in the post-rebellion period there were numerous families against whom no charge could possibly have been brought who shook the dust of the province from their feet and entered the United States. Even among those termed rebels were men whose departure was a loss to the country. What might not Charles Duncombe have given in public service to the province had he not embarked upon the adventure of December,

[30] Francis Hincks, to C. H. Graham, Toronto, May 25, 1838. A photostat of this letter is in the library of the University of Western Ontario. The original is in private hands.

[31] See Francis Hincks, *Reminiscences of His Public Life* (Montreal, 1884), pp. 21-2. Also R. S. Longley, "Emigration and the Crisis of 1837 in Upper Canada," *Canadian Historical Review*, XVII (March, 1836), 29-40.

1837? His reports on education, on prisons, and on the care of the insane influenced legislation after he had become an exile. John Talbot, fiery editor of the *Liberal* at St. Thomas, became in later years a useful and respected citizen of the State of Illinois. Upper Canada could have used his talents to its profit. The Marsh family, with Loyalist background, finding conditions unbearable, removed to Illinois after the Rebellion. There they became rivals of the McCormick family in the manufacture of agricultural implements. Samuel Edison fled from Middlesex County in 1837 to avoid arrest. His grandson, Thomas Alva Edison, became a world-known figure in the field of electrical science. Marshall Spring Bidwell, a man of the noblest character, who was treacherously driven out by Sir Francis Bond Head in 1837, remained a voluntary exile for the rest of his days. Canada was the poorer for his absence from the political scene. Scores of humbler folk also, whose energy and enterprise would have contributed to the development of the province, were made by the events of the thirties to contribute to the upbuilding of states under another flag.[32]

[32] The general question of emigration from Upper Canada to the United States after 1837 is well set forth in M. L. Hansen, *The Mingling of the Canadian and American Peoples* (New Haven, 1940), chap. VI. The border troubles of 1837-8 are intensively examined in A. B. Corey, *The Crisis of 1830-1842 in Canadian-American Relations* (New Haven, 1941).

13: The Anti-Slavery Crusade

Farewell, old master,
Don't come after me.
I'm on my way to Canada
Where colored men are free.
    —Refrain of old Negro song.

During the forty years between the Missouri Compromise of 1820 and the election of Abraham Lincoln the chief issue in American politics was the institution of slavery, and the people of Upper Canada were constantly reminded of their neighbour's problem by the arrival of runaway slaves from the South. The trickle of black folk which began soon after the War of 1812 grew steadily, increasing to large proportions after 1850 when the Fugitive Slave Act sent thousands of Negroes into the British province. Canadian sentiment on the slavery question found expression at that time in the formation of the Anti-Slavery Society of Canada, an organization which continued active until the close of the Civil War.

Slavery in Upper Canada had been disposed of by the first Assembly elected in the province, which in 1793 enacted a measure providing for gradual emancipation. The motives for this action were not entirely humanitarian and some opposition was shown. But slavery was as much out of place in Upper Canada as in New England and it was but a matter of time in any case before it would disappear. There were few slaves in the province in 1793 and no more were brought in afterward so that by 1815 slavery in Upper Canada was gone. But soon other people's slaves began to enter the province, fugitives from the South, aided in their flight to freedom by Quakers and others who viewed slavery as a sin and were quite ready to defy law in order to assist its victims. Soon there were places on the Canadian side of the boundary line which were termini of the "underground railroad" and in the western section of the province, where the Negroes were chiefly to be found, several black colonies were eventually established.

Benjamin Lundy, a pioneer abolitionist, visited Upper Canada in January, 1832. He believed in colonization as a solution for the slavery problem but disagreed with the policy of the American Colonization Society that the Negroes ought to be returned to Africa. Lundy believed that there should be a place for them on the North American continent, somewhere outside the bounds of the United States. In search of such a field for Negro settlement he had already visited Haiti and Mexico before coming to Upper Canada, but after viewing the western portion of the province he prefered it to either of the other locations. Entering at Niagara, Lundy travelled by stage to Detroit, breaking his journey at the village of London to go twenty miles north to a newly-established Negro settlement known as Wilberforce. This colony had been founded about 1829 when enforcement of the Black Laws at Cincinnati caused a considerable number of its free coloured population to emigrate to Canada, assistance being given by friendly Quakers. Lundy was impressed by what he saw at Wilberforce and predicted that the colony would form a nucleus for an extensive emigration of Negroes from the United States. In this he was mistaken as Wilberforce soon ceased to grow, but elsewhere in the province better success attended the effort to place the Negro on the land.[1]

The most successful experiment in the colonization of Negroes in Upper Canada had its beginnings in the late forties. The Rev.William King, an Irish clergyman who had married the daughter of a Southern planter, became after her death the unwilling owner of fifteen slaves. He was troubled in mind over the possession of such property and finally decided to remove the slaves to Upper Canada where they would be legally free and would run no risk of drifting back into thraldom. Laying his plans before the Canada Presbyterian Synod, which showed a friendly interest, a non-sectarian body known as the Elgin Association was formed and a tract of several thousand acres of Crown Lands was purchased in the County of Kent. King's own Negroes arrived in December, 1849, and from then until the close of the Civil War there were frequent additions to the colony which was commonly called Buxton. Land was sold to the Negro settlers in fifty-acre plots at $2.50 per acre, payable in ten annual instalments. Settlers were required to build a house similar to the model house set up by the Association and to proceed with the clearing of their land. The Congressional

---

[1] A description of Wilberforce appeared in Lundy's paper, the *Genius of Universal Emancipation*, issues of March, April, May, 1832. This was reprinted in full by the Ontario Historical Society in its *Papers and Records*, XIX (1922). See also Fred Landon, "Wilberforce, an Experiment in the Colonization of Freed Negroes in Upper Canada," Royal Society of Canada, *Transactions*, XXXI (1937), sec. II.

legislation of 1850, providing more effective machinery for the recovery of fugitives, swelled the migration to Canada and many of those who arrived in the province at that time joined the settlement. By 1852 there were seventy-five families, a year later there were a hundred and thirty families, and when the place was visited by a representative of the New York *Tribune* in 1857 there were said to be two hundred families or about eight hundred souls in all. By this time clearing of land had been much advanced, a church and school had been erected, and the colony was apparently prospering. When Dr. Samuel G. Howe visited Buxton in 1863 as representative of the Freedmen's Inquiry Commission, he was much impressed and his report contained this description of the place:

> *Buxton is certainly a very interesting place. Sixteen years ago it was a wilderness. Now, good highways are laid out in all directions through the forest, and by their side, standing back 33 feet from the road, are about 200 cottages, all built in the same pattern, all looking neat and comfortable; around each one is a cleared place of several acres which is well cultivated. The fences are in good order, the barns are well filled, and cattle and horses, and pigs and poultry abound. There are signs of industry and thrift and comfort everywhere; signs of intemperance, of idleness, of want nowhere. There is no tavern and no groggery; but there is a chapel and a school-house. Most interesting of all are the inhabitants. Twenty years ago most of them were slaves, who owned nothing, not even their children. Now they own themselves; they own their houses and farms; and they have their wives and children about them. They are enfranchised citizens of a government which protects their rights. . . . The present condition of all these colonists as compared with their former one is remarkable.*[2]

In 1852 there were Negro settlements at Buxton, Dawn, Colchester, New Canaan, Sandwich, Wilberforce, and in the Queen's Bush. The first five mentioned were all in the south-western part of the province. Wilberforce was about a hundred and twenty-five miles northeast of the Detroit River, and the Queen's Bush settlers yet farther to the northeast. If the groups scattered here and there in towns and villages were added, there were probably between twenty-five and thirty thousand Negroes

[2] S. G. Howe, *The Refugees from Slavery in Canada West: Report of the Freedmen's Inquiry Commission* (Boston, 1846), pp. 70-1.

in the province. The impelling force behind the more recent growth in numbers was the Fugitive Slave Act of 1850. In order to reclaim a runaway slave the master or his agent was now required merely to present an affidavit of ownership before a federal judge or commissioner. There was no provision for trial by jury and the fugitive might not testify in his own defence. Heavy penalties were provided for any person hindering an arrest or aiding in an escape. A curious provision doubled the fee to the judge if he decided that the fugitive should be returned to slavery. The act placed even free Negroes in serious danger of being seized and sent back into slavery on the mere affidavit of some unscrupulous slave-catcher.

The effects of the legislation were quickly observable in the northern states and in Upper Canada. Newspapers reported the consternation among the coloured people and the frantic exodus to Canada. William Lloyd Garrison collected and printed many such references to the *Liberator*, and the New York *Tribune* also gave much attention to the migration. In its issue of October 5, 1850, the *Tribune* stated that a hundred and fifty Negroes had left Pittsburg for Canada and that others were passing through headed for the same destination. Canadian newspapers along the border soon began to report the arrivals, the most detailed record being set down in the files of a small Negro newspaper, the *Voice of the Fugitive*, published at Sandwich on the Detroit River border by Henry Bibb. In every issue during 1851-2 may be found accounts of the arrival of fugitives, many of them needing immediate assistance. Bibb was active in looking after his people and was generously assisted by Michigan abolitionists who sent money and supplies of food and clothing.

Conditions in the Niagara Peninsula paralleled those in the Detroit River area and in the *Liberator* may be found reports sent from St. Catharines by the Rev. Hiram Wilson. On December 13, 1850, Wilson wrote: "Probably not less than 3,000 have taken refuge in this country since the first of September. . . . In the Niagara District fresh fugitives are numerous. The Methodist church where I preached last Sabbath was thronged with them." At the end of 1851 Bibb estimated that there were three thousand Negroes in his section of the province but during 1852 the accessions increased in number. In July of that year Bibb reported approximately two hundred arriving during one week. Negro immigration continued actively down to the opening of the Civil War, a contingent of nearly two hundred arriving from the State of Illinois as late as the spring of 1861.

The Fugitive Slave Act brought the Anti-Slavery Society of Canada into existence. As early as 1837 sentiment in Upper Canada on the slavery question had produced such an organization[3] but it quickly disappeared in the troubled year that followed. Interest in the question did not lessen, however, but took the practical form of assisting the fugitives who arrived in the province. When the American legislation of 1850 came into force, a new situation was created, an emergency requiring prompt and concerted action. Nine days before President Fillmore signed the Fugitive Slave Bill a public meeting was held in the Toronto Mechanics' Institute "to consider the propriety of taking steps for a public demonstration on behalf of the slaves now flying from bondage to Canada."[4] A second gathering took place on February 26, 1851, in the City Hall, with the Mayor of Toronto in the chair. Four resolutions regarding slavery were presented, the fourth of these proposing the formation of the Anti-Slavery Society of Canada. This was done at once, the Rev. Michael Willis, Principal of Knox Presbyterian College, being elected to the presidency and the Rev. William McClure, a Methodist clergyman of the New Connexion branch, being appointed secretary. Captain Charles Stuart, a romantic figure whose name flits through the records of anti-slavery efforts in the United States, England, and Canada, was made corresponding secretary of the Canadian society.[5] Others who were closely associated with the Society were George Brown, editor of the Toronto *Globe*, at that time the most influential newspaper in the province, and Oliver Mowat, who later became Premier of the province. Through the next decade there was active co-operation between the societies in the United States and Canada, particularly in the matter of exchange of speakers. George Thompson, Frederick Douglass, the Rev. Samuel J.

[3] The Toronto *Constitution*, in its issue of November 16, 1837, reported a meeting of the Upper Canada Anti-Slavery Society which had been held in the City Hall with the Mayor of the city acting as chairman. A speech was delivered by the Rev. Hiram Wilson, agent of the American Anti-Slavery Society, after which resolutions against slavery were passed by the gathering.

[4] President Fillmore signed the Fugitive Slave Bill on October 18, 1850.

[5] Stuart had been the means of converting Theodore Dwight Weld to the anti-slavery cause in the early thirties, thereby bringing in one of the most important figures in the American crusade. See Gilbert H. Barnes, *The Anti-Slavery Impulse, 1830-1844* (New York, 1933), chap. I.

May, and the Rev. J. W. Loguen were among those who visited Canada. Elihu Burritt lectured in Toronto in March, 1857, explaining a proposition for the peaceful extinction of slavery in the United States through the united efforts of both sections of the Union. The Rev. Samuel R. Ward, a Negro who possessed considerable oratorical powers, became a travelling agent for the Canadian society and organized branch societies in the larger towns. The necessity of providing relief and securing employment for the fugitives led also to the organization of women's auxiliaries in a number of places.

The *Globe* and its editor, George Brown, were stout allies. Brown's personal interests in the fugitives was manifested in generous aid for their immediate needs, but a yet greater service to the anti-slavery cause was rendered through the columns of his newspaper. He was outspoken in denunciation of anything that savoured of an alliance with slavery. Canada, he declared, should stand four-square against the whole system of human bondage. "We, too, are Americans," he wrote on one occasion. "On us, as well as on them, lies the duty of preserving the honor of the continent. On us, as on them, rests the noble trust of shielding free institutions."[6]

The general question of colonization of Negroes came before the Canadian Society during its first year of effort. In August, 1851, the Rev. S. Oughten, a Jamaican, visited Toronto and brought the question of West Indian colonization to public notice. The Society placed itself on record as approving the findings of the Great North American Convention of Colored People, which had met in Toronto in the preceding September, that the western part of Upper Canada was the most desirable place of resort for coloured people from the United States, preferable to either the West Indies or Africa. As to the American Colonization Society, the Canadian executive declared that its professions were "altogether delusive." It had originated with slave-holders and was supported by them to rid the country of free Negroes. "A colonizationist and a bitter pro-slavery man are almost convertible terms," it was declared.[7]

The interest of the Canada Presbyterian Synod in the Rev.

---

[6] John Lewis, *George Brown* (Toronto, 1907), p. 114.

[7] Anti-Slavery Society of Canada, *First Annual Report* (Toronto, 1852), pp. 12-13. The American Colonization Society had been founded in 1816 for the purpose of returning Negroes to Africa. The Republic of Liberia was established in 1822 as a home for repatriated Negroes but the scheme was not a success.

William King's colonization scheme has already been noted. In other ways also the Presbyterian body showed itself responsive to the issue which was agitating the people of the United States. In synods held between 1850 and 1860 several resolutions relating to slavery and its effects were proposed, the Synod of 1856 enjoining the presbyteries to be careful in admitting to fellowship Presbyterian ministers from the United States. They should examine them on the subject of slavery to see that their views were in accord with the Synod resolutions of 1851 and 1853 proclaiming non-fellowship with slave-holders.[8] The New Connexion Methodist Church, one of the smaller divisions of Methodism in Canada, took a decided stand on the slavery issue at its Conference in 1852, repudiating "so-called ministers of religion who seek to justify man-stealing from the pulpit."[9] The larger body of Methodists took no positive stand on the question. For this they were severely criticized in pamphlets and broadsides by J. J. E. Linton of Stratford who also raised embarrassing questions concerning the use of Sunday School publications emanating from American churches which were neutral on slavery.[10] The Church of England, most conservative of all Protestant church bodies in the province, while silent on the general question of slavery in the United States, was active on behalf of the fugitives and was able to draw upon funds in England for the support of schools for coloured children. One such school in London was reported in 1856 to have two hundred and fifty children enrolled. As early as 1840 the Rev. John Strachan, at Toronto, had a young Negro in training for work among his own people and had expressed the hope that many of the coloured people might become attached to the Church of England.

Extensive missionary work was carried on among the Negroes under the auspices of the American Missionary Association. Until 1848 the Association limited itself to aiding missionaries already in the field, but from that date missionaries were sent in from the United States. The Association continued its Canadian effort until the close of the Civil War. Its report for 1861 estimated the coloured population in Canada at about

---

[8] Markham (Ontario) *Independent*, November 6, 1856.

[9] *Voice of the Fugitive* (Sandwich), September 23, 1852.

[10] Linton was an ardent abolitionist. He prepared and distributed several numbers of a publication having as title, the *Voice of the Bondsman*, in which he attacked the Wesleyan Methodists in particular. He was also an inveterate writer of letters to the press on the slavery issue.

forty thousand but viewed the prospects for future missionary work as not encouraging. In 1864 the Canadian field was abandoned except for some small support continued to schools for Negro children.

Several historic names appear among the Negroes who came to Canada before the Civil War. Chief among these was Anthony Burns whose arrest and trial as a fugitive in Boston in 1854 was the most sensational case to arise under the workings of the Fugitive Slave Act. An armed force of two thousand guarded Boston's streets while the fugitive was being removed and he was the last Negro taken from the State of Massachusetts. Burns was sent back to his owner in Virginia but soon his freedom was purchased with funds contributed in the North. He attended Oberlin College for a time and in 1860 was pastor of a Negro church in Indianapolis. Finding his position in that city insecure, he crossed into Canada and became pastor of a small coloured Baptist congregation in St. Catharines. He died there in the summer of 1862 and in the local cemetery his gravestone may still be seen, bearing this inscription:

In Memoriam
Rev. Anthony Burns
The fugitive slave of the Boston riots, 1854
Pastor of Zion Baptist Church
Born in Virginia, May 31, 1834
Died in the Triumph of Faith in St. Catharines
July 27th, A.D. 1862

Other famous cases arising under the Fugitive Slave Act also had their endings in Canada. The rescue of Jerry McHenry is one of the best known of these incidents. This Negro, who had been living in Syracuse for some years, was arrested in October, 1851, on the complaint of a slave-owner from Missouri. It happened that on the day of his arrest the Liberty party was holding a convention in Syracuse and the County Agricultural Society's meetings had also contributed to the number of visitors in the city. When word was passed around that a fugitive was under arrest, there was much excitement and indignation. Under the leadership of two prominent abolitionists the court-house was attacked and the police guard overpowered. McHenry was taken out and after being concealed for two or three days was hurried off to Canada. The same year saw the forcible rescue in Boston of a Negro named Shadrack. A mob of Negroes entered the building where he was confined and he was also taken to Canada. Five of the rescuing party were brought to trial but were not convicted.[11] One other incident may be mentioned. In September, 1851, a Maryland slave-holder named Gorsuch came to Lancaster County, Pennsylvania, looking for two runaways from his plantation who had been absent for three years. Accompanied by his son and a federal officer he went to a house where he believed the slaves were being sheltered and demanded their surrender. A mob gathered and in the fighting which ensued Gorsuch was killed and his son wounded. The fugitives escaped and made their way to Canada where they later joined the Elgin Association colony.[12]

Several cases came before the courts of Upper Canada between 1830 and 1860 involving the question of the legal status in the province of runaway slaves. The best known of such cases was that of a Missouri slave, John Anderson, who while attempting to make his escape in 1853, stabbed a white man named Diggs, causing his death. The slave arrived at Windsor in November, 1853, and there told his story to Mrs. Laura S. Haviland, a Michigan woman who was engaged in work among the Negroes in the Detroit River area. He remained unmolested until the autumn of 1860 when he was arrested near Brantford. There was so little evidence against him at that time that he secured his freedom but was later re-arrested upon a warrant sworn out by a Detroit man. His trial took place in Toronto before a court at the head of which was the Chief Justice of the province, Sir John Beverley Robinson. Even while the trial was in progress indignation meetings were being held in Toronto and elsewhere and for fear of violence armed police stood about the court. The three judges who sat on the case disagreed in their judgments and a second trial took place in the Court of Common Pleas where a unanimous judgment was given that the warrant of commitment was bad and that the prisoner could not be remanded in order to have it amended. He was, therefore, given his freedom. In the meantime, however, action had also been taken in the courts of England on behalf of the Negro, the Court of Queen's Bench in London granting a writ of habeas corpus on January 15, 1861. Before news of this English judgment was

---

[11] The Toronto *Globe* early in 1851, reported that Shadrack was in that city. See *National Anti-Slavery Standard*, March 6, 1851.
[12] References to the arrival in Canada of these Negroes appeared in the *Voice of the Fugitive*, June 3, July 1, 1852.

received the case had been disposed of and the whole situation in regard to slavery had been given a new and startling aspect as a result of the election of Lincoln and the secession of South Carolina.

At an earlier date the slavery issue had been a minor factor in Canadian politics. This was in the years 1849-50 when there was a movement for annexation. At that time, however, Washington was too much occupied with the problems arising out of recent territorial acquisitions from Mexico and the status of slavery therein to be much concerned with the possible absorption of the British province to the north. Canadian opponents of annexation quickly saw the opportunity for attack, and the Reform press bitterly assailed the proposal that would make Canada a partner in slavery. The situation was embarrassing for the annexationists who at first sought to ignore the issue and later began to claim that Canada's influence, joined with that of the anti-slavery element in the North, would soon mean the doom of slavery in the Republic. But this argument was laughed out of court, particularly when the South was talking of disunion and civil war. "It would," said the Montreal *Gazette*, "be a sorry instance of our wisdom to make a present of our country to a foreigner, and buy a civil war at the same time. We should have less reluctance to annex to the disunited states than to the present United States."

The enactment of the Fugitive Slave Law, as a part of the great Compromise of 1850, contributed to the ruin of the annexationist party in Canada.

We have hitherto advocated annexation [said the Montreal Witness], *provided certain preparations were made on both sides; but rather than consent to the annexation of Canada to the United States, while this slave-catching law remains in force; rather than the free soil of Canada should be made a hunting ground for the slave-holder and his infamous agents; rather than the fugitive African should be deprived of his last refuge on this continent, we would be willing not only to forego all the advantages of annexation, but to see Canada ten times poorer and worse governed than she is; and we have no doubt this feeling is shared by Annexationists whose objects were higher than mere pecuniary interests.*[13]

[13] Quoted in *British Colonist* (Toronto), October 25, 1850.

Public opinion in Canada, as in the United States, was much influenced by Harriet Beecher Stowe's great novel, *Uncle Tom's Cabin*. First published serially in the *National Era*, an anti-slavery paper at Washington, it appeared in book form early in 1852. Canadian editions in English and French were printed immediately and had a large sale in both Upper and Lower Canada. Sir Wilfrid Laurier, Prime Minister of Canada, declared on one occasion that as a youth he was made an ardent abolitionist by reading Mrs. Stowe's book. Doubtless there were numerous other young Canadians likewise influenced. But a much greater influence upon the public mind was the presence in Upper Canada of the Negro himself, creating a sentiment hostile to slavery. It is true that at times in Canada there were instances of prejudice, fear even of a permanent social problem not of the country's own making, but in general the humanitarian spirit rose above such considerations. A generation ago there were people who still spoke with emotion of the impression that was made upon their hearts and minds by the coming of the fugitive Negroes. The Canadian newspapers, especially during the fifties, frequently printed narratives of the experience of fugitives so that even those who did not have personal contact with the newcomers learned of their condition. Moreover, few American journals gave more intelligent comment on developments in the United States after 1850 than did George Brown of the *Globe*. Other journals might be quite indiffrent to the issue or in some instances lean towards the Southern point of view but their indifference or actual opposition was never so marked as Brown's ceaseless agitation against slavery. The Tory press tended to be indifferent to the abolition movement in the United States but the Reformers found no difficulty in associating anti-slavery views with their programme. A considerable measure of humanitarian spirit was manifest in Canada in this period. The anti-slavery movement had about it much of the attractiveness of a crusade and drew to its ranks men and women who were prepared to make sacrifices for the realization of their ideals. Canadians participated in the work of the "underground railroad" and risked much in its activities. There were even some who ventured into the enemy's country to strike a blow at the thing they hated. Thus, in a variety of ways, the minds of Canadians were educated and influenced so that when the crisis came in the United States with the election of Lincoln and the secession of the slave-holding states there was a considerable measure of public opinion favourable to the Union.[14]

[14] The *Journal of Negro History* (Washington), published since 1916, has printed a number of articles by W. R. Riddell and by the author of this volume dealing with the history of the Negroes in Canada.

14: The Era of the Civil War

That shot fired at Fort Sumter was the signal gun of a new epoch for North America, which told the people of Canada, more plainly than human speech can ever express it, to sleep no more, except on their arms, unless in their sleep they desire to be overtaken and subjugated.

—THOMAS D'ARCY MCGEE (1862)

April 19 – President Lincoln's funeral at noon. All the flags in Toronto were at half mast; all the stores closed from twelve to two. In Zion and Richmond St. churches funeral services were held. Universal horror of the deed, and deep sympathy with the nation was cordially and voluntarily evidenced by the whole people – Catholic and Protestant. Church bells tolled all the time. O what a page in the history of the United States.

—Diary of the REV. WILLIAM MCCLURE (1865)

In a previous chapter it has been shown how the people of Upper Canada were made acquainted with the slavery issue in the United States through the arrival in their midst of large numbers of refugees fleeing from the effects of the Fugitive Slave Act. The process of education was also aided during the decade after 1850 by the publication of *Uncle Tom's Cabin*, by the activities of the Anti-Slavery Society of Canada, and by the succession of dramatic events in the United States itself as the Republic drew near the final catastrophe of war. John Brown's raid on Harper's Ferry in October, 1859, and his subsequent trial before a Virginia court were followed with deep interest by the people of Upper Canada, though it was not generally known that the plans of attack upon the institution of slavery had been formulated at a convention held in the Canadian town of Chatham in May of the previous year. Brown had two reasons for holding this gathering in Canada: to escape observation and to interest the Negroes then in the province in his plans for freeing their fellows from bondage. Although the Chatham convention had been secret, there were some people in Upper Canada who knew that Brown had been meditating a bold stroke and saw at once a connection between Chatham and Harper's Ferry. The raid was reported in detail in the Canadian newspapers and also commented upon editorially. The *Globe* on November 4 printed a leading article of more than a column in length predicting that if Brown were executed, as was now almost certain to be the case, his death could cause him to be long remembered as "a brave man who perilled property, family, life itself, for an alien race." Three weeks later the *Globe* predicted that if tension continued between the two sections of the United States a conflict was inevitable.

When Brown went to the scaffold in early December, mass meetings were held in both Toronto and Montreal. The Toronto demonstration was addressed by Thomas M. Kinnaird, a Negro who had been present at the Chatham convention of the previous year. Money which was collected at this gathering was forwarded to Mrs. Brown. At the Montreal meeting, attended by more than a thousand persons, resolutions of sympathy were ordered to be transmitted to the Brown family. Among those who appeared on the platform were Luther H. Holton, later a prominent figure in Canadian politics, and John Dougall, founder and editor of the Montreal *Witness*. At Chatham and other places in the western part of the province similar meetings took place.

Evidence presented during Brown's trial and in the subsequent senatorial investigation revealed the connection between the Chatham convention and the Harper's Ferry raid; showed also that in Upper Canada there was a considerable sentiment antagonistic to the slavery system and disposed to give protection to runaways. Governor Wise of Virginia referred to this in his message to the state Legislature after the Harper's Ferry incident. "This was no result of ordinary crimes," he said. . . . "It was an extraordinary and actual invasion, by a sectional organization, specially upon slaveholders and upon their property in negro slaves. . . . A provisional government was attempted in a British province, by our own countrymen, united to us in the faith of confederacy, combined with Canadians, to invade the slave-holding states . . . for the purpose of stirring up universal insurrection of slaves throughout the whole south."[1] The Toronto *Weekly Globe* of December 6 further reported Governor Wise as saying: "One most irritating feature of this predatory war is that it has its seat in the British provinces which furnish asylum for our fugitives and send them and their hired outlaws upon us from depots and rendezvous in the bordering states." Later, the Virginia Governor was quoted as declaring to a gathering of medical students who had left Philadelphia in protest: "With God's help we will drive all the disunionists together back into Canada. Let the compact of fanatics and intolerance be confined to British soil."[2]

Actually, in Brown's force on the October Sunday night when the raid took place there was but one man who could in any way be connected with Canada. That was Osborn Perry Anderson, a Negro born free in Pennsylvania who had been working as a printer in Chatham at the time of the convention, and who then threw in his lot with Brown. He escaped capture and later, in a graphic little sketch, *A Voice from Harper's Ferry*, left an account of the events which closed John Brown's career.[3] One other man, Dr. Alexander Milton Ross, of Toronto, by arrangement with Brown, was in Richmond at the time of the raid, presumably with the intention of keeping his leader informed on developments at the state capital. Brown's chief New England supporters, Sanborn, Stearns, and Howe, all fled to Canada immediately after the collapse of his enterprise. There had been some effort in the early part of 1859 to enlist Negro volunteers in Canada but the response was discouraging. Having reached a land which gave them security, the refugees were little inclined to risk death or a return to slavery by joining such an enterprise as was proposed.[4]

Canadian newspapers, particularly the *Globe*, gave close attention to the political developments of the presidential election year. As early as February Lincoln's name was mentioned by the *Globe* though its editor, George Brown, then thought that Seward was more likely to receive the nomination. When Lincoln was chosen the newspaper expressed its confidence in him and by July was predicting his election. The result in November was described as a "triumph of righteousness" and when secessionists began to make valedictory speeches Brown commented: "Since Abraham Lincoln became President we have waded through many speeches delivered by men in and out of Congress, but we have totally failed to find any one good and sufficient reason for destroying the Union." Such were the sentiments of the most influential Reform newspaper in the province but the tone of the *Leader*, a Tory organ also published in Toronto, was in striking contrast. The latter newspaper viewed the Harper's Ferry raid as an insane act and suggested that the South might be ready to

[2] Toronto *Weekly Globe*, December 28, 1859.

[3] Anderson's portrait may be found in Richard J. Hinton, *John Brown and His Men* (New York, 1894), p. 272.

[4] *Ibid.*, pp. 261-3 and Frank B. Sanborn, *Life and Letters of John Brown*, 3rd ed. (Concord, 1910), pp. 536-8, 547.

sacrifice the Union rather than submit to spoliation. When the presidential campaign got under way the *Leader* favoured Breckenridge, the Southern Democratic candidate, and described Lincoln as a mediocre man and fourth-rate lawyer. When Lincoln was elected doubt was expressed whether he would stand by the principles which he had set forth and his elevation to the presidency was described as not the victory of a party but rather the victory of one section over another and one interest over another. In December, 1860, both the *Globe* and the *Leader* found the American slavery issue brought into their own community by the trial of the fugitive Anderson in Toronto. Many newspaper readers must have had their opinions on secession and Southern rights deeply influenced by the question whether Anderson would be surrendered and taken back to Missouri or would remain free in Canada.

The New York *Herald* early in 1861 tried to persuade itself and its readers that a revolution was about to break out in Canada. On alternate days for two weeks articles appeared under such headings as "Canadian Crisis" or "Impending Revolution in Canada." One such article, reprinted in the Stratford *Herald*, said:

> *Probably few persons on the continent imagined that a storm was brewing which, ere half a year had passed away, would threaten to tear from the British crown the last remnants of its possessions in this quarter of the globe. Yet it is undeniable that the contagion of change, which has so rapidly extended from the South to the North since November last has reached the Canadas and that arrangements are already being made there to sunder the connection between the British American colonies and England – amicably if possible, but if needs must be by force of arms.*[5]

The London *Free Press*, commenting upon the outbursts of the *Herald*, pronounced them unmitigated nonsense. "Canadians," it said, "are looking on quietly while the great Republic is splitting into fragments, the prospect offered being such a one as to lead to very little desire to change the political condition we enjoy." The *Globe*'s retort to the *Herald* was that "new and entangling alliances are not in fashion in Canada just now."

The commercial advantages or disadvantages which would

come to Canada in the event of civil war in the United States were stressed in the *Leader* in the last few months before the war. "We see no reason to anticipate any disastrous commercial result to Canada from the revolutionary movement now going on in the Southern states," was its comment on December 31. A fortnight later the *Leader* saw commercial interests at stake in the lessening number of states included in the reciprocity pact and in a tone of sympathy rather unusual expressed its regret "that a great nation which is making a great experiment in self-government should even seem to fail."[6] It soon returned to a more material point of view in predicting that secession would probably turn much European emigration towards Canada which would otherwise have gone to the United States. Through the whole period of the war, the *Leader* continued to display pro-Southern sympathies. It had on its staff for a time one George Sheppard, an Englishman with pronounced views on Southern rights, who eventually was charged by the New York *Times* with being in the pay of Jefferson Davis.[7] The New York *Commercial Advertiser* said of Sheppard's writings: "We are loth to apply any harsh epithets to a part of our Canadian neighbors, much less to all. But if such journals as the Toronto *Leader* were to be accepted as the mouthpiece of public sentiment they would do their best to make us believe hard things of those of whom we have always thought and spoken in the kindest spirit."[8]

The *Leader*'s attitude towards the United States caused some embarrassment to the government, of which it was supposed to be the official organ, and eventually, probably under pressure from above, it issued a statement that it was not to be regarded

---

[6] The *Leader*, January 17, 1861.

[7] Sheppard came to the United States from England in 1850. He was in Canada for part of the next decade but in October, 1860, joined the staff of the Washington *Constitution*. After Lincoln's election this newspaper was removed to the South and Sheppard returned to Canada to join the *Leader*. From 1862 to 1864 he was with the Quebec *Mercury* and later went to the New York *Times* where for a time he was in charge of the editorial page. He died in 1912, in Boston. While connected with the Washington newspaper he wrote several letters to the *Leader* and to the Ottawa *Citizen* on the American political situation. As early as the first week of October, 1860, he wrote privately to a friend in Canada that Lincoln would be elected and expressed a preference for him over either Douglas or Bell. His own sympathies were with Breckenridge. Several of his letters written from Washington are in the Clarke papers in the Ontario Department of Public Records and Archives.

[8] Quoted in the *Globe*, December 27, 1861.

as voicing official government views in its editorials. An example of its bitterness may be quoted from the issue of January 4, 1862, where the Lincoln administration was characterized as " a standing monument of incompetence and wickedness." The apparent occasion of this outburst was the sinking by the federal forces of some old stone-laden hulks to block the entrance to Charleston harbour.

In May, 1861, the *Leader* began to publish the despatches to *The Times* (London), sent by its famous correspondent, W. H. ("Bull Run") Russell. Russell's letters were never pro-slavery, nor were they really pro-Southern, but there was about them a smug complacency, intensely galling to the North, which failed in the earlier stages of the crisis to give the English readers, unacquainted with American conditions, a true picture of the situation. Goldwin Smith, writing from Oxford in January, 1863, said: "I think I never felt so much in this matter [the Civil War in America] the enormous power which the *Times* has, not from the quality of its writing, which of late has been rather poor, but from its exclusive command of publicity and its exclusive access to a vast number of minds. The ignorance in which it has been able to keep a great part of the public is astounding!" Many English readers, believing the North to be so uncertain of its cause that it would let the South go, were later astonished at the manner in which the country sprang to arms in defence of the Union. Russell's despatches provided food for those Canadians who, aping the upper classes in England, cherished hopes that the South would win and that the American democratic experiment would prove a failure. In several cities in the province there were to be found groups of Southerners who had come north to escape the dangers of war. Their presence created a measure of sympathy for their cause. Mrs. John Harris, of London, recorded in her diary both in 1861 and again in 1864 the presence at Niagara Falls of a large number of people from the South, "some very pretty girls amongst them."[9] In Montreal W. H. Russell found "a knot of Southern families, in a sort of American Siberia at a very comfortable hotel, who nurse their wrath against the Yankees to keep it warm and sustain each others' spirits. They form a

---

[9] MSS. diary in the possession of her grandson, Ronald Harris, London. The diary covers the years 1857-77. Selections were printed in the London *Free Press* during 1928.

nucleus for sympathizing society to cluster around."[10] In London, Toronto, St. Catharines, and elsewhere throughout the western section of the province these people were also to be found. Negro women in these Canadian towns found themselves in demand as maids and particularly as cooks, their knowledge of Southern dishes providing them with ready employment.[11]

During the war years there was considerable planning of Confederate operations to be carried out from Canada, these plots centring mainly about the personality of the Hon. Jacob Thompson who arrived in Toronto in 1864.[12] But even before his coming to Canada there had been efforts to organize the Southern sympathizers in the province. Mrs. Harris noted in her diary on July 24, 1862, that her son-in-law, the Hon. Maurice Portman, an Englishman of good family, a son of Lord Portman, spoke of going to Niagara for a gathering of the Southerners in the country, the proposal being to club their means and endeavour to make their way to the Confederacy. Nothing, however, seems to have developed from this plan.

At the same time that Southern refugees from the whirlwind of war were finding a haven in Canada, a much more numerous body, and in general of less desirable character, was coming in from the North. On several occasions Mrs. Harris noted the arrival of large numbers of Americans who were evading military service. On August 6, 1862, she wrote in her diary: "A hundred Americans reached London today and the station-master has been requested to send as many empty cars as he can to Windsor to bring the Americans and their families who are escaping from conscription. They are seeking a home in Canada until the war is over." The St. Catharines *Journal* stated that the number of "skedaddlers" coming to that town was so large that the authorities were beginning to fear for the property, morals, and welfare of the genuine citizens, and that Canadian mechanics and workingmen were feeling the effects of the immigration

---

[10] W. H. Russell, *Canada: Its Defences, Condition and Resources* (Boston, 1865), p. 76.

[11] A Negro woman, Mrs. W. J. Hardin, related that two or three times a week during the war period she would fill a basket with Southern cooking and take it to the rooms of one of the families living in the chief hotel in London. They would then call in the others as their guests (London and Middlesex Historical Society, *Transactions*, part X, 1919, pp. 36-7).

[12] See Wilfrid Bovey, "Confederate Agents in Canada during the American Civil War," *Canadian Historical Review*, II (1921), pp. 46-57.

in a lowering of wages.[13] The *Globe* also made reference to this labour competition in 1863, at the same time pointing out an unfortunate loss of good Canadian population as a result of the war:

> *We observe that some journals are agitating themselves about the number of persons who are leaving Canada for the States. They seem to forget that this exodus has been rendered almost a necessity by the influx from the States to Canada. For the last two years there has been a constant flow of people across the frontier, filling our towns, villages, and townships. The effect of this movement was to overstock the labour market, and make wages low throughout Canada. The drafts on the population from the United States, resulting from the war, having raised wages there, the tide has now begun to turn. The only thing to be regretted is that we have received skedaddling Americans, while the States are taking from us a great many solid and sturdy Britons, who are not liable to the draft, and consequently the most eligible employees in Yankeeland.*[14]

The *Trent* incident in the closing months of 1861 provided a test of Canadian feeling which brought surprising results. When Captain Wilkes, of the United States sloop *San Jacinto*, halted the British steamer *Trent* on the morning of November 8, 1861, and took from her the two Confederate Commissioners, James Murray Mason and John Slidell, the enthusiasm of the North was unbounded. But when, during the next few weeks, this incident brought the United States and England to the verge of war, there were many in the North who realized the mistake that had been made. Likewise in England, hotheads who at first found in the seizure of the two Commissioners food for war talk gradually came to their senses. Lincoln in the United States and the Prince Consort in England were agents for peace and were more powerful in their respective spheres of influence than the warmongers. When the crisis had passed Lady Russell was sufficiently observant to note "the very tempered joy, or rather the ill-concealed disappointment of London society" over the outcome. There were Jingoes in London as well as in Washington in 1861.

---

[13] Quoted in the Stratford *Beacon*, May 8, July 24, 1863.
[14] *Weekly Globe*, October 9, 1863. See also M. L. Hansen, *The Mingling of the Canadian and American Peoples* (New Haven, 1941), chap. VI, for a survey of movements of population during the period of the Civil War.

In Upper Canada there was a surprising burst of patriotism when news came of the "insult" to Britain. It was one of the first clear evidences of the growth of Canadian national feeling which had been under way during the fifties. The confidence in the country which had been shown in business and railway expansion and which had been strengthened by increase in population and trade, now manifested itself in a martial spirit that had hitherto been unsuspected. Everywhere throughout the province militia companies were drilling and new units being proposed. British regiments in the garrison towns were moved nearer to the border and preparations made for defence. "War, war, we hear of nothing but war," Mrs. Harris wrote in her diary on December 17, noting that militia companies were training and new volunteer companies being organized. "Mr. Scott [her son-in-law] thinks of nothing but war," she added. Even in the early months of 1862 the excitement continued. When General Russell and his staff visited London in February, it was announced that two thousand troops would be sent there. All public buildings were requisitioned for barracks and rents quickly doubled. Mrs. Susan Sibbald wrote from Toronto in June, 1862, that "lawyers, varsity students and other professions are forming regiments of volunteers, the same as in England."[15]

The Hon. A. T. Galt, Minister of Finance of Canada, was in Washington during the height of the excitement over the *Trent* incident and was received by Lincoln. The President disclaimed for himself and his Cabinet all thought of aggression towards Canada. Galt was impressed by Lincoln's sincerity and honesty but he brought back to Canada a letter from Lord Lyons, the British Ambassador, urging the necessity of immediate, further preparations for defence.[16]

There is little direct information as to the number of Canadians who were enlisted in the Northern armies. Goldwin Smith has said that he was told by Sir John Macdonald that the number was forty thousand.[17] Upon what basis the computation was

---

[15] F. P. Bett (ed.), *Memoirs of Susan Sibbald, 1783-1866* (London, 1926), p. 318. Mrs. Sibbald, an Englishwoman, was highly contemptuous of Yankees: "The impertinent threats of the Northerners to invade Canada after they 'whipped the secessionists' (which they never can do) has caused all Canadians to scorn and laugh at them."

[16] O. D. Skelton, *Life and Times of Sir Alexander Tilloch Galt* (Toronto, 1920), pp. 314-16. Reprinted in the Carleton Library (1966), pp. 132-34.

[17] *A Selection from Goldwin Smith's Correspondence . . . Collected by his Literary Executor Arnold Haultain* (London, n.d.), p. 377.

made there is no information nor is it clear whether Macdonald included in his estimate former Canadians resident in the United States. That the number who went directly from Upper Canada was large is evident from newspaper references and family records. There are still hundreds of Ontario homes in which the tradition remains of a grandfather or other relative who "went to the war," and in many cases never returned.[18] The bounties which were offered in the later years of the war brought many Canadians into the ranks, some of them, it must be admitted, with no other object than to secure the money and then desert. William Johnson, of Berlin (now Kitchener), received five hundred dollars when he enlisted for three years at Detroit in the summer of 1864. In a letter written to his wife soon after his enlistment he said: "I will not desert. I will come honestly like a brave soldier." He evidently desired to be dissociated from those of his fellow-countrymen who had earned an unsavoury reputation with the American military authorities.[19] There are sufficient records of individuals, however, to make it clear that the bounty-jumpers were but a minority. Numbers of young Canadians joined either for adventure or because of their belief that they were fighting in a good cause. Mrs. Harriet Beecher Stowe's novel had influenced young Canadian minds just as it did young American minds. Newton Woolverton, a Canadian educationist for more than fifty years, was one of five brothers who enlisted at the opening of the war. Though but in his 'teens he was made a captain and served through the whole war, even taking part in the search for John Wilkes Booth after the assassination of Lincoln.[20] Edward William Thomson, Canadian poet and writer, enlisted in a Pennsylvania cavalry regiment at the age of sixteen and served to the close of the war. The Civil War furnished him with the themes of several of his finest poems. The author has pleasant remembrances of evenings spent with him in his home in Ottawa when he told of his experiences as a cavalryman under Sheridan.

Border counties naturally supplied the larger number of recruits. Essex and Lambton sent hundreds of young men to the

---

[18] The writer has tested this by asking groups of people in Western Ontario if any had a relative in the Northern armies. Almost invariably one or more answered affirmatively.

[19] Johnson's wartime letters are in the possession of Miss Hedwig Johnson, of Kitchener.

[20] Newton Woolverton died in Vancouver, British Columbia, in 1932. See obituary in Toronto *Globe*, February 2, 1932.

Michigan regiments while from the Niagara Peninsula equally large numbers joined New York regiments. Popular interest in the war was greatly increased by the fact that so many homes were thus represented. In London during the earlier period of the war it was the practice of the *Free Press*, a morning newspaper, to place on its counter such dispatches as arrived during the day so that the public might have the latest news. An enterprising young printer, John Cameron, took advantage of this interest to establish an evening paper, the *Advertiser*, which first appeared on October 27, 1863. With the large measure of public interest in the war it was an immediate success and was destined to have a life of almost three-quarters of a century, ceasing publication only in the fall of 1936.

It was unfortunate for Canada that British upper class opinion had inclined so strongly towards the South in the earlier years of the Civil War. There was always an element in Canada which looked to England for its views on public questions, and though this element in Canada was but a fraction of the population its attitude did not escape American attention. Canada, as a British dependency, shared the blame for the sarcastic utterances of *The Times*, the wretched cartoons of Lincoln which appeared in *Punch*, and the outspoken sympathy for the South voiced in certain social circles. While there was a decided change in English public opinion after the battle of Gettysburg had sent Lee reeling back into Virginia, the American memory of earlier sneers was not easily eradicated. In Canada, however, a feeling that the North was in the right became more and more deeply implanted as the war passed into its later stages. The figure of Lincoln loomed ever larger in the eyes of Canadians and Emancipation emphasized the great moral issue that lay behind the struggle. "It is a bold step which Mr. Lincoln has taken," said the *Globe* of August 23, 1862, "and it will be keenly criticized. But it is right as well as politic, and it will be sustained by the voice of the civilized world. Four millions of men and women will cease to be chattels and will attain the dignity of human beings. Who shall say that this is too dearly purchased, even by the horrors of civil war." When the election campaign of 1864 came on, Canadian sentiment was generally in agreement with the *Globe*'s tribute to Lincoln's "honesty, patriotism and practical ability." But there were dangers still threatening Canada in 1864 and by none were they more clearly perceived than by the group of Canadian political figures who met, first at Charlottetown and later at Quebec, to devise means for the federation of the British provinces in North America. There were many influences behind the movement for union, but none more dynamic than the fact that within a day's journey the greatest war of the nineteenth century was in progress. The vital question in that year for Canada was, what would happen when the war came to an end?

Canadians had good reason to consider their future in that last year of the war. Russell, *The Times* correspondent, had predicted that the federal government would keep its armies in good humour at the end of the war by annexing the Canadian provinces.[21] As early as July, 1861, the New York *Herald* talked of annexation as if it were but a matter of time, and its bitterness towards England and Canada increased year by year during the war. Edward Blake told Mrs. John Harris, of London, in October, 1864, that he looked for American aggression after the war, and at the close of the year Mrs. Harris wrote in her diary that the probability of invasion in the near future kept her from sleep.[22]

The war came to an end in April 1865, and in the midst of the general rejoicing Lincoln was murdered. "Canada is horrified at the crime," Mrs. Harris wrote on April 15, and that utterance was typical of the general feeling. The loss seemed Canada's own. Governments and municipal bodies everywhere passed resolutions of regret and sympathy and in scores of places memorial services were held.[23] In some towns business was suspended and stores closed while the memorial gatherings were being held. The service which was held in London is stated to have been the largest of its kind in the history of the city. The Toronto City Council appointed three of its members to represent it officially at the funeral in Washington. In the edito-

[21] Russell, *Canada: Its Defences, Condition and Resources*, p. 74.
[22] Edward Blake was at that time the leading member of the legal profession in Upper Canada. Later he was prominent in both provincial and federal politics for many years. He was leader of the Liberal party at Ottawa from 1880 to 1887. Mrs. Harris was an exceedingly well-informed woman and her fears may be regarded as reflecting current public opinion.
[23] The Toronto *Leader*, in its one issue of April 20, 1865, contained reports from twenty-five different places in the province describing memorial services which had been held. In Quebec the stores were closed on the twenty-first. A number of Canadians went from London and other places in the west to Detroit for the memorial services held there on the twenty-fifth.

rial which George Brown wrote for the *Globe* he said: "Almost all of us feel as if we had suffered a personal loss. Mr. Lincoln is spoken of in the same terms as are used towards our familiar friends." The *Leader*, anti-American to the last ditch, thought that the crime must have had some provocation and cited "numberless acts of wickedness" committed in the South by agents of the government, including "fair women violated by a ribald soldiery." But the *Leader* stood alone in Canada in this attitude, everywhere else the Canadian press joined in the tribute to the fallen leader.

These Canadian expressions of sympathy and goodwill did not pass unnoticed in the United States. Even the *Herald* had its belligerency moderated and observed: "These evidences of the appreciation in which our late lamented executive was held will go far to wipe out any cause for resentment that we may have had against the people of the provinces."[24] From other American newspapers came like acknowledgment of Canadian sentiment and this goodwill in the Republic's hour of tragedy may properly be counted as one of the influences which restrained ambitions to embark upon an aggressive policy towards the British provinces.[25] It did not completely dispel the bitterness, as Richard Cartwright noted when in the United States in 1866,[26] and Canadian fears seemed to be well grounded when in that year there was invasion by Fenian forces. But by 1867 both the United States and Canada were entering upon new chapters of their history. The problems of reconstruction after the Civil War, problems not confined alone to the states of the former Confederacy, vexed the Republic and embittered its politics for a decade or more. For the Canadian provinces, hitherto highly localized and isolated communities, the union brought about in 1867 produced a federal government which within three years

[24] Quoted in the *Leader*, April 19, 1865.

[25] John G. Whittier wrote to Dr. Alexander Milton Ross, of Toronto, on May 22, 1865: "The tears which both nations are shedding over the grave of our beloved President, are washing out all bitter memories of misconception and estrangement between them. So good comes of the evil." Whittier appended to his letter two verses of his poem "To Englishmen." The letter and verses appeared in the Toronto *Globe* June 1, 1865.

[26] "I was a good deal in the United States during 1866 and I found their temper exceedingly bitter. They well understood that the sympathy of the governing classes in England had been with the South, and they resented extremely the destruction of their commerce and mercantile marine consequent upon the depredations of the *Alabama* and her consort" (Richard Cartwright, *Reminiscences*, Toronto, 1912, p. 58).

extended from sea to sea. During the years that the United States was fighting its tragic civil war to preserve unity, Canada also was unifying its provinces. National interests were soon to have a place in the thinking of Canadian people, not entirely banishing provincial pride or prejudices, but removing at least a part of the separatism which had hitherto prevailed. The conception of a nation, so eloquently set forth by Thomas D'Arcy McGee during the Confederation era, thus resulted in the frontier becoming more of a political fact than had been the case in the period which has been described in earlier chapters.

15: Reconstruction After 1837

> In the continuous process which we call history, it is all too easy to point to specific dates and to speak of "turning points" when in fact all that happens flows from what has been into what is to be, with a lack of sharp divisions which is annoying to the chronicler but true to all living processes.
>
> —JAMES TRUSLOW ADAMS

At this point it becomes necessary to depart from the chronological sequence of immediately preceding chapters and pick up certain threads in the pattern of life within the province which have not formed part of the narrative. While the forces which have been described in the previous chapters were shaping themselves from the period of the Revolution to that of the Civil War, the social and economic history of Upper Canada was responding to internal growth and development. Forests had given way to farms, some villages had become towns, some towns had arrived at the status of cities; new chapters were being written in the history of education, of religious organization, of local government and political parties. It is with these changes that this chapter will deal.

"A new era has taken place in the politics of the country necessarily growing out of the union of the Provinces – new political parties will spring up – great political changes must be expected." So wrote the editor of the Chatham *Weekly Journal* in the summer of 1841.[1] He might have added that great changes in fields other than politics would also be recorded before the decade had ended, changes in education, in the form of local government, in religion, in trade and commerce, and in many other social and economic fields, constituting something in the nature of a reconstruction period after the political growing pains of the later thirties. Politicians and parties might continue to manœuvre for advantage and power, bills come before Parliament and become law, money be appropriated and spent on public works, but quite outside of such political activities the lives of thousands of people would be affected by processes and influences that were not clearly perceived at the time and which only long after could be analysed and classified.

[1] Issue of July 3, 1841. Upper Canada and Lower Canada were united as the Province of Canada in that year.

Older settled portions of Upper Canada, during the forties, were passing out of the pioneer stage. By 1840 most of the Crown lands in the southern portion of the province had been disposed of by government grants; to secure land now it was necessary to purchase.[2] But though the land had passed out of the government's hands it did not follow that it was all occupied. Hundreds of thousands of acres were held by friends of the earlier administrations or by speculators and land companies. In what is now the County of Elgin two whole townships had been largely withheld from settlement for speculative purposes by Colonel Thomas Talbot.[3] The Canada Company, with its huge tracts of land in the western part of the province, was generally regarded as an obnoxious monopoly and had also been a souce of considerable unrest prior to 1837. Elsewhere in the province there were similar checks to free settlement.

Land speculators might look forward to ultimate profits on their investment but in no other way could wealth in any considerable measure be acquired. John Langton wrote in 1844 that he knew of no money-making business in Canada other than the law, store-keeping, tavern-keeping, and horse-stealing and the latter two he would omit. "Store-keeping," he wrote, "is decidedly the most money-making and is carried on with very little capital, but it appears to me that those who have made it pay are invariably those who have started with next to nothing and have gradually crept up in the world, increasing their business as their capital, custom and experience increased."[4] There was a marked shortage of money in this period and though there was apparent prosperity during the middle forties its evanescent character was revealed when the source was removed by the repeal of the English Corn Laws. Serious depression then descended upon the country. A generation which has witnessed a like succession of boom and depression can have some understanding of the temper of the later forties when annexation to the United States became a lively issue. Yet the country was not stagnant.

One of the important advances of the decade was the

[2] J. J. Talman, former provincial archivist, states that genealogical inquiry can be pursued through the land records of the province down to 1840 but not profitably after that date.

[3] C. O. Ermatinger, *The Talbot Regime, or the First Half Century of the Talbot Settlement* (St. Thomas, 1904), p. 256.

[4] W. A. Langton (ed.), *Early Days in Upper Canada: Letters of John Langton from the Backwoods of Canada and the Audit Office of the Province of Canada* (Toronto, 1926), p. 201.

introduction and development in the province of a new system of local government. It was not England, however, that offered the model. J. L. Hammond has described the English towns in 1835 as "sunk in a condition of barbarism that would have put a citizen of the Roman Empire to the blush." The Municipal Reform Act of 1835 had provided for town councils elected by all the ratepayers to supersede the old governing bodies based on narrow franchise. But this act affected only 179 boroughs and only long after were the local bodies charged with the administration of the social services which are so conspicuous today. Not until quite recent times was there a parallel to the system which Upper Canada fashioned for itself as early as 1849, basing it upon North American forms and experience.

For fifty years after the establishment of Upper Canada local government was carried on chiefly by the ancient English system of local magistrates meeting in Courts of Quarter Sessions. Simcoe aimed to make the system even more autocratic by setting up county lieutenancies, and indeed did so until checked by the home government. The earlier Loyalists, accustomed to the town meeting, introduced the idea on their arrival, to the consternation of some English officials who could see in it only an American, and therefore dangerous, innovation. But the town meeting was too firmly fixed in the minds of Loyalist immigrants to be easily discarded and it persisted, being legalized in 1793 though with no real legislative powers. W. J. Ashley has pointed out that this limitation of powers, differing in that respect from the town meeting in New England, indicates its likeness to the town meeting in New York State whence so many of the Loyalists had come. In that state the county was the original unit of government and the introduction of the township had created a compromise between the town system of the North and the country system of the South. Ashley suggests also that the authority of the magistrates meeting in Quarter Sessions in Upper Canada is probably to be explained at least as much by American traditions as by imitation of England since the justices in Massachusetts, where the town meeting was best established, continued to levy a county rate to the end of the colonial period and even disallowed town by-laws.[5]

Various powers which in New England would have been

[5] W. J. Ashley, Introduction to John M. McEvoy, *The Ontario Township*, University of Toronto Studies in Political Science, 1st series, no. 1 (Toronto, 1889), pp. 8-9.

exercised by the town meeting were in Upper Canada delegated to the Courts of Quarter Sessions. Thus an entirely unrepresentative body had purview of such matters as the building of roads and bridges, erection of jails, fees of district officers, licensing of taverns, and granting of authority to non-Anglican clergy to solemnize marriage. The town meeting, on the other hand, had no powers other than appointing a few township officials, whose duties were of a minor character, and attending to such trivial matters as fixing the legal height of fences and regulating the running at large of farm animals. Had the magistrates been of another type, there might have been less objection to the system, but, as is well shown by examination of their background and qualifications, they were frequently old army officers with pensions, and almost always men of sufficient income from some source to render them indifferent to, and independent of, the hardships and wants of the average hardworking settler. Their qualifications were often meagre and their incompetence was frequently as great as their arrogance.[6] In the end they became an appendage of the Family Compact and their attitude helped swell the unrest before 1837. The events of that year sounded their death knell as masters of local administration in the province.

Records of early town or township meetings which have survived show clearly the limitation upon their powers. The first meeting in Dumfries, in 1819, elected a township clerk, two assessors, a collector, two wardens, four path-masters, and a pound-keeper. The only other business dealt with was to fix regulations for fences and farm animals allowed at large on the roads.[7] Minutes of the town meetings of Lobo Township beginning in 1829 show similar entries. In each year the required height of fences was restated and regulations regarding control of farm stock set down.[8] It was not to be expected that men of independent character would remain content within these bounds while such extensive powers were placed in the hands of appointed magistrates. After 1830 the general agitation for reform included local government as one of its chief objectives. Reform newspapers of the time returned to this subject again

---

[6] McEvoy, *Ontario Township*, p. 22.

[7] James Young, *Reminiscences of the Early History of Galt and the Settlement of Dumfries* . . . (Toronto, 1880), pp. 134-5.

[8] Minute book of the town meetings of the Township of Lobo, in possession of Mrs. Edna Stewart, Byron, Ontario.

and again, charging that among the appointments of magistrates there were many who were utterly unfitted, some who were intemperate, some ready to stir up the mob against Reformers. The St. Thomas *Liberal* also criticized the number of such appointments, pointing out that there were five magistrates in that village and two more within three miles of it.[9] The *Liberal* during 1833 lost no opportunity of exposing the character of appointees to the magistracy and waxed exceedingly sarcastic over the appointment to the Court of Requests of one John O'Neal, picturing this London tavern-keeper and former constable in the following terms:

> *Yesterday O'Neal made proclamation in the Court of Requests and cried "God save the King and their worships," today he, himself, is worshipful and all must do him reverence. At 7 o'clock he attends the horses in the stables, at 11 (the usual hour of opening court) he cleans his hands and presides with the Just-asses in the court. At 8 he lays the toast the steak and eggs for breakfast and is all obsequiousness; at 11 you dare not get between the wind and his nobility! At 10 he mixes grog for six cents a glass, at 11 he soberly ascends the Bench, and administers Justice? Let Justice, with her last breath, as she lies oppressed and degraded, forgive me for using her name in such a connexion, but let her never forgive Mount who placed such a man on the bench.*[10]

In his report on the Canadas Lord Durham had recommended the establishment of municipal institutions as "a matter of vital importance" and made some reference to systems of local administration prevailing in some of the American states. Lord Sydenham, on his arrival as first Governor of the united province, recognized the importance of Durham's recommendation and included a plan in the draft bill for union which he sent to the Colonist Secretary. "Since I have been in these Provinces," he wrote, "I have become more and more satisfied that the capital cause of the misgovernment of them is to be found in the absence of Local Government, and the consequent exercise by the Assembly of powers wholly inappropriate to its functions." He was disappointed when the Colonial Office found it

[9] The *Liberal*, July 18, August 22, 1833. A file of this newspaper for 1833 is in the Public Archives of Canada.
[10] *Ibid.*, September 19, 1833. Roswell Mount was one of the members of the Assembly from Middlesex County.

necessary to drop the local government clauses which he had proposed, but in the new Legislature he was able to accomplish his aim in the District Councils Bill. Conservatives affected to find in the bill a dangerous concession to republicanism while ultra-Reformers contended that it did not go far enough. Although the government continued to exercise considerable influence in local matters, nevertheless a real advance was made by the substitution of the elected district councils for the old Courts of Quarter Sessions. The new district councils were composed for the most part of men known for their energy and ability, and being thoroughly conversant with conditions of the area which they represented they were in a position to judge properly the numerous applications for public improvements.

Sydenham's plan of local government was replaced in 1849 by legislation which bears the name of Robert Baldwin and which in its essential features has continued in force to the present time. Ashley's analysis of this legislation declares it to be similar in all essentials to the so-called "compromise" plan or "township-county system" of New York and some of the northwestern states, with its county board composed of township supervisors.[11] The Baldwin Act gave increased importance to the township by making it an incorporated body with the power, not hitherto enjoyed, of raising money for public works. The township administration consisted of five elected councillors who named one of their number as reeve and another as deputy reeve if the population exceeded five hundred. The reeves and deputy reeves of the several townships in a county constituted the county council and elected one of their number as the warden of the county. It will be seen from the above that the township was made the basic feature. The new county councils took over the duties of the former district councils save in so far as power was delegated to the new township councils. In the course of more than ninety years only minor changes have been found necessary to keep Baldwin's legislation a live instrument. Moreover, it became the basis of legislation in the newer provinces of Western Canada as they in turn had to provide for local administration.

The long and bitter struggle over the issue of church control of education was brought to an end during the forties with the adoption of a comprehensive system of public schools and the freeing of the provincial university from religious limitations.

[11] McEvoy, *Ontario Township*, pp. 9-10.

The new public school system was based upon the experience of Great Britain, Ireland, several countries of Europe, and the eastern states of the American Union. The democratic character of New England's educational ideals was particularly reflected in the changes made in Upper Canada.

In an earlier chapter attention was drawn to the considerable influence exerted upon education in Upper Canada by the system developed in the State of New York. The Commissioners appointed by the provincial Assembly in 1835 to study school systems in the United States found their report rejected by the Legislative Council on the ground that it seemed merely to propose adoption of the New York State system. Despite the opposition of the Council some, if not all, of the Commission's recommendations would doubtless have been accepted had not the whole life of the province been disturbed by the troubles of 1837-8. Not until 1841, under a new constitution and with new leaders in public affairs, was it possible to proceed with alterations in the school system. The changes made by the Act of 1841 improved conditions but little.[12] The influence of New York State was still observable, though little account had been taken of the changes which that state had itself made during the disturbed years in Upper Canada, changes which had corrected some of its weaker features. Not until after 1846 was there genuine advance. The new era in provincial education proceeded from policies proposed by the Rev. Egerton Ryerson who had been appointed Superintendent of Schools in 1844. Immediately following his appointment Ryerson visited the United States and several countries of Europe, the results of his observations being embodied in the Common School Act of 1846, probably the most important piece of educational legislation in the whole history of the province. Ryerson's plans demanded well-qualified teachers, suitable buildings and equipment, regular inspection, and uniform textbooks. From the United States was drawn the thoroughly democratic principle that every child was entitled to the educational privileges provided by the state, and also the idea of local administration through elected school trustees who should have the right to demand from municipal councils the

---

[12] When a bill respecting education was introduced in 1841, the Solicitor-General stated that in Upper Canada the existing schools were caring for only one child in eighteen. See Chatham *Weekly Journal*, August 7, 1841.

funds necessary for educational requirements. Efficiency and responsibility were to be the keynotes of the new system.[13]

Ryerson believed that religion and morality were essential elements in all education. It was important, therefore, that the textbooks placed in the hands of the children should be carefully chosen. As it would require some time to prepare distinctively Canadian texts, Ryerson turned to the series published by the Commissioners of National Education in Ireland and secured authority for their use in Upper Canada. Probably no better choice could have been made at the time. For the next quarter-century the Irish readers were the most familiar school-books in the province and a whole generation made some acquaintance with literature and history through their pages. They were in no respect Canadian in spirit but in the range of their information they were truly cosmopolitan. During the period in which they were in use in Upper Canada the famous McGuffey readers were the most widely used texts in the United States and between the two series interesting comparisons and contrasts could be made. W. Sherwood Fox has pointed out that as compared with the McGuffey readers the Irish texts exhibit a greater measure of balance, restraint, and completeness, qualities which may have been reflected in the characters of those who read them.[14] Both series laid stress upon the cardinal virtues, prudence, justice, temperance, and fortitude.

With the introduction of the Irish readers the use of American textbooks, which had long been under criticism, soon ceased, although the influence of the McGuffey readers may be seen in the native texts which appeared at a later date. Ryerson recognized the support which the McGuffey readers had given to the development of national spirit in the United States and felt the need of similar development in the minds of the youth of Canada. Included in the Ryerson readers of the 1860's are a number of selections which were apparently taken over unchanged from the American series, even the moralizing being retained. The Third Reader of this early Ryerson series has been described as "a strange mixture of United States, Irish and English methods of presenting moral principles to young people." Such stories as that of Brave John Maynard (the lake pilot who gave his life for others), the Poor Little Match Girl, George

[13] Nathaniel Burwash, *Egerton Ryerson* (Toronto, 1906), p. 170.
[14] W. S. Fox, "School Readers as an Educational Force," *Queen's Quarterly* (Kingston), XXXIX (1932), pp. 688-703.

Washington and the Cherry Tree, etc., are among the borrowings from Mc Guffey. Humour is conspicuously absent.

Ryerson's gleanings from American educational theory and practice excited some criticism, chiefly of a political character. Angus Dallas, in a pamphlet published at Toronto in 1855, challenged the new provincial system, however, on the grounds that it was a slavish imitation of the Massachusetts system and that it embodied too much of Horace Mann's Unitarian and republican ideas. "No opportunity," said the writer, "has been permitted to escape wherein it was possible to present the Boston school authorities as embodying the climax of educational wisdom . . . [but since] the conditions for a school system in Massachusetts are diametrically opposed to the conditions for a school system in Canada, where the form of government and the religious communities are altogether dissimilar, the conclusion will be unavoidable that what took place in 1846, namely, the adoption in Canada of the Massachusetts school system, was a palpable mistake."[15]

Secondary education, when established in 1853 as a definite part of the provincial system, was frankly modelled on the American example. In New England the English grammar school had been transformed from its original idea of providing for a privileged few into a high public school supported in the same way as the elementary schools. In Upper Canada the grammar schools, first provided for in 1807, had changed but little in character though made more accessible by increase in their number. In 1853 they became a distinct part of the school system of the province with a well-defined course of instruction and supported by a tax upon property. Henceforth they were known as high schools.

In the realm of higher education American influence has been most noticeable in the idea of the state university, "the greatest contribution made so far by the United States to higher education" in the opinion of Sir Robert Falconer, former President of the University of Toronto. Michigan, one of the first states in the Union to develop a state university, was Upper Canada's nearest neighbour. The University of Michigan was founded in 1837; the year in which the notoriously denominational character of King's College at Toronto was altered by the Legislature of Upper Canada. Teaching was begun at the Uni-

[15] Angus Dallas, *The Common School System: Its Principle, Operation and Results* (Toronto, 1855), pp. iv, v, 15.

versity of Michigan in 1841 and at Toronto in 1843. That the success of the American state university had influence upon the future development of the Canadian university can scarcely be doubted. In 1849 King's College became the University of Toronto providing a system of higher education entirely non-sectarian in character. In more recent times the state or provincial university idea has extended from Ontario into the western provinces of the Dominion.

The zeal for public education which was so marked in the Old Northwest resulted in the establishment of numerous denominational colleges, more indeed than were warranted by the population. In Upper Canada the few denominational colleges which arose resulted from the attempt of the Church of England to maintain control of all higher education in the province. Upper Canada Academy, for example, established by the Methodists in 1836 for the education of young people of every class, was a protest against the exclusive character of Upper Canada College. The Academy secured a royal charter and later, in 1841, blossomed forth as Victoria University. The Rev. Egerton Ryerson, its first President, was not a college graduate but the three other professors on its original staff were men who had received training in the United States and were in touch with American ideas of education. Two later Principals, the Rev. S. S. Nelles and the Rev. Nathaniel Burwash, each received graduate training in a New England college. Victoria University in its earlier history drew extensively upon American example in its curriculum and methods and scarcely at all upon English models.

The advance of the newspaper in Upper Canada during the thirties and forties was governed by much the same conditions as those which prevailed in the American Middle West during the same period. W. S. Wallace has listed one hundred and seventeen newspapers and journals which were established in the province in the period between 1793 and 1840.[16] In the section of the province which lay west of Toronto forty-nine newspapers began publication prior to the year 1841, twenty of these being at Niagara or its vicinity. Moving westward from Niagara, newspapers were established at Dundas in 1818, St.

[16] W. S. Wallace, "The Periodical Literature of Upper Canada," *Canadian Historical Review*, XII (1931), pp. 4-22. See also emendations and additions to this list in the same volume, pp. 181-3.

Catharines in 1826, Ancaster in 1827, Hamilton in 1829, London in 1830, Sandwich in 1831, St. Thomas in 1832, Brantford in 1834, Berlin in 1835, and Woodstock in 1840. During the next decade there was a striking increase in the number of newspapers in the province, particularly in the western counties. Five newspapers began publication in London during this period, at least as many in Chatham, four or more in Hamilton, four in Woodstock, three or more in St. Thomas, and one or more in each of a dozen other places. In their exaggerated partisan bitterness many of them were not far behind their American contemporaries.

Interest in American politics and in events happening in the United States was more noticeable in the Upper Canada press after 1840. The annexation of Texas, the war with Mexico, boundary disputes, commercial developments, and the discovery of gold in California all received attention. Records of crime and of disasters were copied, sometimes at great length. The newspapers drew heavily upon their American exchanges not only for news but also for expressions of editorial opinion. The *Canadian Emigrant* (Sandwich) during 1831-2 had excerpts from more than forty different American newspapers, ranging geographically from New England to the deep South. An examination of the London *Herald* for the first six months of 1843 shows news or editorials taken from the press of Baltimore, New York, New Orleans, and other distant points.

Agricultural journalism had its rise in Upper Canada after 1840. Prior to that time such American journals as the *New England Farmer* (1822), the *Genesee Farmer* (1831), and the *Albany Cultivator* (1834) had circulated widely in the province, while the editors of Upper Canada newspapers had clipped freely from these and other American farm journals for inclusion in their columns.[17] Agricultural journalism in Upper Canada began with the *Canadian Farmer and Mechanic* which was published at Kingston during the summer of 1841 and then died, as the *Genesee Farmer* remarked, "for want of proper care and nourishment." William G. Edmundson, who was associated with this enterprise, thereupon removed to Toronto and established the *British American Cultivator* which was published

---

[17] The *Canadian Emigrant* (Sandwich) during 1831-2 quoted from the *Genesee Farmer* in almost every issue, frequently also from the *New York Farmer* and occasionally from the *New England Farmer*, the *American Farmer*, and other journals of like character.

from 1842 until the end of 1847. Its name indicates the American influence for there were few American publications better known in Upper Canada than the *Albany Cultivator*. In the nature of its articles the new Canadian journal differed little from its American contemporaries from which it quoted copiously. Other farm journals established in the province during the decade were the *Newcastle Farmer* (1846), the *Canada Farmer* (1847), the *Farmer and Mechanic* (1848), and the *Canadian Agriculturist* (1849), the latter being a consolidation of the earlier *British American Cultivator* and the *Canada Farmer*.[18] These journals reflected the more scientific spirit which was influencing the farming practices of the province. They all stressed the value of agricultural education and the application of science to the problems of the farm.

Religious journalism in Upper Canada began with the publication by the Rev. John Strachan in 1819 of the *Christian Recorder*, an Anglican monthly which lasted two years. It contained much news of the Missionary and Bible Societies. Ten years later, in 1829, the Methodists established the *Christian Guardian*, a powerful organ for the advancement of their views on public questions and for the edification of their own people. Prior to the establishment of the *Guardian*, the *Christian Advocate*, published at New York, had circulated in Canada among the Methodist preachers and people.[19] The *Church*, the official organ of the Church of England, first appeared in May, 1837, and in the controversies of the day crossed rapiers regularly with the *Christian Guardian*. Other religious journals which appeared in the thirties were the *Canadian Wesleyan* (1831), the *Upper Canada Baptist Missionary Magazine* (1836), the *Canadian Christian Examiner and Presbyterian Review* (1836), and the *Canada Baptist Magazine and Missionary Register* (1837). The latter journal was the organ of the Baptists in the eastern section of the province and in Montreal. During the 1840's a number of other religious journals appeared, some of them short-lived. Several religious publications having their offices at Montreal enjoyed considerable circulation in Upper Canada while smaller religious groups, such as the Universalists and the Christian

[18] For further details concerning these journals see Fred Landon, "The Agricultural Journals of Upper Canada (Ontario)," *Agricultural History*, IX (1935), pp. 167-75.

[19] See G. F. Playter, *The History of Methodism in Canada* . . . (Toronto, 1862), pp. 165-6, 288. The *Christian Advocate*, published by the Methodist Episcopal Church in the United States, first appeared in 1826.

Church, depended almost entirely upon American publications. The Methodists made much use of Sunday School papers published at New York. There was a marked similarity between the contents of these Canadian religious journals and that of their American contemporaries, an example being the numerous descriptions of ecstatic death scenes. Such records were apparently regarded as having high moral value for readers. In a majority of cases the ecstasy would appear to have been related to the last stages of tuberculosis.

The Reform party in Upper Canada, despite the charges of disloyalty lodged by its political opponents (charges widely believed in England), quickly recovered its place after the union of the provinces in 1841. During the forties it was led by Robert Baldwin, who, though ready to fight to the last ditch for what he believed to be the right, was in no sense an extremist. Within the party, however, there was a radical wing whose political programme was definitely influenced by American theory and practice. To this group the name Clear Grit was applied, at first derisively but later in more respectful manner. Boastful of their democracy, the Clear Grits demanded wider suffrage, the secret ballot, and abolition of property qualifications for candidates for Parliament. They also called for biennial Parliaments, popular election of many officials, abolition of all special privilege to any group, and direct taxation. This programme, with its American tinge, was regarded in conservative circles as radical and dangerous, and was even viewed with suspicion by many within the Reform party itself. George Brown, editor of the *Globe*, once described the group as "a miserable clique of office-seeking, bunkum-talking cormorants" and on another occasion classified them as "radicals, republicans and annexationists." By the early 1850's, however, he had cast in his lot with them and soon became their recognized leader. The chief area of circulation of the *Globe* was the western peninsula and it was there that Clear Grit sentiment was most in evidence. Among the Scottish farmers, so numerous in this section, the *Globe*'s views were read and accepted as having almost inspired authority. In the cities Clear Grit principles made little headway and it was noticeable also that they were less in evidence as one travelled eastward, becoming almost non-existent in the more easterly counties of the province. The party's suspicion of cities and bankers and railway interests bears a likeness to other progressive and agrarian movements in Canada and the United States. As F. H. Underhill has observed: ". . . the essential thing about the *Globe* and the movement it led is that it represented the aspirations and the general outlook on life of the pioneer Upper Canadian farmer. The 'Clear Grit' party in Upper Canada was an expression of the 'frontier' in our Canadian politics just as Jacksonian Democracy or Lincoln Republicanism was in the politics of the United States. It was to 'the intelligent yeomanry of Upper Canada' that the *Globe* consciously made its appeal."[20] An added characteristic of the Clear Grit movement after Brown assumed leadership was its hostility to the Roman Catholic Church. This anti-Romanist attitude bore some resemblance to that of the contemporary Know Nothing party in the United States but there is no evidence that the Upper Canadian group was influenced by the American propaganda, though Thomas D'Arcy McGee noted the influence in another direction. In a letter written to the *Globe* in 1861, he said: "Since the era of the Know Nothing movement the last vestige of political preference for the United States has disappeared among the Irish."[21]

For a time John A. Macdonald, Brown's chief opponent, was inclined to minimize the effects of the Clear Grit movement but by the end of 1856 he was less sanguine. Writing to the editor of the Montreal *Gazette*, he said: "The Peninsula must not get control of the ship. It is occupied by Yankees and Covenanters, in fact the most yeasty and unsafe of populations."[22] Macdonald here recognized what the Toronto *Leader* had once described as the "eternal restlessness of the Peninsula," a temper of mind in which democratic ideas found congenial soil.

The Reform convention of 1859, the first great party convention ever held in Canada, clearly demonstrated where the strength of the Clear Grit movement lay. If the "Peninsula" did not have control of the ship of state, a danger which Macdonald had suggested, it did at least have numerical control of the convention of 1859, for of the 520 delegates who attended no less than 273 were from the western counties and the Niagara Peninsula, with 178 others from York and the central counties and less than 70 from the eastern section of the province. It was

[20] F. H. Underhill, "Some Aspects of Upper Canadian Radical Opinion in the Decade before Confederation," *Canadian Historical Association, Report of the Annual Meeting 1927*, p. 47.

[21] The *Globe*, December 27, 1861.

[22] Public Archives of Canada, Chamberlin Papers, John A. Macdonald to Brown Chamberlin, Toronto, January 21, 1856.

a clear proof that Clear Grit strength was greatest where most remote from Montreal.[23] Another interesting aspect of the convention was the prominence in it of the newspaper editors of the province. The notice calling the convention was signed by sixty-two persons, of whom no less than forty-two were connected in some way with newspapers. Editors were likewise prominent in the convention itself. The *Globe* specifically mentioned twenty-eight in its list of delegates and there is good reason to believe that there were others present who were not so identified.[24] Of the twenty-eight mentioned by the *Globe*, twenty-three were from what Macdonald called "the Peninsula."

The Reform convention of 1859 is one of the turning points in Canadian political history and its decisions form one of the milestones on the high road towards the federation of 1867. The union of Upper and Lower Canada brought about in 1841 had long been a cause of heart-burning to the Clear Grits who believed their province to be the victim of an unscrupulous and unprincipled government which maintained itself in power by gross corruption and the votes of Lower Canada. "Were human ingenuity," said the *Globe*, "exercised to the utmost to discover a political machine by which one section — and that section Lower Canada — should inflict the greatest possible amount of insult, injury, and costly injustice upon its partner in the business of legislation, no better contrivance than the union could be devised." Reform newspapers boiled over with charges of governmental extravagance, railroad peculation, tariff discrimination against the farmer in favour of the commercial class, and general cynical indifference to the farming class and its needs. Criticism was extended even to the representative of the Crown. When Sir Edmund Head in 1858 gave sanction to the famous "Double Shuffle," Brown and his friends waxed highly indignant and in the London *Free Press* its editor Josiah Blackburn wrote:

The governor-general ought to keep in mind that acts such as the black one so recently chronicled in Canadian history have a very complex bearing and might have a direful issue. Loyal as we Canadians are, we are not intoxicated with crowns; and, indeed, it is a notorious fact that in this age crowns are not

---

[23] See George Brown, "The Grit Party and the Great Reform Convention of 1859," *Canadian Historical Review*, XVI (1935), pp. 245-65.

[24] The name of Josiah Blackburn, editor of the London *Free Press*, does not appear in the list though he was present at all sessions and wrote lengthy reports of the proceedings for his newspaper.

ascending in power and value. . . . We can be independent – we might prosper as an independent power, and less than a "heads or tails" may decide the issue of events. The cords that bind us to England are strong, but they can be severed, and what if Governor Head is teaching us to sharpen the scissors.[25]

The Reform convention of 1859, following closely upon the political scandal of 1858, assembled in a mood far from complacent. Rather, it was "a political avalanche of outraged virtue" which descended upon Toronto. The convening circular stated that its object would be to consider the whole aspect of public affairs and seek the best remedy for the evils complained of "unfettered by any restriction." Opportunity was to be afforded for the discussion of written constitutions,[26] dissolution of the union of the two provinces, a federal union of all the British North American provinces, a federal system for the united province of Canada alone "or any other plan calculated . . . to meet the existing evils."

Of the several alternatives to be presented to the convention, dissolution of the union was by far the most dangerous. Adoption of this idea would promptly have split the Reform party in two since the whole eastern section of the province was economically dependent upon Montreal. Moreover, it would leave the province cut off from a sea port and thereby produce a situation where it would tend at once to move down an inclined plane into close relations with the United States. The chief protagonist of dissolution was George Sheppard and chief support for this radical proposal came from the delegates representing the western section of the province. But even they were by no means unanimous. Hope Mackenzie, of Sarnia, expressed the opinion that dissolution was supported only by those holding "American ideas" and he predicted that dissolution would create a desire for annexation to the United States. This view also found

---

[25] London *Free Press*, August 10, 1858. In the same issue the *Free Press* remarked: "United States party politics have always been deemed the most tricky and contemptible. But the late proceedings under Governor Head eclipse Yankeedom hollow. The Detroit *Advertiser* evidently feels that we are taking the wind out of their sails in this particular. Alluding to the schemes of the governor-general it says: 'This looks sharp enough for Yankee politics.' "

[26] The London *Free Press*, during the weeks preceding the convention, busied itself with showing the weaknesses of written constitutions, citing examples of abuses from neighbouring states. "A mere system is but a poor substitute for morality," was one of its comments.

expression in the editorial columns of the London *Free Press*. To George Brown, however, must go the chief credit for heading off a proposal which would have been disastrous to the Reform party and probably also to the country. It was one of his great services to Canada. As a recent writer on this period has observed:

> *The stake was high – nothing less than half a continent, but if the union of the provinces was dissolved, if the Grit party turned its eyes inward to fight the battle of constitutional reform within the bounds of Upper Canada, everything might be lost. The unity of the party on some basis of co-operation with Lower Canada was the one essential of the moment to be preserved at all costs. To imagine that Brown saw nothing of this is to him an impossible injustice and indeed the whole record of these months makes it clear that this was his guiding principle.*[27]

Sheppard, as the chief advocate of dissolution, deserves some attention. An Englishman of radical views, he had migrated to America in 1850 where, after an unsuccessful colonizing venture in the West, he became associate editor of the *Daily Republican* at Washington. In 1857 he was in Toronto as editor of the *Daily Colonist* but soon transferred his energies to the *Globe*. To that newspaper, during the summer of 1859, he contributed a series of editorials enunciating policies which were more extreme than George Brown himself favoured. Sheppard was an ardent admirer of the political institutions of the United States and firmly convinced that the Grit party must commit itself whole-heartedly to the cause of constitutional reform even though that meant the damning of its prospects for office. Sheppard's influence, as exercised during the summer of 1859, was distinctly mischievous, as Brown was to find out during the Reform convention.

Brown and the more conservative element in the party favoured the idea of a federal system for Upper and Lower Canada by themselves, believing that a federation of all the provinces in British North America was a still somewhat remote possibility. Resolutions along this line were presented to the convention on the evening of the first day and precipitated a debate that lasted until eleven o'clock on the following evening. Of that debate it has been written:

[27] Brown, "Grit Party and the Great Reform Convention," p. 250.

. . . every phase of Grit thinking was elaborated at length. One cannot but be struck by the fact that the voice of the assembly was that of an agrarian democracy. There were present many town-dwellers, but the movement was essentially of the soil. Here we listen to the farmer of Canada West voicing his suspicions of merchants, bankers and politicians who fattened themselves at the expense of the honest toilers of the frontier. There was a sturdy belief in the essential virtue of a free and enfranchised citizenry. Government, it was felt, should be near at hand and always under the scrutinizing eye of the sovereign people: it should be simple, inexpensive, and entrusted with as few responsibilities and powers as possible.[28]

This was Jeffersonian democracy in earnest. Government was to rest in the hands of the producing class where intelligence and sanity chiefly dwelt, and democratic progress was to be attained by preserving and extending political and economic liberty. "A government vigorous, frugal and simple," Jefferson's formula in the election of 1800, was what the Clear Grits of 1859 hoped to see achieved. It was not easy to keep American political theory out of the discussions but any mention of annexation met with immediate disapproval while generous applause greeted all expressions of loyalty to the British connection. The Reform convention of 1859, like many Reform gatherings since, had to be on guard against statements that might be twisted by political opponents into some semblance of disloyalty.[29]

Sheppard's speech was the critical point in the convention. "I appear here as the advocate of the simple, unadulterated dissolution of the Union," was his introductory sentence, and as he pursued his way through the subject it was clear that he was the voice of a large section of the delegates present. His amendment favouring complete dissolution of the Union with Lower Canada meant a split in the party if it were accepted. This the leaders of the party knew full well. Reform ranks would be broken on almost straight geographical lines since the more easterly portion of the province, with its close ties to Montreal, was bound to reject a proposal that meant economic ruin.

In the end the Reform convention of 1859 did exactly what

[28] *Ibid.*, pp. 253-4.

[29] "One noticeable thing in the debates was that the idea of annexation to the United States, once very current in Upper Canada, seems to have few, if any, supporters" (New York *Tribune*, quoted in the London *Free Press*, November 21, 1859).

conventions of later days and of both parties have done in the face of a troublesome issue – it compromised on an amendment which offered a means of saving its face. And, as has so often happened since, the amendment which offered a way out was carried with "immense enthusiasm." What the convention approved after long hours of debate was a proposal that there should be two or more local governments to care for matters of local sectional character with "some joint authority" charged with the care of matters of common interest. The whole proceeding bore the stamp of practical party tactics. Words were uttered but none could define precisely what they meant – their value lay in their vagueness. Nevertheless, Brown's success in securing adoption of the rather meaningless amendment meant a victory over Sheppard and those who favoured dissolution. Their policy would have left the western wing of the party divorced from the central and eastern groups. Brown's success in carrying the convention forestalled the possibility of Upper Canada being separated from Lower Canada and forced into closer relations with the United States by being cut off from the sea. However vague might be the ideas of federation enunciated in 1859, there was embraced in them a principle which was to widen out during the next few years to take in not merely two but all the British provinces. Here may be seen the importance of the decisions arrived at in 1859. Upper Canada Reformers had clearly grown in their political thinking. The Reform convention of 1857 had seen only one feasible solution for its woes, representation by population. Two years had changed the point of view. This is clearly seen in the editorials which appeared in the *Globe* during the summer of 1858. Brown and his party were becoming more national in outlook and it was such an outlook that coloured his speech before the Reform delegates assembled in 1859. "I do hope," he said on that occasion, "that there is not one Canadian in this Assembly who does not look forward with high hope to the day when these northern colonies shall stand out among the nations of the world as one great confederation." He could scarcely dream as he uttered those words that within ten years this high hope would be realized and that in its accomplishment he would be one of the leading figures. The decisions arrived at by the Reform convention under the influence of his convincing arguments were a prelude to greater developments to come and determined the road along which these developments were to proceed.

16: The Organization of Labour

When the full story of self-government in America is written, review-ing the commonplace no less than the spectacular, pages on the cellular growth of local craft unions will be placed beside the record of town meetings; while chapters on the formation of national labour structures will complement the sections on the origin and develop-ment of the federal Constitution.

—CHARLES A. BEARD

Labour organization in Upper Canada began within the ranks of the printing trade. As early as 1833 there was a species of union in Toronto, its chief objects being to maintain wages and to limit the number of apprentices in any shop. From Toronto the union idea was carried to Hamilton where organi-zation was also effected in 1833. The Toronto workmen seem to have been in trouble with their employers in 1836, a notice in the *Patriot* stating: "The Journeymen Printers, having recon-sidered their decision to live idle, have wisely rescinded the same, and returned to their vocations, on condition of a general amnesty, which has been freely accorded by the employers and the hatchet is buried."[1] The Toronto printers' union disappeared during the troubles of 1837-8 but was reorganized in 1844, almost at once coming into conflict with Peter Brown, proprietor of the *Banner*, a Presbyterian publication, who had declared for an open shop. The Union presented its case in a printed docu-ment entitled *Plain Statement of Facts* and also communicated with the Buffalo Typographical Society, probably the first instance of international co-operation affecting Canada.

Both in Toronto and elsewhere throughout the province there were, no doubt, other trade organizations in existence at this time, though records of their activities are few. The London [U.C.] *Times* of January 3, 1846, reported a meeting of carpen-ters held at the British Coffee House "to take into consideration whether machinery would be a benefit or an injury to the Trade and Town generally." It was agreed that it would be a great injury and a resolution to that effect was unanimously carried. Efforts to correct abuses affecting the trades formed the chief activities of these early unions, the apprenticeship system and prison labour being given particular attention. Until the middle

[1] See St. Catharines *Journal*, December 8, 1836.

of the century, however, such labour organizations as appeared in Upper Canada were quite unconnected with any foreign body. They were purely local in character and consequently lacked strength. The change came in 1850 when the Amalgamated Society of Engineers, an English organization, established itself, first in Toronto, then at Hamilton, Stratford, and London. Ten years later the Amalgamated Society of Carpenters and Joiners, also of English origin, organized locals at Toronto, Hamilton, and London. After 1860 branches of various American labour organizations appeared in such trades as printing, iron moulding, cigarmaking, coopering, and among railroad workers. The spectacular rise during the sixties of the oil-refining industry in the western part of the province explains the appearance of the London branch of the International Journeymen Coopers, one of the most vigorous and progressive of the labour bodies. Canada was represented at the cigarmakers' national convention in Baltimore in 1860, and at the Buffalo convention a year later the name of the union was changed so as to embrace the Canadian locals.

The Order of the Knights of St. Crispin, founded in 1867 at Milwaukee as a protest against the introduction of shoe-making machinery, had seventeen locals in Canada by 1870 and in 1873 held a provincial session at Toronto. Locals were to be found at Toronto, Guelph, Hamilton, Windsor, Georgetown, and elsewhere, some of these being linked with state lodges; Georgetown, for example, being regarded as a unit of the Michigan district. In the United States the Crispins set up co-operative shoe-making shops and also co-operative stores but almost nothing of this kind appears to have been attempted in Canada.[2] Labour organizations in Canada lagged behind the United States. The factory system did not develop to any degree until after 1867 but when it did appear there were immediate signs of the diverging interests of employers and workmen. The movement for the nine-hour day was in full swing in Ontario by the spring of 1872, great demonstrations in its favour being held in Toronto, Hamilton, Guelph, St. Catharines, and other places. The *Ontario Workman*, an early Canadian labour paper, which began publication at Toronto in April, 1872, made the nine-hour day its chief interest, basing its arguments chiefly

[2] See H. A. Logan, *History of Trade Union Organization in Canada* (Chicago, 1928), p. 18. Also Herbert Harris, *American Labor* (New Haven, 1939), pp. 71-2.

upon the British movement in order to avoid the inevitable cry of "Yankeeism" but drawing attention also to the contemporary demand for an eight-hour day in the United States. "While in Canada the agitation for the nine-hour system is being vigorously prosecuted, across the line the movement for eight hours is being even more vigorously followed up," said the *Workman* in 1872.

Curiously, out of the agitation for the nine-hour day, labour in Canada made the most notable gain recorded to that time, though in another field. In March, 1872, there had been a printers' strike in Toronto and on the day following the nine-hour demonstrations mentioned above the Master Printers' Association, the employers, caused the arrest of the whole committee of the Typographical Union, twenty-four in all, on a charge of seditious conspiracy. Prominent in this high-handed action was the Hon. George Brown, proprietor of the *Globe*, who in his newspaper had vigorously attacked unionism as a breeder of discontent. As he was an outstanding figure in the Liberal party the affair at once assumed political significance and furnished excellent capital for the Conservative party under Sir John Macdonald. A bill introduced by Macdonald during the session of Parliament then under way, and based on recent British legislation, not only gave unions a legal basis of existence but also recognized their right to strike. The enactment of this legislation knocked the props from under the charges laid against the leaders of the Toronto strikers and in June a nine-hour day for Toronto printers was adopted.[3] Though acceptance of the nine-hour day in other trades was far from general, and was sometimes vigorously combated by employers, the agitation concerning it increased the solidarity in labour ranks and was a contributory factor in the establishment in 1873 of the Canadian Labour Union. This body proposed to hold annual congresses to which any trade union might send delegates, but only two such meetings were ever held, that at Ottawa in 1874 at which sixteen delegates were present and that at St. Catharines in 1875 with yet fewer in attendance, after which the organization ceased to function.

While new local unions continued to appear during the 1880's the striking feature of that decade was the entry and

---

[3] In September, 1872, the International Typographical Union held its twenty-third annual session in Montreal, an occasion which was marked by gratification over the gains which labour had made in that year.

rapid growth of the Knights of Labor, in many respects the most interesting labour organization in American history. The first local assembly of the Knights of Labor in Canada was established at Hamilton in 1881 and from that city the Order spread rapidly throughout the province. The General Assembly for the United States and Canada held its ninth session at Hamilton in 1885, Master Workman Terence V. Powderley being in the chair. At that time there were locals in Hamilton, organized as a District Assembly, and having a membership of 362. In all forty-four Canadian locals were reported, two in British Columbia, three in Quebec, one in Manitoba, and thirty-eight in Ontario, the majority of these being in the western section of the province. At the General Assembly of 1887 it was reported that the 174 Canadian locals had a membership of 12,553. At this meeting a resolution was presented asking that a legislative committee be appointed, representing the several provinces, with authority to send a delegate to Ottawa during each session of the Canadian Parliament to watch legislation. The resolution was approved and Master Workman Powderley was instructed to name the committee.[4]

The Haymarket Riot at Chicago in May, 1886, was disastrous to the Knights of Labor in the United States. Reactionary interests at once connected the Knights with the outrage and in the following two years tens of thousands deserted its ranks. The repercussion was almost as sharp in Canada as in the United States, the tone of the press in the two countries being almost indistinguishable. The Toronto *Daily Mail* of May 5 had carried a lengthy account of the Haymarket affair under a heading: "Labour war. The workingmen's battle for an eight-hour day" but three days later it swung far to the right and found in the affair "Satanic doctrines," creeds of "No God, no master," and a power aiming at "the destruction of church, state and capital." The *Globe* was more conservative in its comments upon the affair and had a good word for Master Workman Powderley of the Knights of Labor, who, it said, "with his peaceful urgency, his quiet systematic organization, and his continued appeals to the highest instincts of his fellow-workmen and to the enlightened self-interest and love of fair play on the part of employers, is showing himself to be the true friend of labour and of

[4] General Assembly of the Knights of Labor of America, *Proceedings of the Eleventh Regular Session*, 1887, pp. 1819-20.

humanity as well."[5] The trial of the Chicago anarchists was fully reported in the Canadian press. On the day following the executions the *Mail* devoted nine columns to details of the affair with additional lengthy editorial comment. The *Globe* printed four columns on the execution with pictures of seven of the condemned men. The *Mail* in its comment said: "It was absolutely necessary that the movement should receive a vigorous check, and that an example should be made of some of the wavers of the red flag of revolution, rapine and murder. This has been done, and at the same time justice has had her due."[6]

Decline in the membership of the Knights in Canada was less marked than in the United States so that even at the turn of the century, when the Order had sunk to comparative obscurity in the Republic, new locals were still being formed in Canada. The American Federation of Labor was not yet an aggressive force in the Canadian labour field and the nature of Canadian economic life in this period made it easier in many places to form local assemblies of the Knights of Labor than to organize craft unions. Canada continued to be represented at the annual sessions of the General Assembly and at the meeting of 1900, held at Birmingham, Alabama, the long hours of Canadian postal clerks and letter carriers received attention, a resolution of protest being sent to the Canadian government.[7] Canadian delegates were present at the Indianapolis meeting in 1901 when A. B. McGillivray of Glace Bay was elected to the office of General Worthy Foreman. On several previous occasions Canadians had been elected as members of the Executive Board of the Order.

During the 1880's the Knights in Canada exercised some influence in politics, particularly during the federal election of 1887 when both major parties courted the labour vote.[8] It was not without significance that the interest of the federal political parties in labour matters coincided in point of time with the outburst of industrial conflicts in the United States commonly known as the "Great Upheaval." The prosperity which had

---

[5] The *Globe*, May 6, 1886.

[6] The *Mail*, November 12, 1887.

[7] *Report of the Proceedings of the Regular Session of the General Assembly at Birmingham, Alabama*, 1900, p. 56.

[8] Sir John Macdonald had a series of speeches on labour questions prepared by a Toronto newspaper man for use during the election campaigning of 1887. His speech to the Workingmen's Liberal-Conservative Association of Ottawa and Le Cercle Lafontaine on October 8, 1886, was printed and used as a campaign document in 1887.

followed the return of the Liberal-Conservatives to power in 1878, chiefly due to the pump-priming effects of extensive railroad construction, had pretty well evaporated by 1885 and such matters as unemployment, long hours, low wages, and delayed factory legislation were live issues when the election of 1887 came on.[9] There were two labour candidates in the city of Toronto in 1887 but neither was successful. To the surprise of its Liberal opponents, probably even to its own surprise, the Conservative administration was returned to power with a majority of more than thirty seats. Having successfully weathered the gale, it quickly lost interest in labour matters. When Friedrich Engels visited Canada in 1888 he recorded that at first he thought he was back in Europe but later felt that he had entered a decaying and retrogressive country which would one day be ripe for annexation by the United States.[10]

The disappearance of the Knights of Labor in Canada was inevitable with the decline of the Order in the United States, though the process in Canada was gradual. In the very year in which the first local was established at Hamilton the seeds of disintegration had been sown in the United States by the organization of "The Federation of Organized Trades and Labor Unions of the United States and Canada." While the activities of the Knights in Canada had given a definite American tinge to labour organization, there was always a feeling that Canadian labour organization should be national, a sentiment which had been shown in the formation of the Canadian Labour Union in 1873. Short-lived though it was, this organization had the germ idea which was revived in 1886 when 109 delegates met in Toronto and effected a permanent organization under the name of the Trades and Labour Congress of Canada. With the exception of one delegate representing a Knights of Labor assembly in Quebec City, the gathering was made up entirely of Ontario representatives.

In its earlier days the Congress sought to harmonize the trades unions and the Knights of Labor, regarding them as complementary. Neither group was able to dominate the conventions during the 1880's and the Knights displayed considerable strength as late as 1894 when at the Ottawa Convention

---

[9] Factory legislation had been announced in both the parliamentary sessions of 1883 and 1884 but had not been proceeded with.

[10] Gustav Mayer, *Friedrich Engels, a Biography* (New York, 1936), pp. 294-5.

they had twenty-six delegates present, only one less than the unions. Within a few years, however, it became evident that the situation would have to be clarified and a more logical definition given of Canadian labour's relation to organized American labour. At the convention of 1901 the presiding officer suggested that a federation of American unions, represented by a national union, and a federation of Canadian unions, represented by a national union, each working with the other in special cases, would be a great advantage over having local unions in Canada connected with the national unions of the United States. He thought also that the presentation of Canadian matters by Canadian leaders, and *vice versa*, by American leaders, would lead to greater success and would not in any way prevent a federation of the national bodies.

It was becoming increasingly evident that in a contest of strength the Canadian body was no match for the American Federation of Labor. Indeed, at this time the first Vice-President of the Congress was the chief organizer in Canada for the American Federation and under him were other fully paid organizers actively at work.[11] At the 1902 meeting warning was given by one of the officers that unless something were soon done the organization would become entirely American. The climax came at the Berlin (Kitchener) meeting in 1902 when the constitution was so amended that all assemblies of the Knights of Labor and all central labour unions were excluded, as were all national unions organized where international unions also existed. The Congress thus became definitely allied to, and dependent upon, international unionism. An immediate result was the organization at Berlin in September, 1902, of the Canadian Federation of Labour. Though professing at first merely a desire to retain national autonomy, the new body soon took an attitude of hostility to the American Federation and stressed patriotism as the basis for its own existence.

During the period 1886-1900 the Trades and Labour Congress presented a programme of reforms affecting the welfare of labour, chiefly similar in character to those which were advocated in the United States. Government ownership was strongly advocated in 1890 in a resolution which called for the taking over by the Dominion of railways, telegraphs, and telephones, an echo probably of agrarian programmes in the United States. Labour Day, authorized as a national holiday by the United

[11] See Logan, *History of Trade Union Organization in Canada* pp. 75-6.

States Congress in 1894, was in the same year declared a Canadian national holiday by Parliament. The almost immediate adoption of this American idea was the result of a vigorous lobby carried on at Ottawa by Alexander W. Wright, a former Ontario newspaper man who had been editor of the *Journal* of the Knights of Labor and who returned to Canada to agitate for this recognition of labour's place in national life. Logan attributes to Knights of Labor influence a recommendation of the Executive Committee of the Congress in 1895 declaring the monetary system to blame for the industrial depression then existing, and calling for the issue of all money by the government, the banks to be limited to the deposit function. The Congress approved this suggestion. At the same meeting approval was given to the principle of the single tax as set forth by Henry George.

17: Farms and Farmers

That slovenly cultivation is generally apparent in Upper Canada as well as in all the British colonies cannot be denied; neither do the early settlers willingly relinquish old and rude modes of husbandry. In new countries, however, time and example are sure to accomplish improvements.

—JOHN M'GREGOR (1828)

The production of wheat has, for a long time, been the principal aim of the farmers in Ontario. But I was told by some of the most intelligent among them that the time was now come when it would be more profitable to produce beef, butter, cheese, mutton and pork than to depend so much on wheat.

—GEORGE EASTON (1869)

Agriculture in Upper Canada during the first half-century after 1791 followed with but little deviation the pattern set by the older states of the neighbouring Republic, making no improvement in the inefficient and primitive husbandry. The system borrowed has been described as based "largely on the knowledge and practices of English farmers of the early seventeenth century, but in many ways much less advanced than the agriculture of the motherland even at that early date."[1] There was little disposition shown either in the United States or in Upper Canada to adopt the new ideas and processes which had been introduced into English agriculture, and a routine of continuous cropping of the same grains, with neglect of fertilizers, inevitably threatened sterilization of the land. As late as 1833 Timothy Flint remarked of the American West: "The people are not given to experiment; [they] continue to farm in the beaten way. Agricultural improvement proceeds at a slow pace." Similar comment was made with respect to Upper Canada during the thirties, though in the province, as also in any state, there was bound to be wide variations in the efficiency of farming operations.

Some of the defects in the agriculture of the province during the thirties may be attributed to the presence of a class of settlers who were merely land-clearers, waiting only for a purchaser for their acres before moving on to another location. A farmer living near Elora wrote in 1835 of the land-clearing type: "Of

[1] L. B. Schmidt and E. D. Ross, *Readings in the Economic History of American Agriculture* (New York, 1925), p. 173.

improving their farms and increasing their produce and stock, in the way of regular industry and careful experiment, they have no idea. They only like to clear land, and at this they work very hard. When the land is cleared, they throw in the seed in seed-time, and reap in the harvest; and this is the extent of their farming."[2] A more favourable view, however, was expressed by A. J. Christie, writing at an earlier date. He regarded the American farmer, with all his disposition to sell out and move on, as having a definite place in the economy of the country. Contrasting this type with the British emigrant, Christie wrote:

How soon a farmer from the old country gets his farm cleared and under a proper state of cultivation, he sits down quietly for the remainder of his life, to enjoy the fruits of his labour. With him, his farm constitutes his fortune, on which he lives; with the United States farmer on the contrary, his farm is an article of merchandise, which he will sell to the best advantage and with the money he gets lay in a new stock of the same kind of goods as quick as possible. It is scarcely necessary to add that the latter forms a character of great utility in a country such as this is; and it cannot be denied that Canadian agriculture has reaped very important benefits from the labours of such men.[3]

Settlers coming from overseas were impressed by the energy of the American farmers. "When Yankees work, they do so very hard," said one observer in 1838, "they rise at four in the morning, milk the cows (this the men do here, which you will think queer), and in summer they do not end their labour till darkness compels them. The quantity of wheat they cut down in a day is astonishing, and we require considerable practice with their scythe (which is a grand tool) before we can match them; but on the dunghill (which they pay little attention to), at the flail, or the plough, we can beat the best of them."[4] The energy and enterprise of the American emigrant farmer in Canada were also noted by Sir James Alexander. His contact with this class was probably not extensive but he gives this description of the

[2] *Counsel for Emigrants, and Interesting Information from Numerous Sources Concerning British America, the United States, and New South Wales,* &c, &c. 3rd ed. (Aberdeen, 1838), pp. 99-100.
[3] A. J. Christie, *The Emigrant's Assistant: or Remarks on the Agricultural Interest of the Canadas . . . with an Appendix* (Montreal, 1821), pp. 18-20.
[4] *Counsel for Emigrants,* p. 144.

American method of clearing wooded land and beginning farming operations:

> *When an American comes over to Canada to take out a location-ticket, he immediately sets to work, in the fall of the year, and slashes [fells] and burns the wood on perhaps eight acres of land; then, walking through his new field among the stumps, with a bag of Indian corn seed about his neck, and his axe in his hand, he makes a hole in the ground with it, and dropping two or three seeds into it, he closes the hole with his foot, and he thus disposes of his whole seed. He then, perhaps, returns to the States, or hires himself out to work till the time of harvest comes around, when he returns to his field and reaps it. He may now think of building a log-house: he prepares the timber, the neighbours collect in "a bee," and assist him to erect his dwelling; he roofs and floors it with bark, the doors and windows are cut out, the hinges are of wood, as are sometimes the locks, the light is admitted through oiled paper, the table is a rough board, and the stools cuts of round logs. He brings his wife and a barrel or two of pork; more land is cleared; pigs, poultry and cattle are seen to increase; the log hut is converted into a stable, and a frame house is substituted.[5]*

The growth in the population of Upper Canada during the thirties was reflected in an increased acreage under culture and in the larger number of horses and cattle.[6] During the forties signs of the coming of a more scientific agriculture could be noted. Attention was being given to drainage, fertilizers, the breeding of stock, and the improvement of grains and vegetables. Canadian farm journals made their appearance at this time, though American farm journals had been circulating in the province for some time and still continued to circulate extensively. Agricultural societies were also active, and new types of farm machinery were being introduced. Good times, during the middle of the decade, gave encouragement to better farming but the depression in agriculture at the end of the period was severe.

The fifties saw expansion in both agricultural and industrial

[5] J. E. Alexander, *Transatlantic Sketches or Visits to the Most Interesting Scenes in N. and S. America and West Indies, with Notes on Slavery and Canadian Emigration* (London, 1833), II, 220-1.

[6] Cultivated acreage, which was 818,416 in 1831, rose to 1,713,163 by 1840 and the occupied but uncultivated acreage increased from 3,569,361 to 5,298,573.

lines. It was the era of railroad building in Upper Canada and the stimulus given to general business activity was shared by the farmers. The chief feature of Upper Canada's agriculture at this time was the rapid expansion of the wheat acreage, due to the prevailing high prices, the stimulus of railroad-building, and the additional demands for foodstuffs arising out of the Crimean War. Though the acreage was greatly increased in this period, the average yield fell because of the ravages of the wheat midge, the loss from this cause in 1857 being estimated at $8,000,000. The financial crisis of 1857 also caused distress by the sharp fall in the price of wheat in the English market and at the end of the decade the agricultural population was again experiencing sharp depression.

James Caird's writings, extolling the advantages of the Illinois prairies, exerted some influence upon emigration from the province in the early sixties. The *Lower Canada Agriculturist* spoke in 1862 of Canadians farmers being "seduced" by the glowing description drawn by Caird of prairie farming and of their disappointment with actual conditions. This journal said also that agents of the Illinois Central Railway had flooded the recent provincial exhibition at Kingston with their books and pamphlets, seeking to draw people to the lands owned by the railroad. The depression with which the decade of the fifties had closed led many Upper Canadians to give thought to the American West, but the decade of the sixties was scarcely more than entered upon before a situation arose which was to have profound influence upon Canadian agriculture and, indeed, upon Canadian nationhood.

At the opening of the Civil War Upper Canadian farmers might reasonably have expected increased demand and a profitable price for their wheat. "In the present condition of the world," said the *Canadian Agriculturist*, "we see no prospect of prices ruling low, and there is every motive for our Canadian farmers to get in as large a breadth of wheat as possible the coming autumn, with a reasonable prospect of remunerative returns."[7] In this expectation, however, the farmers of Upper Canada were grievously disappointed. The United States was able both to meet its own extraordinary wartime needs and to supply the deficiencies of European harvests, paying for munitions in England with wheat instead of cotton. In the war years, during which the loyal states and territories greatly increased their wheat production, Upper Canada found itself with crops below average and with prices prevailing during 1862, 1863, and 1864 that were less than those between 1858 and 1861. Only by the sale of other products were Canadian farmers able to profit materially in the Civil War years. Horses were much in demand and cattle exports also increased sharply, reaching a peak in 1865 in anticipation of the approaching termination of the Reciprocity Treaty. Wool was another export that expanded with the war demands, the need of this commodity for army clothing being so great that all available supplies were quickly bought up.

Despite the ready market for various other products the farmers of Upper Canada were startled by the failure of their wheat market, and through the press and agricultural journals and in the agricultural societies there was widespread discussion of the situation. Was the province moving in the same direction as Lower Canada, where wheat production now scarcely met local needs? Today we can see that Upper Canada was repeating the experience of neighbouring New York State where wheat production, formerly the chief occupation of the farmers, had since the early thirties been giving way to dairying, livestock, and the production of grains such as corn, oats, barley, and rye which could be used to feed livestock for the larger markets. Factors entering into this change in eastern New York were soil depletion, rust, insect pests, and the competition of the western section of the state whose grain could be sent eastward via the Erie Canal. By the forties and early fifties the same factors which had produced changes in the eastern section of the state were operating in the western counties. Soil was losing its strength, the wheat midge had by 1840 reached every western county, rust had appeared, and the Hessian fly had become a scourge in all parts of the state. Moreover, western New York, which had supplanted eastern New York in wheat growing, now found itself threatened by the competition of the more distant West whose products also went eastward by the Erie Canal. New York State's agricultural changes during the forties and fifties were to be repeated in Upper Canada during the sixties.

The farmers were becoming thoroughly awakened to their situation by 1864. In the reports of the agricultural societies for that year and the immediately succeeding years the warning note appears frequently. At the annual meeting of the Provincial Agricultural Association in 1864 President E. W. Thomson said:

"The most valuable crop produced in Upper Canada, as shown by the census returns, is undoubtedly wheat. Although it is likely to continue a staple production in Upper Canada, it is doubtful whether we have not sacrificed too much and are not sacrificing too much in its production. It is asserted by competent judges that in the State of New York much of the land which formerly yielded good crops of wheat has by over-cropping been rendered incapable of producing it any longer. And this is the inevitable result to which the same vicious system, if practiced in Canada, would lead." President J. C. Rykert mentioned the subject a year later in his annual address. "We no longer find the main dependence of the cultivation of the soil to be the wheat crop," he said. "The question has been seriously asked whether it would not be advantageous to abandon its cultivation for a limited period, with a view to extirpate that much dreaded enemy, the midge." Rykert mentioned also in his address the growth of the cheese industry and the larger production of flax as substitutes for wheat farming.

The annual reports of the district agricultural societies during these years reveal the changes that were taking place, affecting the character of future farming operations. Of these changes, none was of such far-reaching importance as the turn to dairying and especially the introduction from New York State of the factory system of cheese production. Oxford County was the first in Canada to adopt this system, a fact which is recorded on a bronze tablet erected in Ingersoll by the Historic Sites and Monuments Board of Canada. Oxford, in the early 1860's, was experiencing crop failures, insect pests, and depletion of soil fertility. Its salvation came through the introduction and spread of the co-operative cheese factory idea. It was inevitable that this system, so successful in New York State, should eventually be adopted in Canada, but Oxford County was specially favoured in that a highly experienced American cheese-maker, Harvey Farrington, came to the county in 1864 and by his advice and counsel placed the industry on a sound basis. His enthusiasm was contagious and in the county which became his adopted home his name remains honoured and revered. From Oxford the factory system spread far and wide.

The change from wheat-growing to dairying was not effected overnight. It was aided by the efforts of bankers and businessmen who associated themselves with the farmers to spread the gospel of dairy farming. An outstanding dairying authority, Professor Arnold, of Utica, was brought to Oxford County to give a course of lectures. These lectures – three each day for a solid week – were given to farmer audiences that crowded the Ingersoll town hall. The marketing problem was next tackled and arrangements made for co-operative marketing under the brand name "Ingersoll District Cheese." By 1867 the importance of the industry was such that the Canadian Dairymen's Association was organized at a meeting in Ingersoll, its birth coinciding with the creation of the new Dominion.

No other change in agriculture was quite so spectacular in results as the new methods in the cheese-making industry. In the Niagara District, however, where the wheat crop of 1863 was ruined by insect pests, it was reported in the following year that the farmers were turning more and more to the growing of fruit for which the area had long been famous. The traveller Goldie described the cherry trees planted by the roadside when he was there in 1819. G. W. Warr, who visited the district in the early forties, spoke of Niagara where there were "whole orchards of peach trees bearing the most tempting descriptions of that excellent fruit." He noticed also that the settlers made vast quantities of preserves and had it on the table at every meal. This was the beginning of the future canning industry.[8] The Vine Growers' Association, chiefly made up of farmers in the Niagara District, received a charter from the provincial Legislature in 1866.

From the early thirties on, occasional mention appears of a crop which, in recent years, has become one of the great staples of Western Ontario – tobacco. Its introduction in the southwestern section of the province, principally along the Detroit River, has been attributed to the early French settlers from Quebec, but with the arrival of runaway slaves, some of whom had been employed on southern tobacco plantations, methods of production were improved. The *Canadian Emigrant* (Sandwich) pointed out in 1832 that for some years past tobacco was the only crop that had not been ravaged by the Hessian fly. Production increased in succeeding years as larger numbers of Negroes entered the province and Henry Bibb, at Windsor, was able to write in 1851: "We have good crops of tobacco raised here every year for market; and sweet potatoes, a root which

[8] G. W. Warr, *Canada as It Is; or, the Emigrant's Friend and Guide to Upper Canada* (London, 1847), pp. 49-50.

requires a warm climate, grow and do well in the southern part of Canada West."[9]

One important influence of the Civil War upon Upper Canada's farming operations was the speeding up of the use of agricultural implements. This was due in some degree to a shortage of labour. The Commissioner of Agriculture for the province, in his annual report for 1868, had this to say:

> It is an encouraging fact that during the last year in particular, mowers and reapers and labour-saving implements have not only increased in the older districts, but have found their way into new ones, and into places where they were before practically unknown. This beneficial result has, no doubt, mainly arisen from the difficulty, or rather, in some cases, impossibility of getting labour at any price; but in consequence of the operations of agricultural societies, and the information so widely and cheaply diffused by the press, there is an increasing desire felt by farmers to avail themselves of the valuable aid of the mechanic, whose skill and enterprise will be found adequate to meet any increased demand of this nature that may arise.

The introduction in Upper Canada of new machines or of improvements to older ones was usually later than in neighbouring New York, due to the delayed state of land-clearing. Not until the stumps and larger stones had been removed was it possible to use many of the machines available. When these did come into use they were usually the product of factories in Rochester, Buffalo, and Albany.[10] Oshawa, lying directly across the lake from Rochester, was one of the first towns in the province in which a branch of an American firm was located. The earlier ploughs made in Upper Canada held to old country models but harrows, rollers, scarifiers, and cultivators were invariably of the American type. This was true also of seed drills which were in common use in the United States by the middle of the century. The farmers of the province were slow to adopt the new harvesting machinery which was widely used in the United States by the 1850's. Both Hussey and McCormick reapers were imported but one of the judges at the Provincial

---

[9] *Voice of the Fugitive* (Windsor), March 12, 1851. Bibb was himself a Negro refugee from the South.

[10] See unpublished thesis by Charles C. Toon, "Some Aspects of the History of Agriculture in Canada West and Ontario between 1850 and 1870" (University of Western Ontario, 1938).

Exhibition in 1851 said after trying both reapers he had gone back to cradling. At late as 1853 George Buckland, editor of the *Canadian Agriculturist*, remarked that reapers were not at all popular with the farmers. American implements were sometimes copied by Canadian blacksmiths and small iron-working establishments and Canadian firms also acted as agents for American makers. In 1852, a Port Hope firm, John Helm & Son, were producing "Hussey's American Champion Reaper" and also acting as agents for "Ketchum's Mowing Machine." The introduction of farm machinery in Upper Canada owes much, however, to the establishment of warehouses, and later of factories, under the guiding and stimulating influence of New York State manufacturers.[11] To enumerate the New York firms which had connections with the implement industry in the province would be tedious. Around 1850 John Rapalje, of Rochester, established a branch factory and warehouse at Port Hope. At the Provincial Exhibition of 1851 the implements handled by this branch took all the important prizes in the foreign implement section and repeated this success for several years, as well as taking prizes in the domestic branch. Joseph Hall, of Rochester, established a branch of his business in Oshawa in 1851 which was for many years one of the leading firms of the province. Its advertisements in the *Canada Farmer* during 1864 listed five different reapers and mowers, as well as other machinery in wide variety.

Farmers in Canada had, from early days, shown a disposition to organize for common effort. The "bee," at which the community gathered for the raising of a barn or the harvesting of a crop, was an early manifestation of this spirit. Later came agricultural societies and farmers' clubs of various kinds, the latter having no definite model for their organization but much alike in their aims and procedure. They furnished the background into which American agrarian organizations such as the Grange fitted with ease when they crossed the international border.[12] The Patrons of Husbandry entered Canada in 1872, the torchbearer of the movement being Eben Thompson, a Vermont youth who had just graduated from Dartmouth College. Although the Grange had grown up chiefly in the middle

[11] *Ibid.*, p. 158.

[12] See L. A. Wood, *A History of the Farmers' Movements in Canada* (Toronto, 1924), for an account of the introduction of the Patrons of Husbandry in Canada.

West and might have been expected to enter Canada from that quarter, it actually entered the provinces by way of New England. In Ontario the first "grange" was established at L'Orignal on the Ottawa River early in 1874, Eben Thompson again being the active agent. It was the western section of the province, however, which was to prove the most fruitful soil for the American movement. Thompson came to London in February, 1874, to find the ground well prepared by the good offices of William Weld, who in his journal, the *Farmer's Advocate*, had taken note of the recent establishment of granges in Quebec and had urged that they should be given a trial in Ontario. Through Weld's help, arrangements were made for a meeting to be held in the Township of Westminster, immediately south of London, and there on February 27, 1874, Advance Grange, the first in the western section of the province, was founded. A second grange was established in Yarmouth Township, Elgin County, during the next month. Thompson then went to Grey County where he instituted three granges in less than a week. It was evident that Ontario farmers were interested, though as usual there were some who feared the movement. Party politicians were probably responsible for rumours that the movement was annexationist in sentiment. This was indignantly denied by Weld and by others who were interested in the possibilities for good which they believed lay in the Order.

The rapid increase in the number of Canadian granges brought to the front the question of their future government, particularly the question whether they were to continue as a part of the American Order or were to be autonomous. Weld, while offering no criticism of international connections, thought the Grange in Canada should maintain its own identity, particularly in all financial matters. Action was taken at a meeting held in London on June 2, 1874, when a resolution was passed declaring that the time had arrived for the organization of a Dominion Grange and that those present should consider themselves the Dominion Grange. It was also resolved that a general meeting of representatives of all locals in Canada should be held in Toronto in September. The declaration of principles which was adopted was chiefly composed of sections of the declaration of purposes of the National Grange as accepted at the St. Louis meeting in February, 1874. The action taken at the London meeting was somewhat revolutionary since the delegates in attendance, twenty-five in all, were entirely from the western section of the province. There appears to have been no objection shown, however, when the first annual meeting was convened in Toronto with seventy-three delegates present, including a small representation from Quebec. The action taken by the Canadian granges in cutting loose from the parent organization was severely criticized at the next meeting of the National Grange held at Charleston, South Carolina, but within a year the defection was accepted. From mere acceptance of the Canadian position, the National Grange soon took a more friendly attitude and before long fraternal delegates were appearing at the annual meetings in each country.

The Grange in Canada followed the example of the parent organization in the United States by engaging in a variety of economic activities, but while the midwest American granges viewed the railroads as Public Enemy No. 1, it was the middleman who occupied that position in Canada. It was an era when the farm was personally visited by salesmen for sewing machines, agricultural implements, fruit trees, and other goods and the farmer had the idea that the agent's commission on sales ran anywhere from 25 to 100 per cent of the selling price. Complaint was also made that the country storekeeper set his prices too high, but the latter had always the defence argument that since credit was customarily extended to farmers for a year or longer he had to have some compensation for such methods of doing business. When co-operative methods of buying were inaugurated, country storekeepers countered by offering lower prices to those who would pay cash. In one county a company was formed which not only bought goods for its constituent members but also engaged in marketing activities. A store was opened in Toronto and for several years favourable reports were presented annually, but eventually it was wound up. From time to time it was proposed that the Grange should engage in production of some of the chief farm necessities but apart from the formation of a salt company, which was fought bitterly by its competitors, nothing was accomplished. An experiment in the field of fire insurance was likewise unsuccessful. The Grange even entered the banking field, the Grange Trust, Limited, being incorporated in Ontario in 1879. It did a small business for a few years but was wound up in 1887 without loss to anyone.

Following the American example, the Grange in Canada manifested much interest in legislation and was able to achieve some definite gains. There was this difference, however, that whereas in the United States the Order entered actively into politics, in Canada the Grange confined itself to criticism and suggestion. It is true that members of the Order were sometimes candidates for public office but they did so not as representatives of the Grange but as individuals. From time to time representations were made to the federal government on the subject of the tariff but it was in the provincial field that influence could more effectively be brought to bear and the Grange deserves the credit for securing in Ontario the passing of the Noxious Weed Act, legislation with respect to loans for tile drainage, and the abolition of the market fees imposed by municipalities.

More spectacular in its activities than the Grange was the organization known as the Patrons of Industry which entered Western Ontario in 1889, just two years after its beginning in the neighbouring state of Michigan.[18] The founders of the Michigan organization were all residents of Port Huron, directly opposite Sarnia, so that their programme became quickly known in neighbouring counties of Ontario. In the summer of 1889 the first primary lodge in Canada was organized at Mandaumin, a small village eight miles east of Sarnia. Other lodges were quickly added in the counties of Lambton, Kent, and Middlesex, and in May the Canadian lodges received papers of incorporation from the provincial government.

Soon a situation arose paralleling that of the Grange at an earlier date, namely the question whether Ontario lodges formed a part of the American organization or were autonomous. To settle this question a convention met at Sarnia in February, 1891, where, with eighteen counties represented, a resolution was passed declaring for independent existence. Those present at Sarnia proceeded at once to form a Grand Association of the Patrons of Industry of Ontario. The American organization at first objected but soon realized that nothing could be done about it. The organization of the Ontario Association coincided with the federal election of 1891 and two Patron candidates promptly appeared in the field. In Bothwell, Alexander McLartey came last in a three-cornered contest, though leading his competitors in twelve rural subdivisions, while in North Middlesex W. E.

---

[18] See Sidney Glazier, "Patrons of Industry in Michigan," *Mississippi Valley Historical Review*, XXIV (September, 1937), 185-94. Also Wood, *History of Farmers' Movements*, chap. X.

Taylor, a Liberal but endorsed by the Patrons, was defeated by but six votes.[14]

A platform which had been hastily prepared for the use of McLartey's supporters in Bothwell was now sent out to more than three hundred lodges in the province for criticism and suggestion. The replies, when examined and consolidated, were presented at a special meeting of the Grand Association held at London in September, 1891, and adopted with little change as the general platform of the body. When the Grand Association held its annual meeting in Toronto in February, 1892, it was evident that the movement was sweeping the rural sections of the province. Delegates were present from no less than thirty county associations and the paid-up membership was reported to be thirty thousand. The peak was reached in 1894 with a membership variously estimated from fifty thousand upwards. In this peak year the Patrons gained their most spectacular victory when they elected seventeen members to the provincial Legislature, ten of these being from the western counties, seven from elsewhere in the province. The Patrons had hoped to hold the balance of power in the newly-elected Legislature but in this they were disappointed. Nor were they at all influential in the actual business of the Assembly. When another provincial election came in 1898 one single Patron candidate was elected. By the turn of the century little was left of the organization.

The Patrons, like the Grange, embarked upon various economic ventures but with no better success. They were sufficiently numerous, however, to influence legislation coming before the Assembly, but on many public questions, temperance for example, they seemed unable to show a united front. Considerable interest was displayed in the single tax when Henry George visited Canada in 1895, though no public stand was taken by the Order. In 1893 there seemed to be a possibility that the Patrons would join with labour, as had been done in the Populist convention at Omaha of 1892. At a conference in Toronto in March, 1893, representatives were present from the Patrons of Industry, the Dominion Grange, the Trades and Labour Congress of Canada, the Toronto Trades and Labour Council, and the District Assembly of the Knights of Labor. While some interest was shown in the idea of the farmer and the trade unionist uniting forces in politics, nothing came of it, one reason being that the Grange members could not, by their

14 Wood, *History of Farmers' Movements*, p. 113.

constitution, take part in political activities. It is of interest to note that both the Patrons of Husbandry and the Patrons of Industry, each of them an importation from the United States, received support chiefly from the farmers in the western counties, the section lying between the Niagara and Detroit rivers which from the very beginnings of the province had been most susceptible to American influences.

At the same time that the Patrons were seeking political power another importation from the United States appeared on the Ontario scene which while not agrarian in character affected the fortunes of the Patrons since the two were sometimes confused. The American Protective Association, an organization hostile to the Roman Catholic Church, was organized in Ontario under the name of the Protestant Protective Association and in the provincial election of 1890 attacked the Mowat government. As many farmers were members of both organizations, the officers of the Patrons of Industry found it necessary to issue a denial of any alliance between the two, though they made it clear that they were not denouncing the activities of the P.P.A. In the provincial election of 1894 no less than seven P.P.A. candidates announced themselves as having Patron support. Based as it was on secrecy and prejudice, the P.P.A. did not last long in the province.[15]

One other phase of Ontario agriculture deserves mention because of the conspicuous influence of the United States. In the 1840's Professor George Buckland, of Kent, England, came to the province as Professor of Agriculture in the provincial university. His influence was most beneficial and among the improvements which he advocated was the establishment of a school of agriculture and an experimental farm. He was not able to secure these aids to agriculture but the seed which he had sown bore fruit later. When the agricultural changes of the sixties began to be publicly discussed, the Hon. John Carling, Commissioner of Agriculture for the province, sent the Rev. W. F. Clarke, former editor of the *Canada Farmer*, to the United States to inquire into agricultural education. His report was so favourable with respect to the educational developments in the United States that it was decided to establish an institution for agricultural instruction in Ontario. The Ontario School of

[15] See Toronto *Week*, February 2, 1894. An article in the Toronto *Mail* of November 24, 1893, set forth the principles, membership and position of the P.P.A. at that time.

Agriculture was opened at Guelph in May, 1874, with an enrolment of thirty or more students and later developed into the Ontario Agricultural College, one of the great institutions of its kind on the continent.

18: Neighbours and Friends

Sir, these countries touch each other for thousands of miles; we have many interlacing, many common, and some conflicting interests; spite of all obstructions we mingle and exchange largely still; and, besides we come of the same stock and speak the same tongue. In every respect we are too close to each other to be indifferent; we must be friends or enemies; and it is the highest interest of Canada and the empire that we should be good friends.

—EDWARD BLAKE (Speech at Toronto, 1897)

When Benjamin Lundy, pioneer American abolitionist, travelled through Upper Canada from Queenston to Detroit in January, 1832, his experiences were not unlike those of an American tourist making the same journey today. There were customs officers at Niagara, keepers of inns and dispensers of food along the way, contacts with fellow-travellers and with residents of the province, exchange of experiences and ideas, some impressions taken away and some memories left behind. From Lundy's day to the present the roads crossing Western Ontario have provided a short cut between East and West. Every day hundreds of American citizens are traversing the peninsula in automobiles, buses, or by steam railroad lines. In dining cars and at wayside lunch-rooms, in coaches and smoking compartments, at hotels and tourist homes, these travellers exchange news and views with Canadians. During summer months automobiles from almost every state in the union may be seen on the provincial highways. At times they seem almost to outnumber those with Ontario licence plates.

The railroads within this area learned long ago that among the most popular points to which excursions may be run are Detroit and Buffalo. By boat similar holiday crowds are taken to Cleveland and other lake ports. No other portion of Canadian territory has such easy access to great American cities, and the main streets of these American cities are mentioned with the same familiarity as those of the capital city of Toronto. The seeming Americanization of southwestern Ontario is at times deplored – even by visitors from the United States. A leading American publicist told a Canadian audience not long since that, coming from Detroit, he did not feel that he had really entered Canada until he was east of London.[1] Had he come from Buffalo and journeyed westward he would probably have had to make some similar reference to the American influence.

In this study an attempt has been made to picture the variety of ways in which the western section of the province has from its very beginning been subject to influences from the neighbouring Republic. For more than a generation the early population was largely derived from the United States, as Loyalists or as plain land-seeking immigrants. These people brought with them their own technique of agriculture and methods of doing business, their theories of education, and their forms of religion. They brought also political ideas which ran counter to the eighteenth-century system of John Graves Simcoe and his successors. The clash of ideas had important consequences for the British province. In the end new forms of government were evolved which embodied some of the best features of both English and American experience.[2]

Federation of the British provinces in 1867 broadened the interests of the people of old Upper Canada. The great Northwest became a challenge to the efforts of the coming generation. Some of the issues which had long vexed the province seemed to fold up in this era and though new ones soon took their place there was gain in the passing of that over which men had for so long differed seriously. New leaders appeared on the scene, new economic ideas were heard, yet, in many ways, life in the province changed but little during the period from the sixties until the turn of the century.

Confederation made no radical change in the field of education. Ontario's school system, evolved at an earlier date under the direction of Egerton Ryerson, had garnered what seemed in his day to be the most valuable features of British, European, and American practice. If there was a weakness in the system, it lay in the complacent belief of its administrators that it was the best in the world, an opinion in which they were further confirmed when at the Centennial Exhibition of 1876 certain features of the Ontario system received high commendation. The twentieth century brought a more searching spirit in educational practice and considerable revision of curricula and methods,

[1] Toronto *Star*, October 29, 1938. The speaker was W. J. Cameron, publicity representative for the Ford Motor Company.
[2] See W. B. Munro, *American Influences on Canadian Government* (Toronto, 1929), chap. I.

but here the influence of the United States was less than might have been expected. In matters of building and equipment the American example has been widely followed but there has been a marked tendency to view with critical eye the courses of study, the textbooks, and the educational technique of American primary and secondary schools.

In the field of higher education the University of Western Ontario, at London, has shown a disposition to adopt some of the tried features of American university experience and practice. Its courses in Business Administration have been modelled upon those of Harvard and have been taught chiefly by men with Harvard training. The American system of "credits" for courses is in use in the Arts faculty and "clinics" deal with the cases of students who are not maintaining proper grades. The University of Western Ontario was the first in Canada to provide a full year's course in the history of the United States.[3]

Union of the provinces in 1867 may have promoted the idea of union in the churches. Methodist and Presbyterian groups, hitherto autonomous, came together in 1874 and 1875 respectively to form the Methodist Church of Canada and the Presbyterian Church in Canada. A yet larger Methodist union was brought about in 1883. Down to the turn of the century this united Methodism changed but little from the Methodism of the forties and fifties, stressing conversion as a definite experience, utilizing the class meeting for the training and strengthening spiritually of its members, placing definite restrictions upon such amusements as dancing, theatre-going, and card-playing, and adding to its numbers by revivals differing scarcely at all from those of pioneer days save in the absence of some of the hysteria of the earlier period. Except for temperance, in which the Methodists were always crusaders, there was comparatively little interest shown in social questions. These had not yet really entered the public consciousness, and as late as 1900 evangelical preachers had no solution for social problems other than a contention that wrong and injustice would disappear automatically if men were but converted. For the most part Methodism continued to be a church of the common folk. There were few wealthy men in its pews until the decade of prosperity after the turn of the century brought an accession of industrialists, stock-

[3] See Sir Robert Falconer, "American Influences on the Higher Education of Canada," Royal Society of Canada, *Transactions*, XXIV, sec. II pp. 23-38.

brokers, and real-estate promoters. Only in some of the larger city churches could Wesleyan tradition and influence be discerned. Preachers were occasionally brought from the British Isles to fill city pulpits. But the greater number of Methodist churches, in towns and villages, retained the pioneer characteristics, with revivalism ever to the fore and the Sunday School as an agency for the conversion of the young. Pioneer Methodism was still recalled by occasional pious exclamations from the pews; "Amen," "Praise God," and "Hallelujah" did not disappear from many Methodist services till late in the century.

The strong hold which early Methodism had taken upon the western section of the province was clearly seen in the church assemblies. At the first general conference of the Methodist Church of Canada, following the union of 1874, 98 of the 186 ministers present were from the London and Toronto districts while at the second general conference four years later, 140 of the 225 ministers were from the same areas. With the consummation of union British Wesleyanism as such receded into the background and Canadian Methodists thought of themselves as a completely separate body, not only autonomous but even national in spirit.

Lingering traces of the old animosity between Methodism and the Church of England were still in evidence late in the century, each body tending to remain aloof from the other. Yet the Anglican body in Upper Canada had itself been affected by its North American environment and through the years had developed a democracy that was not always understood even by its own people. As late as 1907, on the occasion of the fiftieth anniversary of the creation of the Diocese of Huron, Bishop David Williams felt constrained to say:

We are not — what we are so often alleged by others to be — an antiquated piece of aristocracy transplanted to a foreign soil and unable to take root in a new country; but . . . while retaining unbroken connection with the past, we are, nevertheless, a thoroughly democratic Church, resting absolutely upon the people, and existing solely to promote their good and the glory of God. The Church of England is like the English constitution, monarchical only in form, thoroughly democratic in essence. Her form is monarchical through the Episcopate, and linked with the Apostolic age; by her Episcopal elections, by her Synods and Vestries, she is also directly representative of the people.

Let it never be forgotten that the Anglican church in Canada is a church of the people. It has no state connections, no prescriptive or traditional rights, nor does it aspire to have any of these things.[4]

The Church of England in Canada had travelled far from the early position of the Rev. John Strachan, first Bishop of Toronto, who had contended that the Church of England was, by law, the established church in the province. The change which had come during the years was nowhere more in evidence than in the history of the Diocese of Huron, comprising the western counties of the province. In this area, since the early thirties, a "low" church tendency had been in evidence and was one factor in producing the demand after 1850 that the western counties be formed into a separate diocese. When this new diocese was created in 1857, the method of selection of a bishop reflected the democratizing influences which had been at work, for there took place in the little city of London the first Episcopal election ever known in the British Empire. The influence of the Bishop of Toronto, Tory and reactionary in his politics and "high" church in his tendencies, failed to secure the election of Archdeacon A. N. Bethune, his choice of the candidates; instead the choice fell upon the Rev. Benjamin Cronyn, who had spent his whole Canadian ministerial career of twenty-five years as rector at London. It was significant that while the clerical vote was closely divided between "high" and "low" candidates, the lay vote was decidedly in favour of the "low" church candidate. The example thus set was continued in the choice of later Bishops of Huron, all of whom have been "low" church men. Moreover, in the early sixties, Bishop Cronyn established at London a theological college for the training of his clergy, contending that the teachings of Trinity College, the creation of Bishop Strachan, were erroneous. Such connections as the Diocese of Huron has since maintained with England have been with the evangelical church element.

Unlike Methodism, which retained so many of its early American characteristics, the Presbyterian Church in Ontario soon lost all noticeable American features and turned to the Scottish tradition. The first churches established in the Niagara Peninsula had used revival methods and in the singing of hymns and in the use of Sunday Schools had resembled the Methodists.

[4] *What the Church Stands For* (London, 1907), pp. 16-17.

But after 1840, when Scottish Presbyterianism became dominant, a more severe type of religious service prevailed and for many years there were Presbyterian churches in which no organ was allowed nor were any hymns sung – only the Psalms and paraphrases, a precentor leading the congregation in this portion of the religious exercises.[5]

Baptist churches retained one point of contact with the United States until 1866, their missionary work being carried on through the agency of the American Baptist Missionary Union. In the sixties a movement was inaugurated to form a Canadian auxiliary and eight years later the Regular Baptist Missionary Society of Ontario and Quebec was organized, entirely independent of the American Union.

Fraternal temperance organizations, particularly strong in the rural districts because of their social and educational features, reached their greatest strength in the last quarter of the century and thereafter diminished in importance and influence. Before their decline had really begun, however, a new and vigorous organization came in from the United States in the Woman's Christian Temperance Union. It happened that an Ontario woman, Mrs. Letitia Youmans, was present at the inaugural meeting in 1874. She returned to her home in Picton and at once organized a branch of the society there. But preceding her by a few weeks, another Ontario woman, Mrs. R. J. Doyle, had organized a society at Owen Sound under the name of the Woman's Prohibition League. In later years Mrs. Youmans was President of the W.C.T.U. in Canada and was closely associated with Miss Frances Willard in the international activities of the organization.

The foregoing examples in the field of religion and humanitarian effort further illustrate how imponderable, how little subject to any formula, were the American social influences which played upon Upper Canada during the nineteenth century. In the case of Methodism certain early American characteristics persisted over a long period. In the case of Presbyterianism they quickly disappeared under the pressure of influences from another land. It would be of interest to follow through, more closely than has yet been done, the effect of the North American

---

[5] The London *Free Press* of June 9, 1939, contained an account of the South Kinloss Presbyterian Church where the psalms alone were still used, where a precentor led the congregation and where there was a three-day preparatory service before communion.

environment upon the Church of England in Canada, some little indication of which has been given in the record of the Diocese of Huron.

The major determinants in the history of Western Ontario have been its geographical situation, the sort of people who settled in it and the nature of the culture which they brought with them. A glance at a map of the province shows its unique situation, not only as the most southerly portion of the whole Dominion but as wedged down into nearby American states. As for the ingredients of its population, people of Ontario little realize how predominant was the American strain during the first generation of colonization. The Loyalists were scarcely more than settled on the lands set aside for them by a benevolent government before there came an influx of mere land-seekers, a part of the great westward movement which peopled the frontier states. Western Ontario received far more land-seekers than Loyalists.

When we speak, however, of "the sort of people" who came to Upper Canada, the phrase can have no implication other than cultural since there was no biological difference between the two early groups of Americans nor between these groups and the people who came later from the British Isles. Such distinctions as have often been drawn between Loyalist and non-Loyalist have, for the most part, no validity. The question of loyalty itself has no place in this discussion and it is probably true that descendants of Loyalists have emphasized much more than did their forefathers the extent of the sacrifice made on behalf of British allegiance. There were no marked differences in religion between Loyalists and non-Loyalists, nor did they differ much in social stature. The culture which was brought to Canada by land-hungry immigrants differed not at all from the culture which had been brought by those whose presence in the province had been determined by the outcome of the American War for Independence.

It remained for the decades of the thirties and forties to change both the racial mixture and in some degree the character of the culture within the province. By 1830 emigration from the British Isles to Upper Canada was in full flood, the western counties being particularly affected by the large Scottish immigration of the period. Whole townships seemed to fill up as shiploads of people from Argyleshire, Sutherlandshire, and other portions of Scotland took up land. The effect of their coming upon the Presbyterianism of the province has already been noted. The tenacity with which they held to their land, once it had been received, was in contrast to the earlier American and Canadian farmers, always ready to sell out and move on to another bush lot. In politics there was a considerable sympathy between these Scottish settlers and the native Reform element so that when the Clear Grit party came into being its greatest strength was among the farmers in the western counties, the "Yankees and Covenanters" as John A. Macdonald described them in 1856.

The early American immigration to Upper Canada contributed one element which has retained its particular culture even to the present. German and Swiss settlers who came to Pennsylvania, Virginia, and North Carolina in the first half of the eighteenth century had a reputation even in colonial days for thrifty, intensive farming. More than a century later Harriet Martineau, describing life in America, wrote of them: "There is one certain test of the permanent fitness of any district of country for agricultural purposes; the settlement of any large number of Germans in it. They are much smiled at by the vivacious and enterprising Americans for their plodding, their attachment to their own methods. . . . Nothing can be more thriving than the settlements of Germans."[6] People of this stock, so-called Pennsylvania Dutch, moved into Upper Canada around the year 1800 and took up land in what is now Waterloo County. Their Mennonite religion separated them from the Scottish immigrants who came later and the cultural heritage which they brought with them from Pennsylvania has largely persisted in spite of all that might be expected to weaken it. The pattern in Canada has been exactly the same as in the United States where the Anglo-Americans proved to be a people who could use natural resources best to immediate advantage but the German-Americans a type who could improve them for posterity.[7]

The Mennonite settlers in Waterloo County and elsewhere in the province were people who had a tradition of agricultural lore reaching back for centuries. An example of their long-range view of agriculture may be found in the treatment of their woodlots. While their neighbours were slashing down the forest

[6] Harriet Martineau, *Society in America* (New York, 1837), I, 297-8.
[7] See R. H. Shyrock, "Cultural Factors in the History of the South," *Journal of Southern History*, V (1939), p. 343.

with no thought but the immediate clearing, these Mennonite farmers were leaving reserves of wood and timber lots from which they have been systematically cutting the "ripe" trees for more than a hundred years. There is one sawmill in Waterloo County which has operated continuously in one location for almost a century, drawing steadily upon the conserved woodlots.[8]

The physical heritage may seem to be of great importance but it is less important than the social heritage passed on by those who have gone before. The social heritage of the Canadian people is derived from many sources. France made rich contributions in the first century and a half of the nation's history and the descendants of her colonists, multiplying greatly in number, have preserved almost intact that which she gave. Conservation in this instance has been facilitated by the bonds of religion and language. The English colonies along the Atlantic coast made the next great contribution when, at the close of the War for Independence, a migration took place to the British provinces of those people in whose hearts allegiance to England outweighed material considerations. They brought with them to Upper Canada and to Nova Scotia ideas of self-government which were not always relished by some of the British administrators. Insistence upon self-government wrought startling changes in the political machinery of British North America. Following close upon the Loyalists there came to Upper Canada many others from the old colonies, moved by no special desire to be under the rule of England but drawn chiefly by the report of cheap land and the desire to better their material condition. Their contribution to the life of the province was most marked in the western area between the Niagara and Detroit rivers. From their own experience they taught others how to live in the new land. They introduced social processes, some of which disappeared, while others became a part of the common life. Large movements of people from older lands in turn added their contribution so that the social fabric of the province is of many strands, sometimes indistinguishable as to their origin.

This study, having been restricted in its scope to a particular section of one province, may seem to be local history. But only as we are able to see the working out of our social institutions in separate localities and can compare the results one with another will we be able to obtain a clear perspective of the whole. Canadians, like Americans, have been a mobile people. Tens of

[8] London *Free Press*, September 1, 1939.

thousands of men and women from older Ontario were pioneers in the Canadian Northwest. They took with them the social ideas under which they had lived and gave them root in new soil. No one, therefore, can properly understand the social and political growth of the Canadian West without some knowledge of the source from which it was derived. Nor can the social and political institutions of Ontario be explained merely in terms of acts of Parliament and Assemblies. These were, in most cases, the responses to popular demands arising from forces and influences explainable only when the past could be surveyed from the summit of years. The same is true of movements and events. No proper explanation of the Duncombe uprising in 1837 is possible without an understanding of the conflict between the farming population and the petty Family Compact of Colonel Talbot and his friends. The character of Canadian Methodism was largely determined by the first forty years of its existence in the province, and even the Church of England in Canada shows the results of its contacts with North American conditions. The great Dr. Johnson once remarked that the use of travelling was to regulate imagination by reality, and instead of seeing how things might be to see them as they are. So also travel in time enables us to place our present in some relation to the past and to give to existing institutions and practices a meaning that they may otherwise lack.

Bibliography*

This study, being concerned with but a portion of a single Canadian province, deals less with the policies of government or the vicissitudes of large commercial ventures than with the activities and attitudes of three generations of common people. The materials upon which it is based have been drawn from a variety of sources, including manuscripts, newspapers, religious and agricultural journals, contemporary or nearly contemporary books and pamphlets, and government reports and other official publications. Certain portions of the *G Series* and the *Q Series* in the Public Archives of Canada have been utilized, as also the *Chamberlin Papers*, the miscellaneous papers relating to trials for sedition at London in 1837, portions of the *Upper Canada Duplicate Dispatches*, and some minor collections. Manuscript material from the library of the University of Western Ontario includes the minute book of the London District Quarter Sessions, 1800-8, and the minute books and papers of the Commissions on Rebellion Losses Claims in the London and Western districts. Various correspondence relating to Upper Canada affairs in 1837-8 was made accessible through the courtesy of Miss Elsie Sumner, of Ingersoll, Ontario. Miss Amelia Harris, of London, permitted the use of the diary of her grandmother, Mrs. John Harris, while Colonel Ibbotson Leonard, also of London, gave similar permission for the use of the manuscript diary of Elijah Woodman, a participant in the events of 1837-8. Some use has also been made of the valuable collections of papers of the Rev. John Strachan and the Honourable Charles Clarke in the Department of Archives of the Province of Ontario, while extensive use has been made of the large collection of documentary material relating to the London District in the possession of the London and Middlesex Historical Society and deposited in the library of the University of Western Ontario.

PRINTED SOURCES

Much documentary material has been printed and published in recent years, making readily accessible portions of the treasures contained in the Public Archives of Canada and in

* This bibliography reproduces that in the original edition except that a selection of works appearing since 1940 has been added to the sections entitled "Monographs" and "Articles."

other collections. Such are the Durham Papers (*Report* of the Public Archives for the year 1923), the *Elgin-Grey Papers, 1846-1852,* edited by Sir Arthur Doughty (4 vols., Ottawa, 1937), the letters and papers of John Graves Simcoe in five volumes, edited by E. A. Cruikshank and published by the Ontario Historical Society (Toronto, 1923-31), and the collection of documents relating to the War of 1812, edited by Lieutenant-Colonel William Wood and published in four volumes by the Champlain Society (Toronto, 1920-8). Of the *Territorial Papers of the United States,* published by authority of Congress, volume II (Washington, 1934) has some relation to this study.

Other printed sources of distinct value include the *Papers and Records* of the Ontario Historical Society (Toronto, 1899-1939), the annual reports of the Ontario Bureau of Archives (1903-33), and the Michigan Historical Collections, 40 volumes (Lansing, 1874-1929). Much use has been made of the publications of the local historical societies in Western Ontario, notably those of the London and Middlesex, Niagara, Lundy's Lane, Welland, Waterloo, Elgin, Kent, and Essex societies. Certain county histories have also yielded information.

The appendices to the *Journals* of the Legislative Assembly of the province contain an abundance of useful and varied reports and form a source which no investigator should overlook.

NEWSPAPERS AND PERIODICALS

Contemporary newspapers and periodicals present a lively picture of the daily life of the communities through their news items and their advertisements. As early as 1793 a newspaper had appeared at Niagara, and elsewhere in this volume will be found some account of the development of the press in Western Ontario. Most early newspapers were ephemeral and usually only scattered numbers have survived. But even single copies have been found well worth examination. To find as much as a year of the St. Thomas *Liberal* of 1832-3 or of the Sandwich *Western Herald* for 1838-9 is to uncover a rich vein of information on the earlier social history of the province. Radical activities in the London District in the period before 1837 stand more clearly revealed in surviving issues of the St. Thomas *Liberal* than in any other source examined.

Agricultural journals first appeared in Upper Canada in the

1840's, and the religious bodies, with publications as early as the *Christian Recorder* of 1819, the *Christian Guardian* of 1829, and the *Catholic* of 1830, now increased their printing activities and put forth a variety of denominational publications. Both groups of journals have been found of value in dealing with the social life of Upper Canada, though often the useful reference lies buried under a mass of material irrelevant to this study.

Newspapers which have been consulted include the following fairly extensive runs:

Chatham *Journal*, 1841
Chatham *Freeman*, 1848
Chatham *Chronicle*, 1849-50
Chatham *Western Planet*, 1854-6
London *Herald*, 1843
London *Times*, 1846-8
London *Canadian Free Press*, 1849-52
London *Free Press*, 1856, and various later years
St. Catharines *British American Journal*, 1834-5
St. Catharines *Journal*, 1835-40
St. Thomas *Liberal*, 1832-3
Sandwich *Canadian Emigrant*, 1831-4
Sandwich *Western Herald*, 1838-9
Sandwich *Voice of the Fugitive*, 1851-2
Simcoe *Norfolk Observer*, 1840-1
Toronto *Palladium*, 1837-8
Toronto *Globe*, 1850-60
Toronto *News of the Week*, 1852-4
Toronto *Leader*, 1860-4

CONTEMPORARY AND NEARLY CONTEMPORARY WORKS

Descriptions of early Upper Canada came in considerable number from the pens of travellers who visited the province, but a majority of these writers saw little of the country west of the Niagara River, the area most distinctively American in character. Their comments, therefore, tend to be based chiefly upon what they saw at Niagara, Toronto, and Kingston and along the banks of the St. Lawrence. Those who did penetrate the western districts usually noted the likeness of this Canadian area to neighbouring portions of the United States. Numerous guide-books were published in the thirties and forties but these were sometimes subsidized by land companies and in general painted altogether too rosy a picture of conditions in Upper Canada. If used with caution, however, they provide some description of the life of the period.

In this study considerable attention has been given to the religious bodies which entered Upper Canada from the United States and to the religious and moral movements emanating from the same source which found a foothold. There is a considerable body of religious biography and experience having to do with the period under discussion while the reports of missionary societies and of humanitarian organizations also reward careful examination.

ALEXANDER, J. E. *Transatlantic sketches, or visits to the most interesting scenes in North and South America, and the West Indies. With notes on slavery and Canadian emigration.* London, 1833. 2 vols.

BARCLAY, Captain [of Ury]. *Agricultural tour in the United States and Canada, with miscellaneous notices.* Edinburgh, 1842.

BETT, F. P. (ed.). *Memoirs of Susan Sibbald, 1783-1866.* London, 1926.

BIGSBY, JOHN J. *The shoe and canoe, or pictures of travel in the Canadas . . . with facts and opinions on emigration, state policy and other points of public interest.* London, 1850. 2 vols.

BIRKBECK, MORRIS. *Notes on a journey in America, from the coast of Virginia to the territory of Illinois.* Philadelphia, 1818.

BONNYCASTLE, SIR RICHARD. *Canada, as it was, is, and may be.* London, 1852. 2 vols.

BURNET, JACOB. *Notes on the early settlement of the North-Western territory.* New York, 1847.

BUTTRICK, TILLY. *Voyages, travels and discoveries of Tilly Buttrick Jr. Boston, 1831.* Reprinted in REUBEN GOLD THWAITES (ed.), *Early western travels, 1748-1846,* vol. VIII. Cleveland, 1904.

CAIRD, JAMES. *Prairie farming in America; with notes by the way on Canada and the United States.* New York, 1859.

CAMPBELL, PATRICK. *Travels in the interior inhabited parts of North America in the years 1791 and 1792.* Edited with an introduction by H. H. LANGTON. Toronto, 1937.

CARROLL, JOHN. *"Father Corson"; or the old style Canadian itinerant: embracing the life and gospel labours of the Rev. Robert Corson, fifty-six years a minister in connection with the central Methodism of Upper Canada.* Toronto, 1879.

CARTWRIGHT, C. E. (ed.). *Life and letters of the late Hon. Richard Cartwright.* . . . Toronto, 1876.

CHAMBERS, WILLIAM. *Things as they are in America.* Edinburgh, 1854.

CHRISTIE, A. J. *The emigrant's assistant: or remarks on the agricultural interest in the Canadas.* . . . Montreal, 1821.

Counsel for emigrants, and interesting information from numerous sources concerning British America, the United States and New South Wales, etc. etc. 3rd ed. with a supplement. Aberdeen, 1838.

COX, F. A. and HOBY, J. *The Baptists in America; a narrative of the deputation from the Baptist union in England to the United States and Canada.* 2nd ed., rev. London, 1836.

CRUIKSHANK, E. A. (ed.). *Documentary history of the campaigns upon the Niagara frontier, 1812-1814,* Lundy's Lane Historical Society Publications, vol. III, parts I-IX, 1902-8.

DAVIS, ROBERT. *The Canadian farmer's travels in the United States of America in which remarks are made on the arbitrary policy practised in Canada, and the free and equal rights and happy effect of the liberal institutions and astonishing enterprise of the United States.* Buffalo, 1837.

DAY, S. P. *English America, or pictures of Canadian places and people.* London, 1864. 2 vols. in 1.

DUNLOP, WILLIAM. *Statistical sketches of Upper Canada, for the use of emigrants, by a backwoodsman.* London, 1832. Reprinted in the New Canadian Library, 1967.

DURHAM, JOHN GEORGE LAMBTON, 1st Earl of. *Report on the affairs of British North America from the Earl of Durham, Her Majesty's High Commissioner.* Toronto, 1839.

FERGUSSON, ADAM. *Practical notes made during a tour in Canada and a portion of the United States in MDCCCXXXI.* Edinburgh, 1834.

(A) *Few plain directions for persons intending to proceed as settlers to His Majesty's province of Upper Canada in North America.* . . . *By an English farmer settled in America.* London, 1820.

FIDLER, REV. ISAAC. *Observations on professions, literature, manners and emigration in the United States and Canada during a residence there in 1832*. New York, 1833.

GODLEY, JOHN R. *Letters from America*. London, 1844. 2 vols.

GOLDIE, JOHN. *Diary of a journey through Upper Canada and some of the New England states, 1819*. Toronto, 1897.

GRAY, HUGH. *Letters from Canada, written during a residence there in the years 1806, 1807 and 1808. . . .* London, 1809.

HEAD, F. B. *A narrative*. London, 1839.

HENRY, MRS. P. A. *Memoir of Rev. Thomas Henry, Christian minister, York pioneer and soldier of 1812*. Toronto, 1880.

HINCKS, FRANCIS. *Reminiscences of his public life*. Montreal, 1884.

HIND, H. Y. *et al. Eighty years progress of British North America. . . .* Toronto, 1863.

HOSMER, REV. WILLIAM (ed.). *Autobiography of Rev. Alvin Torry, first missionary to the Six Nations Indians and the northwestern tribes of British North America*. Auburn, 1864.

HOWE, S. G. *The refugees from slavery in Canada West:* Report of the Freedmen's Inquiry Commission. Boston, 1864.

HOWISON, JOHN. *Sketches of Upper Canada, domestic, local, and characteristic: to which are added practical details for the information of emigrants of every class; and some recollections of the United States of America*. Edinburgh, 1821.

(An) *Impartial and authentic account of the Civil War in the Canadas. . . .* London, 1838.

JAMESON, ANNA. *Letters and friendships 1812-1860*, (ed.) Mrs. Stuart Erskine. London, 1915.

——*Winter studies and summer rambles in Canada*. New York, 1839. 2 vols. Reprinted in a shortened version in the New Canadian Library, 1965.

LANGTON, W. A. (ed.). *Early days in Upper Canada: letters of John Langton from the backwoods of Upper Canada and the Audit Office of the province of Canada*. Toronto, 1926.

LATROBE, C. J. *The rambler in North America 1832-1833*. 2nd ed. London, 1836. 2 vols.

LINDSEY, CHARLES. *The life and times of William Lyon Mackenzie. With an account of the Canadian Rebellion of 1837, and the subsequent frontier disturbances, chiefly from unpublished documents*. Toronto, 1862. 2 vols.

MACTAGGART, JOHN. *Three years in Canada: an account of the actual state of the country in 1826-7-8. Comprehending its resources, productions, improvements, and capabilities; and including sketches of the state of society, advice to emigrants, etc.* London, 1829.

MAGRATH, T. W. *Authentic letters from Upper Canada; with an account of Canadian field sports.* Dublin, 1833.

MARTINEAU, HARRIET. *Society in America.* New York, 1837. 2 vols.

MAUDE, JOHN. *A visit to the Falls of Niagara, in 1800.* London, 1826.

MERRITT, J. P. *Biography of the Hon. W. H. Merritt, M.P., of Lincoln, District of Niagara, including an account of the origin, progress and completion of some of the most important public works in Canada. Compiled chiefly from his original diary and correspondence.* St. Catharines, 1875.

NORTON, L. A. *Life and adventures of Colonel L. A. Norton, written by himself.* Oakland, Cal., 1887.

PLAYTER, GEORGE F. *The history of Methodism in Canada: with an account of the rise and progress of the work of God among the Canadian Indian tribes, and occasional notices of the civil affairs of the province.* Toronto, 1862.

PRESTON, T. R. *Three years residence in Canada, from 1837 to 1839, with notes of a winter voyage to New York, and journey thence to the British possessions: to which is added, a review of the condition of the Canadian people.* London, 1840. 2 vols.

ROLPH, THOMAS. *A brief account, together with observations, made during a visit in the West Indies, and a tour through the United States of America, in parts of the years 1832-3; together with a statistical account of Upper Canada.* Dundas, U.C., 1836.

RUSSELL, W. H. *Canada: its defences, condition and resources.* Boston, 1865.

SCHULTZ, CHRISTIAN. *Travels on an inland voyage through the states of New-York, Pennsylvania, Virginia, Ohio, Kentucky and Tennessee, and through the territories of Indiana, Louisiana, Mississippi and New-Orleans; performed in the years 1807 and 1808; including a tour of nearly six thousand miles.* New York, 1810. 2 vols.

SHIRREFF, PATRICK. *A tour through North America; together with a comprehensive view of the Canadas and the United*

States. As adapted for agricultural emigration. Edinburgh, 1835.

Six years in the bush, or extracts from the journal of a settler in Upper Canada, 1832-38. Huntingdon, England, 1838.

SMITH, MICHAEL. *A geographical view, of the province of Upper Canada, and promiscuous remarks upon the government.* . . . Hartford, 1813.

STUART, CHARLES. *The emigrant's guide to Upper Canada; or, sketches of the present state of that province, collected from a residence there during the years 1817, 1818, 1819.* . . . London, 1820.

TALBOT, E. A. *Five years residence in the Canadas, including a tour through part of the United States in 1823.* London, 1824. 2 vols.

TAYLOR, JAMES. *Narrative of a voyage to, and travels in Upper Canada, with accounts of the customs, character and dialect of the country, also remarks on emigration agriculture, etc.* Hull, 1846.

THELLER, E. A. *Canada in 1837-38, showing by historical facts, the causes of the late attempted revolution, and its failure; the present condition of the people, and their future prospects, together with personal adventures of the author, and others who were connected with the revolution.* Philadelphia, 1841. 2 vols.

THOMPSON, SAMUEL. *Reminiscences of a Canadian pioneer, for the last fifty years: an autobiography.* Toronto, 1884.

WADDILOVE, REV. W. J. D. (ed.). *The Stewart missions; a series of letters and journals calculated to exhibit the spiritual destitution of the emigrants who settled in the remote parts of Upper Canada.* London, 1838.

WARR, G. W. *Canada as it is; or, the emigrant's friend and guide to Upper Canada: being a sketch of the country.* . . . London, 1847.

WEBSTER, THOMAS. *Life of Rev. James Richardson, a bishop of the Methodist Episcopal Church in Canada.* Toronto, 1876.

WELD, ISAAC. *Travels through the States of North America and the provinces of Upper and Lower Canada in 1795-1797.* 4th ed. London, 1800.

WILKIE, DAVID. *Sketches of a summer trip to New York and the Canadas.* Edinburgh, 1837.

WOOD, JOHN. *Memoir of Henry Wilkes, D.D., LL.D., his life and times.* Montreal, 1887.

MONOGRAPHS

BURKHOLDER, L. J. *A brief history of the Mennonites in Ontario, giving a description of conditions in early Ontario, the coming of the Mennonites into Canada, settlements, congregations, conferences, other activities. . . .* Toronto, 1935.

BURT, A. L. *The United States, Great Britain and British North America from the Revolution to the establishment of peace after the War of 1812.* New Haven, 1940.

CANNIFF, WILLIAM. *The medical profession in Upper Canada, 1783-1850. An historical narrative with original documents relating to the profession, including some brief biographies.* Toronto, 1894.

CLARK, MARTHA. *Simcoe's Economic Policy.* Unpublished thesis, University of Toronto, 1923.

CLARK, S. D. *Movements of Political Protest in Canada, 1640-1840.* Toronto, 1959.

COREY, A. B. *The Crisis of 1830 to 1842 in Canadian-American Relations.* New Haven, 1941.

COWAN, HELEN I. *British Emigration to North America, 1783-1837.* Toronto, 1928.

——*British Emigration to British North America: the First Hundred Years.* Toronto, 1961.

CRAIG, G. M. *Early Travellers in The Canadas, 1791-1867.* Toronto, 1955.

——*Upper Canada: The Formative Years, 1784-1841.* Toronto, 1963.

CREIGHTON, D. G. *The Commercial Empire of the St. Lawrence, 1760-1850.* Toronto, 1937.

——*The Road to Confederation: the Emergence of Canada, 1863-1867.* Toronto, 1964.

DORLAND, A. G. *A History of the Society of Friends (Quakers) in Canada.* Toronto, 1927.

DUNHAM, AILEEN. *Political Unrest in Upper Canada, 1815-1836.* London, 1927. Reprinted in the Carleton Library, 1963.

ERMATINGER, C. O. *The Talbot Regime; or the first half century of the Talbot settlement.* St. Thomas, 1904.

FRENCH, G. S. *Parsons and Politics: the Role of the Wesleyan Methodists in Upper Canada and the Maritimes from 1780 to 1855.* Toronto, 1962.

GRAHAM, W. H. *The Tiger of Canada West.* Toronto, 1965.

HAMIL, F. C. *Lake Erie Baron: the Story of Colonel Thomas Talbot*. Toronto, 1955.

——*The Valley of the Lower Thames, 1640 to 1850*. Toronto, 1951.

HAMILTON, M. W. *The Country Printer, New York State, 1785-1830*. New York, 1936.

HANSEN, MARCUS LEE. *The Mingling of the Canadian and American Peoples*. Vol. I Historical. New Haven, 1940.

HARRIS, HERBERT. *American Labor*. New Haven, 1939.

IVISON, E. H. S. and ROSSER, FRED. *The Baptists in Upper and Lower Canada before 1820*. Toronto, 1956.

JONES, R. L. *History of Agriculture in Ontario, 1613-1880*. Toronto, 1946.

KILBOURN, WILLIAM. *The Firebrand: William Lyon Mackenzie and the Rebellion in Upper Canada*. Toronto, 1956.

KINCHEN, O. A. *The Rise and Fall of the Patriot Hunters*. New York, 1956.

LANDON, FRED. *An Exile from Canada to Van Dieman's Land*. Toronto, 1960.

LOGAN, H. A. *The History of Trade-Union Organization in Canada*. Chicago, 1928.

MCCRIMMON, A. L. *The Educational Policy of the Baptists of Ontario and Quebec. . . .* Toronto, 1920.

MCEVOY, JOHN M. *The Ontario Township*. University of Toronto Studies in Political Science. First series, no. 1. Toronto, 1889.

MAYO, A. D. *The American Common School in New York, New Jersey and Pennsylvania*. Report, U. S. Commissioner of Education, 1895-6.

MOIR, J. S. *Church and State in Canada West: Three Studies in the Relation of Denominationalism and Nationalism, 1841-1867*. Toronto, 1959.

MUNRO, W. B. *American Influences on Canadian Government*. Toronto, 1929.

PRATT, J. W. *Expansionists of 1812*. New York, 1925.

RIDDELL, W. R. *The Life of John Graves Simcoe, First Lieutenant-Governor of the Province of Upper Canada, 1792-96*. Toronto, 1926.

RYERSON, EGERTON. *The Loyalists of America and Their Times, from 1620 to 1816*. Toronto, 1880. 2 vols.

SANDERSON, C. R. *Sir George Arthur, a vindication*. Unpublished thesis, University of Toronto, 1940.

SANDERSON, J. E. *The First Century of Methodism in Canada.* Toronto, 1908. 2 vols.

SISSONS, C. B. *Egerton Ryerson: His life and letters.* Toronto, 2 vols., 1937, 1949.

SKELTON, O. D. *The Life and Times of Sir Alexander Tilloch Galt.* Toronto, 1920. Reprinted in the Carleton Library, 1966.

SPRAGGE, G. W. *The John Strachan Letter Book: 1812-1834.* Toronto, 1946.

SWEET, W. W. *Religion on the American Frontier: The Baptists, 1783-1830.* New York, 1931.

——*Religion on the American Frontier: II. The Presbyterians, 1783-1840, a collection of source materials.* New York, 1936.

——*The Story of Religions in America.* New York, 1930.

TEMPLIN, HUGH. *Fergus and the Rebellion of 1837* (condensed from a series of articles printed by the Fergus *News-Record*, December, 1937).

TOON, CHARLES C. *Some Aspects of the History of Agriculture in Canada West and Ontario Between 1850 and 1870.* Unpublished thesis, University of Western Ontario, 1938.

WOOD, LOUIS A. *A History of Farmers' Movements in Canada.* Toronto, 1924.

YOUNG, JAMES. *Early History of Galt and the Settlement of Dumfries in the Province of Ontario.* Toronto, 1880.

ZASLOW, MORRIS (ed.). *The Defended Border: Upper Canada and the War of 1812.* Toronto, 1964.

ARTICLES

AITCHISON, J. H., "The Municipal Corporations Act of 1849," *Canadian Historical Review*, XXX (June, 1949), 107-122.

BANKS, JOHN, "American Presbyterianism in the Niagara Peninsula," *Ontario History*, LVII (September, 1965), 135-140.

BOVEY, WILFRID, "Confederate Agents in Canada during the American Civil War," *Canadian Historical Review*, II (March, 1921), 46-57.

BROWN, GEORGE, "The Grit Party and the Great Reform Convention of 1859," *Canadian Historical Review*, XVI (June, 1935), 245-265.

——"Canadian Letters: Description of a tour thro' the provinces of Lower and Upper Canada, in the course of the years 1792 and '93," *Canadian Antiquarian and Numismatic Journal*, IX (July-October, 1912).

COLQUHOUN, A. H. U., "The Career of Joseph Willcocks," *Canadian Historical Review*, VII (December, 1926), 287-293.

CORNELL, P. G., "The Alignment of Political Groups with the United Province of Canada, 1854-64," *Canadian Historical Review*, XXX (March, 1949), 22-46.

CRAIG, G. M., "The American Impact on the Upper Canadian Reform Movement before 1837," *Canadian Historical Review*, XXIX (December, 1948), 333-352.

CREIGHTON, D. G., "The United States and Canadian Confederation," *Canadian Historical Review*, XXXIX (September, 1958), 209-222.

CRUIKSHANK, E. A., "Immigration from the United States into Canada, 1784-1812, its Character and Results," *Proceedings* of the Ontario Educational Association (Toronto, 1900).

DAVIS, LEROY G., "Some Frontier Words and Phrases," *Minnesota History*, XIX (September, 1938), 241-246.

EARL, D. W. L., "British Views of Colonial Upper Canada, 1791-1841," *Ontario History*, LIII (June, 1961), 117-136.

FALCONER, SIR ROBERT, "American Influences on the Higher Education of Canada," *Transactions* of the Royal Society of Canada, XXIV (1930), 23-38.

FOX, W. S., "School Readers as an Educational Force," *Queen's Quarterly*, XXXIX (November, 1932), 688-703.

GATES, L. F., "Mackenzie's Gazette: An Aspect of W. L. Mackenzie's American Years," *Canadian Historical Review*, XLVI (December, 1965), 323-345.

GLAZIER, SIDNEY, "Patrons of Industry in Michigan," *Mississippi Valley Historical Review*, XXIV (September, 1937) 185-194.

GOODMAN, W. H., "The Origins of the War of 1812: A Survey of Changing Interpretations," *Mississippi Valley Historical Review*, XXVIII (September, 1941), 171-186.

HARVEY, D. C., "The Intellectual Awakening of Nova Scotia," *Dalhousie Review*, XIII (April, 1933), 1-22; Reprinted in G. A. RAWLYK (ed.), *Historical Essays on the Atlantic Provinces*, Carleton Library, 1967.

JACKSON, ERIC, "Organization of Upper Canadian Reformers 1818-1867," *Ontario History*, LIII (June, 1961), 95-115.

JOHNSTON, C. M., "An Outline of Early Settlement in the Grand River Valley," *Ontario History*, LIV (March, 1962), 43-67.

KERR, W. B., "Colonel Anthony Von Egmond and the Rebellion of 1837 in Huron County," a series of articles contributed to the Goderich *Signal* between October 1 and December 24, 1931.

LANDON, FRED, "The Agricultural Journals of Upper Canada, (Ontario)," *Agricultural History*, IX (October, 1935), 167-175.

——"Wilberforce, an Experiment in the Colonization of Freed Negroes in Upper Canada," *Transactions* of the Royal Society of Canada, XXXI (1937), 69-78.

LONGLEY, R. S., "Emigration and the Crisis of 1837 in Upper Canada," *Canadian Historical Review*, XVII (March, 1936), 29-40.

MACKAY, R. A., "The Political Ideas of William Lyon Mackenzie," *Canadian Journal of Economics and Political Science*, III (February, 1937), 1-22.

MEALING, S. R., "The Enthusiasms of John Graves Simcoe," *Report* of the Canadian Historical Association (1958), pp. 50-62.

MOIR, J. S., "Early Methodism in the Niagara Peninsula," *Ontario History*, XLIII (April, 1951), 51-58.

——"Settlement of the Clergy Reserves," *Canadian Historical Review*, XXXVII (March, 1956), 46-62.

PATTERSON, W. J., "The Long Point Furnace," *Canadian Mining Journal*, LX (September, 1939), 544-549.

PEASE, T. C., "The Ordinance of 1787," *Mississippi Valley Historical Review*, XXV (September, 1938), 167-180.

PHILP, JOHN, "The Economic and Social Effects of the British Garrisons on the Development of Western Upper Canada," *Ontario History*, XLI (March, 1949), 37-48.

REGEHR, T. D., "Land Ownership in Upper Canada, 1783-1796: A Background to the First Table of Fees," *Ontario History*, LV (March, 1963), 35-48.

RICHARDS, J. H., "Lands and Policies: Attitudes and Controls in the Alienation of Lands in Ontario During the First Century of Settlement," *Ontario History*, L (Autumn, 1958), 193-209.

RIDDELL, W. R., "The First Canadian Prohibition Measure," *Canadian Historical Review*, I (June, 1920), 187-190.

SHYROCK, R. H., "Cultural Factors in the History of the South," *Journal of Southern History*, V (1939).

SPRAGGE, G. W., "John Strachan's Contribution to Education, 1800-1823," *Canadian Historical Review*, XXII (June, 1941), 147-158.

STACEY, C. P., "A Private Report of General Winfield Scott on the Border Situation in 1839," *Canadian Historical Review*, XXI (December, 1940), 407-414.

STILL, BAYRD, "An Interpretation of the Statehood Process, 1800 to 1850," *Mississippi Valley Historical Review*, XXIII (September, 1936), 189-204.

TALMAN, J. J., "The Newspaper Press of Canada West, 1850-60," *Transactions* of the Royal Society of Canada, XXXIII (1939), 149-172.

TAYLOR, G. R., "Agrarian Discontent in the Mississippi Valley Preceding the War of 1812," *Journal of Political Economy*, XXXIX (August, 1931), 471-505.

——"Prices in the Mississippi Valley Preceding the War of 1812," *Journal of Economic and Business History*, III 1930), 148-163.

UNDERHILL, F. H., "Some Aspects of Upper Canadian Radical Opinion in the Decade before Confederation," *Report* of the Canadian Historical Association (1927), 46-61.

WALLACE, W. S., "The First Journalists in Upper Canada," *Canadian Historical Review*, XXVII (December, 1945), 372-380.

——"The Periodical Literature of Upper Canada," *Canadian Historical Review*, XII (March, 1931), 4-22.

WATKIN-JONES, H., "Methodist Thought in Contact with Modern History," *Hibbert Journal*, XXXVI (October, 1937), 56-68.

WILSON, G. A., "The Clergy Reserves: 'Economical Mischiefs' or Sectarian Issue?," *Canadian Historical Review*, XLII (December, 1961), 281-299.

SUGGESTIONS FOR
FURTHER READING

There is as yet no comprehensive history of Western Ontario though several of its individual counties such as Norfolk, Bruce, Essex, Lambton and Kent have been studied in considerable detail by local historians and local historical societies. For the period before 1815 there are biographies of Governor John Graves Simcoe by D. B. READ (Toronto, 1890), DUNCAN CAMPBELL SCOTT (Toronto, 1905) and W. R. RIDDELL (Toronto, 1926) while his voluminous letters and papers have been published in four volumes by the Ontario Historical Society (Toronto, 1923-26). For political conditions after the War of 1812 see G. M. CRAIG, *Upper Canada: The Formative Years, 1784-1841* (Toronto, 1963). On the war itself a book of essays has recently been compiled by MORRIS ZASLOW: *The Defended Border: Upper Canada and the War of 1812* (Toronto, 1964). M. L. HANSEN and J. B. BREBNER, *The Mingling of the Canadian and American Peoples* (New Haven and Toronto, 1940) is an intensive study of population movements between the two countries.

The religious differences which long disturbed Upper Canada centre about the careers of two men, the Anglican John Strachan and the Methodist Egerton Ryerson. There is as yet no definitive biography of Strachan but Ryerson has been comprehensively dealt with by C. B. SISSONS in two volumes (Toronto, 1937, 1949). For the role of the Methodists, see GOLDWIN S. FRENCH, *Parsons and Politics* (Toronto, 1962). STUART IVISON and FRED ROSSER have recorded early Baptist activity in Upper Canada in *The Baptists in Upper and Lower Canada Before 1820* (Toronto, 1956).

Much has been written on the Rebellion of 1837 and on the disturbing border conditions of the time. See WILLIAM KILBOURN, *The Firebrand, William Lyon Mackenzie and the Rebellion in Upper Canada* (Toronto, 1956), and AILEEN DUNHAM, *Political Unrest in Upper Canada, 1815-1836* (Carleton Library, 1963). The general political troubles of the time and their sequel are dealt with in CHESTER NEW's biography of Lord Durham. The Canadian portion of this book, entitled *Lord Durham's Mission to Canada*, is available in the Carleton Library (1963). An abridgement of Lord Durham's *Report* is also included in the same series (1963).

NOTE ON THE AUTHOR

Fred Landon was born in London, Ontario, in 1880 and educated at the University of Western Ontario. He served as Ottawa correspondent of the London *Free Press* before becoming, successively, Librarian of the London Public Library and the University of Western Ontario. In the latter post he also lectured in the Department of History. From 1946 to his retirement in 1950 he was Vice-President and Dean of Graduate Studies at the University of Western Ontario.

Among Dr. Landon's honours are the presidency of the Canadian Historical Association in 1941-42, the Tyrrell Medal for Canadian historical writing given by the Royal Society of Canada, and honorary degrees from Western Ontario and McMaster universities. For a number of years Dr. Landon was Chairman of the Historic Sites and Monuments Board of Canada.

Besides *Western Ontario and the American Frontier* (1941) Fred Landon has written *Lake Huron* (1944) and *An Exile from Canada to Van Dieman's Land* (1960). In 1928 he collaborated with J. E. Middleton in a four-volume work, *The Province of Ontario, a History, 1615-1927*. He has also contributed numerous articles to Canadian and American journals on the joint relations of the two nations, on slavery and the anti-slavery controversy and on the Great Lakes.

THE CARLETON LIBRARY